ACCESSING HUMAN SERVICES

SOCIAL SERVICE DELIVERY SYSTEMS
An International Annual

MEETING HUMAN NEEDS
1: An Overview of Nine Countries
edited by DANIEL THURSZ and JOSEPH L. VIGILANTE
Volume 1   1975   ISBN 0-8039-0314-6 hardcover   ISBN 0-8039-0589-0 softcover

MEETING HUMAN NEEDS
2: Additional Perspectives from Thirteen Countries
edited by DANIEL THURSZ and JOSEPH L. VIGILANTE
Volume 2   1976   ISBN 0-8039-0590-4 hardcover   ISBN 0-8039-0591-2 softcover

REACHING PEOPLE
The Structure of Neighborhood Services
edited by DANIEL THURSZ and JOSEPH L. VIGILANTE
Volume 3   1978   ISBN 0-8039-0817-2 hardcover   ISBN 0-8039-0818-0 softcover

REACHING THE AGED
Social Services in Forty-Four Countries
edited by MORTON I. TEICHER, DANIEL THURSZ, and JOSEPH L. VIGILANTE
Volume 4   1979   ISBN 0-8039-1365-6 hardcover   ISBN 0-8039-1366-4 softcover

LINKING HEALTH CARE AND SOCIAL SERVICES
International Perspectives
edited by MERL C. HOKENSTAD, Jr., and ROGER A. RITVO
Volume 5   1982   ISBN 0-8039-1819-4 hardcover   ISBN 0-8039-1820-8 softcover

REDISCOVERING SELF-HELP
Its Role in Social Care
edited by DIANE L. PANCOAST, PAUL PARKER, and CHARLES FROLAND
Volume 6   1983   ISBN 0-8039-1990-5 hardcover   ISBN 0-8039-1993-X softcover

ACCESSING HUMAN SERVICES
International Perspectives
edited by RISHA W. LEVINSON and KAREN S. HAYNES
Volume 7   1984   ISBN 0-8039-2388-0 hardcover   ISBN 0-8039-2389-9 softcover

SOCIAL SERVICE DELIVERY SYSTEMS
An International Annual
Volume 7

ACCESSING HUMAN SERVICES

International Perspectives

WITHDRAWN

Editors
RISHA W. LEVINSON
and
KAREN S. HAYNES

Foreword by Joseph L. Vigilante

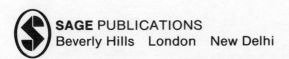

SAGE PUBLICATIONS
Beverly Hills   London   New Delhi

To Gerald and Kingsley

For information address:

SAGE Publications, Inc.
275 South Beverly Drive
Beverly Hills, California 90212

SAGE Publications India Pvt. Ltd.
C-236 Defence Colony
New Delhi 110 024, India

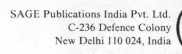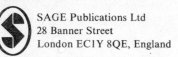

SAGE Publications Ltd
28 Banner Street
London EC1Y 8QE, England

Printed in the United States of America

Library of Congress Cataloging in Publication Data

Main entry under title:

Accessing human services.

   (Social service delivery systems ; v. 7)
   Includes index.
   1. Social service—Information services—Addresses,
essays, lectures. 2. Information networks—Addresses,
essays, lectures. I. Levinson, Risha W. II. Haynes,
Karen S. III. Series: Social service delivery
systems ; vol. 7.
HV37.A18   1984   361'.007   84-16012
ISBN 0-8039-2388-0
ISBN 0-8039-2389-9 (pbk.)

FIRST PRINTING

CONTENTS

Foreword
Joseph L. Vigilante 7

Preface 11

Introduction: Comparative Access Models
Risha W. Levinson and Karen S. Haynes 15

I. Citizens Advice Bureaus: CAB Model 23

1. The British Citizens Advice Bureau: Entry
to the Social Services System
Alex Eastabrook 29

2. The Community Information Project:
A British Resource Center
Grainne Morby 57

3. The Development of Citizens Advice Bureaus in
New Zealand
Neil Smith 77

4. Implementing a CAB System in Cyprus:
Prospects and Problems
Eleni Wiltcher 95

5. Citizens Advice Bureaus in a Changing Society:
An Israeli Report
Yemina Barneis and Ofra Fisher 105

6. Networks of Access Systems in Israel:
A Conceptual Analysis
Abraham Doron and Eli Frenkel 119

II. Information and Referral Services Systems: I&R Model 135

7. Model I&R Systems in the United States:
Public Policy Issues in Capacity Building
John J. Gargan and James L. Shanahan 141

8. Technological Advances in I&R: An
   American Report
   William Garrett   171

9. Impact of Advanced Technology on I&R in
   a Canadian Provincial Context
   Donald F. Bellamy and Donald J. Forgie   199

10. AID of Edmonton: An Expanding
    Canadian I&R Service
    Barbara Ann Olsen   217

III. Other Access Systems: Variations and Modifications   **239**

11. Access to Social Services in Poland
    Irene Sienko   245

12. Community Welfare Volunteers in Japan:
    the Minsei-Iin System
    Atsuko Matsuoka   259

13. CAB in New Delhi, India: "In the Service
    of the Citizen"
    Ramesh Chandra Mishra and Meera Agarwal   275

14. The Ombudsman: Watchdog of Legality and Equity
    in Administration
    Ulf Lundvik   287

    Addendum: The International Ombudsman Institute
    Randall E. Ivany   303

    Conclusions
    Risha W. Levinson and Karen S. Haynes   307

Index   310

About the Authors   316

FOREWORD

JOSEPH L. VIGILANTE

This seventh volume of this series, Social Service Delivery Systems: An International Annual, is enthusiastically welcomed by the Series' Editors. As originally conceived by the Editors, Social Service Delivery Systems has had three major purposes: to provide information to students, scholars and professional practitioners in the human services about the methods of human service delivery throughout the world; to report these services through first hand accounts from those involved; and to suggest similarities and differences in systems while opening opportunities for research and cross-national communication. We are delighted that Professors Levinson and Haynes have produced this volume within the context of these purposes.

Since it has been a long-established pattern of this series that there be minimal editing of manuscripts in order to reflect the writing style and literary qualities of the contributors, which in themselves should suggest something about the country, we are twice grateful: The chapters do indeed reflect both the unique literary styles as expressed by the authors and the cultural differences of the countries they represent, an essential requirement for understanding service delivery systems.

The availability of human services can only be meaningful if there are concomitant guarantees of access. The past twenty years have witnessed a burgeoning concern throughout the world regarding not only the volume of human services but also in relation to access as a highly significant component of social service delivery systems. Levinson's and Haynes' comparative analysis of access systems has therefore made a major contribution. This book strongly underscores the significance of access.

7

Levinson and Haynes have identified two major forms of access in
nine developed and developing countries[1]: The United Kingdom's
Citizens Advice Bureau (CAB) as described in this book was developed during World War II and represents a pioneer model in the
operation of a universal access system. In North America, the Information and Referral Model (I&R) emerged in the 1960s in the United
States and Canada as an organized response to consumerism and the
need for improved access to the complex bureaucracies of social
welfare institutions. In the introductory chapter of this comparative
study, the reader is provided with an excellent graphic instrument to
study systems of access services in one's own country. Following the
reports of selected access systems in the nine countries under review,
the editors conclude with a thoughtful analysis of commonalities and
diversities of the CAB and I&R models. This volume should facilitate
and enhance ongoing efforts in cross-national analyses as new access
systems continue to develop throughout the world.

Further, in the tradition of the series, the editors of this volume
have cited the importance of specific socioeconomic and geographic
variables both in their selection of the countries included as well as in
their comments preceding each of the three parts of the book. Our
fascination with the work grows from its recognition of the combination of cultural traditions and the development of new institutional
approaches to access systems.

Levinson and Haynes have emphasized the vital roles of the
professional and the volunteer in designing and conducting access
systems in the public and voluntary sectors. Not the least is their
recognition of the ombudsman role in access. We draw the implication
from their work that social institutions, both governmental and non-
governmental, have the capability of providing access through the use
of the ombudsman, who serves both as an advocate for clients and an
outreach agent for potential clients. The opportunity for the development of the ombudsman role in this regard would seem to be
quite promising, and suggests yet another model for access to services.

This volume should prove to be useful to direct service practitioners in many other social welfare settings as well as to workers in
access services. As an introduction to comparative cross-national
studies of diverse access systems, this volume should also provide
teachers, and students, and more advanced scholars of the human

service professions with a textual and bibliographical source for intensive study and research.

—Joseph L. Vigilante
—Daniel Thursz
Series Editors

NOTE

1. The countries under study are Canada, Cyprus, Great Britain, India, Israel, Japan, New Zealand, Poland, and the United States.

PREFACE

All citizens in an industrial society require human services to maintain a desirable standard of physical and social well-being. In the development of the complex and highly bureaucratized health and social welfare systems in most industrialized countries, however, little attention has been given to assuring access to resources.

This book, which is the seventh volume in Sage's series of international annuals, *Social Services Delivery Systems,* deals specifically with reports on organized access systems that operate in selected countries.

The major purpose of this cross-national report is to promote familiarity with the diverse access systems that have developed in many parts of the world. These systems generally aim to achieve two major objectives: (a) to link persons in need of services with appropriate resources and (b) to utilize the data reports of these access systems for purposes of policy formulation and social planning. Because of the recency and rapidity with which this newly emerging field has developed, the introduction to the book offers a general description of access systems and presents a comparative analysis of two basic models: the British CAB Model (Citizens Advice Bureau) and the American I&R Model (Information and Referral).

These cross-national reports from developed and developing countries are examples of access systems that are designed as either citizens advice bureaus or information and referral services or represent hybrids or unique blends of these two basic models.

The reports of individual countries are organized in the three major sections of this book. In Parts I and II, the reader will be introduced to selected reports of the two dominant models of access systems: CABs and I&R Services. Part III includes examples of access systems that reflect some of the aspects of the British and American models but also represent variations that are unique to the particular country under study.

The content of the 14 chapters, which report on nine individual countries, explores various dimensions of access systems, such as historical development, organizational auspices, service delivery, agency resources, and future directions. The concluding chapter offers a retrospective view of some of the common elements that have emerged from this cross-national report and also calls attention to the diversities that are apparent in this initial effort to study access systems in the international arena.

This cross-national study grew out of the editors' mutual interest in the development and operation of access system in the United States and abroad. Dr. Karen Haynes's international work and studies in job satisfaction and professional employment have been a springboard for her continued study of international social welfare and international social work education. Her earlier work on taxonomic issues in human services further added to her professional interest in international access. Dr. Risha Levinson's research in the development and operation of I&R service systems in the United States and abroad has extended over a 15-year period. Her study of the CAB system in the United Kingdom was sparked by her five-week visit to the United Kingdom while on sabbatical leave (1980-1981), during which she conducted ten site visits to CAB agencies and interviewed 40 selected staff members of the National Association of CABs in England, Scotland, and Wales.

We are very grateful for the enthusiastic interest and cooperation of our 20 contributors, who have given generously of their time and efforts to report on their respective access systems within the time constraints and despite inevitable delays that occur in overseas communications.

The development of this international interest has been greatly aided through the kind cooperation of the staff of the National Association of Citizens Advice Bureaus (NACAB)—notably, Mr. Jeremy Leighton, former Executive Director of NACAB, and Mrs. Sheila Bellamy, former Overseas Correspondence and Visitors' Programmes Officer at NACAB. Through Mrs. Bellamy's guidance and assistance it was possible to establish communication with a wide variety of CABs and I&R service organizations in Africa, Asia, Australia, Canada, New Zealand, the Canal Zone, and Israel, as well as in various European countries. We are indeed grateful to our British colleagues for their helpful cooperation and sharing of information.

We are also very appreciative of the administrative supports that each of our schools of social work have extended to us: the Adelphi University School of Social Work and the Indiana University School of Social Work. The extraordinary helpfulness of our secretaries, Ann Mallinson at Adelphi University and Philip Coffin at Indiana

University, deserves special thanks, as does the assistance of Beth Rosenthal, doctoral student at Adelphi, and Janine Gauthier, student assistant at Indiana University.

This volume is designed to be of interest to a wide range of readers, representing many disciplines, a variety of service organizations, diverse fields of human services, and the academic community. In view of the fact that the largest proportion of CAB and I&R providers are paraprofessionals and volunteers, this report should be of interest to nonprofessionals as well as professional service providers. The rapid expansion of CABs and I&Rs, both in the United States and abroad, has generated growing public interest in the experiences of a variety of international settings in which access systems operate. We hope that this volume will represent a source of information on access systems that formerly has not been available to faculty and students who are interested in the organization and delivery of human services. These cross-national reports on access systems can provide a source of instructional materials, as well as a springboard for research and program development.

We are hopeful that these endeavors will further promote and broaden international interest in the continued development of organized access systems that provide linkages to human services.

Risha W. Levinson
Karen S. Haynes

INTRODUCTION
Comparative Access Models

RISHA W. LEVINSON
KAREN S. HAYNES

Our postindustrial society has been characterized as a service society. The planless proliferation of services has resulted in a society that is "overserviced but underserved." Notwithstanding the expansion of service agencies, impediments to gaining access to services have persisted. The problems of entry to needed services in complex service bureaucracies have resulted in service inadequacies, insufficiencies, and gross inequities. Extended delays, restricted admissions, communication gaps, and discriminatory practices have seriously compounded the problem of inaccessibility to services. Even where services exist, knowing where and how to qualify for benefits and entitlements is often perplexing. In search of help, inquirers are often shunted from one agency to another in a wasteful and frustrating "ping-ponging" process. Where to turn for help is especially problematic for the economically disadvantaged, the chronically ill, and the elderly.

RESPONSE TO SERVICE BARRIERS:
ACCESS SYSTEMS

One organizational response to facilitate linking the citizen-consumer with available services has been the development of organized access systems in many of the developed and developing countries throughout the world. The concept of access as an organized system for entry into human services has been given various emphases, depending upon the historical development of the human welfare services and the national cultural life of the particular country.

Access systems reflect an emerging field of human services that is characterized by great diversity in its structures, operations, range of services and organizational settings. Access systems may be located in libraries, storefronts, train stations, health departments, social agencies, and, in fact, wherever people tend to congregate. Operationally, access systems may exist in formal organizations and informal groups, and may provide general or specialized information, advice, and referral services. Levels of staff may include professionals, paraprofessionals, and volunteers in varying proportions, or a mix of all of these staff levels.

For purposes of analysis, there are two major models of access systems: the Citizens Advice Bureau (CAB) Model and the Information and Referral (I&R) Model. CABs developed in the United Kingdom in 1939 and the early 1940s in response to emergency war conditions during World War II. Thereafter, CABs became established as an important feature of the British welfare system as information, advice and advocacy centers for the local citizens. To date, over 900 CABs operate in England, Wales, Scotland and Northern Ireland. Many countries associated with the British Commonwealth have established CAB-type access systems with various adaptations and modifications depending upon the particular demands for services, available resources, and unique preferences of the providers and consumers of human resources.

While the beginnings of Information and Referral (I&R) have been traced to the Social Service Exchanges of the late nineteenth century, which were operated by Charity Organization Societies, organized I&R programs were shaped by the emerging community councils in the 1920s that were sponsored by the United Community Funds and Councils of America (currently identified as the United Way of America). Spearheaded by the United States Administration on Aging and the profusion of new social service programs in the 1960s, I&R services were established to facilitate access to human service systems. Under the social service legislation of Title XX in the mid-1970s, funds for program development and training became available and consequently I&R services proliferated on all levels, including national, state and local. It should also be noted that the enormous advances in information systems and automation contributed to the rapid growth of I&R services in North America, both in the U.S. and in Canada. It is estimated that approximately 10,000 I&R programs are currently operating in the United States and Canada, though this estimate may actually represent an under-report of operative access systems.

WHAT CONSTITUTES AN ACCESS SYSTEM?

Although marked differences exist in the organization and operation of CABs and I&R services, there is general agreement that these entry services represent a universal doorway to existing resources, available free of charge, and aimed at promoting access through an organized, updated and retrievable information, referral and follow-up system. The aim of a CAB or I&R service is to provide a reliable and responsible entry to services as close to the consumer's locality as possible. Essentially, these locality-based services represent an attempt to overcome some of the problems of mobility and alienation in an industrial society.

The underpinning of an access system is the resource file which provides selected and systematized data on resources to meet human service needs. As for essential functions, information, advice and referrals to resources are essential service components, and also include appropriate follow-up to ensure accountability. Levels of counseling and the extent of advocacy usually depend upon the agency mission and staff capabilities in maintaining a broad and universal entry to services. Various collateral services associated with access systems may include transportation and escort services, legal assistance, crisis-intervention services, health education, and any variety of service-related programs. Based on its resource files and the reporting system for service statistics, access systems also provide a valuable information base for health and social planning.

CAB AND I&R MODELS:
SIMILARITIES AND DIFFERENCES

Bearing in mind that the British CABs predated American I&R services by over twenty years, there are some interesting similarities as well as sharp differences between these two major access systems. While the British CAB and American I&R services share the common goal of facilitating access to services, there are significant differences between these two models that pertain to organizational structures, the delivery of services, staffing, technology, and policy-planning capabilities, as illustrated in the accompanying table.

Both CABs and I&R services require a universal entry to services that is nonsectarian, nonpolitical and nondiscriminatory. Both the British and American access systems acknowledge the importance of providing a broad range of information to inquirers, and aim to link the

TABLE 1 Comparative Analysis of the British CAB Model and the American I&R Model

Aspects: Access Systems		CAB Model	I&R Model
I.	Organization		
	Auspices	Local authority	Local, state or national auspices
	Governance	Local management committee	Varied: depends on auspices and funding
	Accountability	Hierarchical structure local, area committee national association	May be autonomous, or related to municipal, state, regional, and/or national organization
	Funding	Primarily local funding; contributory funds from NACAB	Multiple funding sources: public, voluntary, proprietary
	Centralization/decentralization	Centralized functions assumed by the national association (NACAB), decentralized local CAB service	No national centralized network; decentralized I&R service may be part of a centralized system
II.	Delivery of Services		
	Mode of entry	Primarily walk-in services	Primarily telephone services
	Staffing	Predominantly volunteers	Mix of volunteers, paraprofessionals, professionals
	Training	Mandatory training	Optional training
	Technology	Uniform Information System application of national Prestel system	No common language, diverse information systems
	Generic/Specialized services	Traditionally generic; trend toward specialized services	Traditionally specialized; trend toward generic services
	Legal services	Volunteer solicitors	Lawyers not directly involved
III.	Policy-Planning		
	Policy	Participation in national policy formulation	No national policy
	Planning	Consultation to other agencies for planning, evaluation and research	Limited planning and research
	Program development	Development of CAB programs; standards and criteria enforced	Suggested standards; no regulatory measures

user with an appropriate resource. In addition to providing direct service to inquirers with safeguards for confidentiality and privacy, CAB and I&R programs also are designed to provide feedback and an organized data base that is useful for the purpose of policy formulation, social planning, legislative action and policy advocacy. As a universal point of entry, I&R and CAB services are designed to serve their local constituents without a service charge.

A common concern of all access services is to provide a balanced program that offers basic generic and specialized services that can meet the particular information, advice and referral needs of target populations. A balance is also sought between strictly adhering to the principle of neutrality and non-partisanship and possibly also carrying out an advocacy program on behalf of individual users or aggregates of users as may be indicated.

The location of CABs and I&R agencies often reflect a maldistribution of their respective services and a dearth of services in congested urban areas and sparsely populated rural areas. Also, the arrival of new ethnic minorities in the United States and United Kingdom has generated unprecedented needs that call for effectively linking the new immigrant with existing resources through organized access systems.

There are, however, also some marked differences between these service systems, as would be expected in countries that differ so vastly in geographic size and population. It should be noted that the United Kingdom does not have the subdivisions of states comparable to the level of state governments in the U.S. and therefore can maintain more direct accountability between the national government and local jurisdictions. Central government funds for CAB operations are granted directly to the National Association of Citizens Advice Bureaus (NACAB), which represents the central hub of all local CAB operations. Unlike the major financial support provided by local authorities to the British CABs, funding for I&R programs in the United States is usually supplied by a wide variety of multiple voluntary and public sources, often with little or no contributions from the local jurisdictional unit, and consequently with no significant investment by the local community. In the United States, no national policy has been formulated to promote centralized access systems, and federal funds to develop or support I&R operations are very limited. The only federally mandated I&R program that has promoted the establishment of I&R services and I&R systems consistently has been sponsored by the United States Administration on Aging.

Unlike the usual arbitrary training programs for I&R staff, a major strength of the British CAB system is the mandatory training program provided for all volunteers and other levels of staff, thereby providing a well-trained and well-informed work force. American observers have been impressed with the extensive utilization of large numbers of volunteers in CAB operations who receive systematic training in information, advice and advocacy programs in accordance with established standards and procedures. The benefits of a predominantly volunteer staff that is responsible for the delivery of direct services have proved not only cost-efficient but also service-effective, given the required training and staff monitoring that the CAB system provides.

One of the major differences between these two systems is the availability of a uniform information system, which NACAB has developed and supplies to every CAB in Britain, thereby ensuring standardization, regular updating and efficient retrieval of information. In contrast to the British system, American I&R programs operate under a myriad of information systems and diverse classification systems, thereby rendering comparability almost impossible. NACAB is empowered to accredit each CAB in accordance with established standards of operation. Although standards for I&R in the United States have been formulated and published through the joint collaborative efforts of the Alliance of Information and Referral Systems (AIRS) and the United Way of America, no regulatory mechanisms exist to ensure that these standards are implemented and enforced according to prescribed procedures.

In the United States there is no parallel to the hierarchical levels of organization that operate in the CAB system, with its established system of accountability that emanates from the individual bureau and its local management committee to the regional CAB Area Committee and ultimately to NACAB. Nor is there a centralized national resource such as the British Community Information Project, which was established in 1977 to provide a repository of information on operational access systems and a data base for research and experimentation to promote improved access systems.

In view of expanding social needs and shrinking resources, as have occurred since the mid-1970s in both the United States and the United Kingdom, it has become abundantly clear that interorganizational coordination and interagency collaboration of access systems with other human service systems are essential to facilitate organized entries to available services.

A GROWING LITERATURE

The growing literature in both Britain and the United States reflects a groundswell in the reported expansion of access systems. The largest volume of research reports on I&R systems in the United States have to date been conducted under the auspices of the U.S. Administration on Aging. In the voluntary sector, the United Way of America has historically been a major proponent of I&R services and has published a variety of materials on program development and staff training.

The United Way has developed a basic classification system for human services (identified as the United Way of America Service Identification System, or UWASIS), which has been adopted by a large number of I&R agencies. Since its founding in 1973, the national Alliance of Information and Referral Systems Inc. (AIRS) has been an important source of information on access systems through its published I&R directories, annual conference proceedings, official AIRS newsletter and publication of the professional *I&R Journal* since 1979. Through the collaborative efforts of the United Way of America and AIRS in the U.S. and Canada, national standards for information and referral were published in 1983.

As reported in Chapter 1 of this volume, NACAB has published a variety of occasional papers on research reports and special studies and has sponsored innovative programs to promote access to services. The publication of a newsletter, *The Owl*, and the availability of a variety of training manuals have provided information on CAB procedures and program development. Since 1977, the Community Information Project, described in Chapter 2, has become a national resource and repository for research studies, special studies and other published materials relevant to access systems in the United Kingdom.

While the state of the art in organized access services has advanced dramatically during the past decade, no comprehensive updated history or overview of the developments of CABs and I&R services is currently available. The 1966 study of CABs reported by Kahn and his associates in the monograph on *Neighborhood Information Centers* has exerted a profound influence on the development of I&R services in the U.S. based on an analysis of the CAB system in Britain and the recommendations suggested for the development of access systems in the U.S.

The only other cross-national report of access services is the series of unpublished papers presented at the Conference of European Social Development Programs that was held in Washington, D.C., in October 1979. This "Tenth National Group Conference on Access to Social Services," which was co-sponsored by the American Public Welfare Association and the United Nations, recommended expansion of multi-national communication and exchange of information on access to human services.

We hope this volume will contribute to the emerging literature and help to generate a continued and expanded interest in access systems in the international arena.

NOTES

1. An overview and analysis of I&R service systems in the U.S. will be reported by Risha W. Levinson in a forthcoming book, *Doorways to Human Services: I&R.* (Springer Publications, in process).

2. For discussion of CAB systems in Britain and options for the United States see *Neighborhood Information Centers: A Study and Some Proposals* (New York: Columbia University School of Social Work, 1966).

3. Four background papers were presented at the United Nations European Social Development Program (ESDP) Expert Group Meeting on Access to Social Services in October 1979. The authors of the papers were David M. Austin, Raymond T. Clarke, Alfred Kutzik, and Toshio Tatara.

I

CITIZENS ADVICE BUREAUS: CAB MODEL

All of the chapters in Part I deal with variations of the Citizens Advice Bureau Model as originally developed in the United Kingdom during World War II. The British CAB, as established in the early 1940s, represents the earliest model of an original access system designed to serve dual purposes: to facilitate access to needed services for the local citizen and to provide an information base for policy formulation and social planning.

The CAB system as it operates currently in England, Wales, Scotland, and Northern Ireland represents the most highly organized network of an entry system to human services because of its hierarchical structure and multiple levels of accountability. More specifically, the individual CAB is accountable to its local management committee and to a regional area committee which, in turn, is represented in the National Association of Citizens Advice Bureaus. The decentralized operations of CABs provide the direct services of information, advice, advocacy and referral to local users and rely on the local authority for major funding. On a national level, the centralized functions of the National Association of CABs (NACAB) include the use of a standard information system, staff training programs, standard setting, planned program development, and contributory funding to the local CABs.

In Chapter 1, Alex Eastabrook presents an overview of the British CAB system dating from its beginnings during World War II to its current operation in over 900 local bureaus. His major concern is the delivery of high-quality service through the implementation of national standards that are formulated and regulated by the central office of NACAB. The volunteer staff member who is described as "the first-line general practitioner" is required to undergo a planfully structured training program in preparation for the direct service role which volunteers assume in response to inquirers at local bureaus.

In discussing the second major aim of the CAB system, namely the social policy aspects of the CAB, Eastabrook calls for a more aggressive role on the part of NACAB in social policy formulation and social planning. While NACAB has, at times, served as a consultant at the request of Parliament, Eastabrook assigns greater responsibility to CAB leadership in promoting social legislation and social action.

Although Eastabrook points to the paucity of research in access systems, it is to his credit that he has served as the series editor for the publication of fifteen occasional papers by NACAB that deal with a wide range of research efforts pertaining to the social welfare system, the health care system, the legal system, and advocacy programs. New approaches to service delivery in the work place and in rural areas are reported as additional areas of interest and experimentation in facilitating access to services.

In the report on the British Community Information Project (CIP) in Chapter 2, the CAB system is referred to as but one of many access systems that operate in the United Kingdom. During the five-year period from 1977 to 1982, the CIP was transformed from a research program for community information located in the central office of the British Library System into a national resource center. The author suggests that the original association of the CIP with the British Library system has given the project a "neutral stance" and has fostered interagency collaborations and networking. The CIP has succeeded in developing positive working relationships and interagency cooperation with a wide variety of access systems including consumer advice centers, law centers, village contact programs, and new modes of service delivery, including mobile advice centers, telephone advice services, and experimental programs in the application of computer technology. CIP has been eminently successful in involving agencies with a minimum of professional resistances. Despite differences in organizational structure and styles of service delivery, competition for funding, and basic service philosophies, the CIP has been successful in developing a national network of service organizations that includes NACAB as well as other access systems. The project has succeeded in linking up with such varied organizations as the Association of Housing Aid, the Law Centers Federation, and, more recently, a newly formed network known as DIAL (the Disabled Information and Advice line). CIP has also been an important unifying force in the Federation of Independent Advice Centers.

In addition to its own program of community research, the CIP also has assisted researchers in devising service classifications, preparing information packets for service providers, and assisting with information materials for the Asian-speaking population. CIP also has been a major distributor of published materials on access systems, including bibliographies, handbooks and specialist guides and other resource materials. By offering personal consultant programs, CIP has established a two-way flow of information through its interagency contacts and promoted research studies and program initiatives in new settings and new areas, including the application of computer technology in the human services.

In tracing the ten-year experience of CABs in New Zealand (1973-1983) in Chapter 3, Neil G. Smith traces the development of CABs from local bureau operations to regional structures and the concurrent emergence of a national association. As in the British system, the pivotal provider of direct services is the trained volunteer, whom Smith regards as the information expert and "the enabler" rather than the "advice giver." In Smith's judgment, the volunteer tends to be more responsive to the service inquirer than is the professional social worker, whom Smith critically regards as being "professionally" overinvolved with bureaucratic requirements and organizational constraints. Smith concurs with Eastabrook on the importance of utilizing an access system to generate social action programs, citing the effectiveness of the CAB provider in dealing with the housing problem in New Zealand. While CABs are basically viewed as a generalist service, Smith anticipates that CABs may compete with the growing number of specialist crisis centers, a pattern which has recently become evident in Great Britain.

The chapter on Cyprus reported by Eleni Wiltcher, offers important lessons on the critical role of leadership and the need for community readiness in establishing citizen advice bureaus. Trained in the British tradition of the CAB model, Wiltcher reports on her leadership role and her limited success in transposing the British model to Cyprus. The initial enthusiasm of interested groups was apparently short-lived and insufficient to carry out the project of a CAB system from the initial planning phase to successful implementation. The reluctance on the part of the community leaders at the point of start-up, and the limited time available to Wiltcher to follow through with her initial efforts in leadership presented serious constraints in the launching of a CAB system in Cyprus. Nevertheless, the reported organizational case history remains instructive.

As a background to the CAB system in Israel in Chapter 5, Yemina Barneis and Ofra Fisher offer a brief overview of the relatively recent history of the Israeli state. The authors trace the development of the CAB network from its early organizational structure as a voluntary agency to its current operation, which is under the auspices of the National Department of the Ministry of Social Welfare. Thus, the CAB system, which began as an experimental project, has become a government-sponsored project that operates on a national level. Similar to the British CAB, the Israeli CAB system offers direct services at the local level, as well as accountability on the regional and national levels. Other similarities include the mandatory training programs for volunteers, who apparently are held in the same high esteem in Israel as in Britain. Volunteers are primarily senior citizens and are described as central to the "impartial system of peer counseling."

The authors call attention to two major problems that affect the Israel CAB system: firstly, that when social problems become most acute and services are urgently needed, CAB services tend to be cut back; and secondly, that because many immigrant-citizens with multi-cultural backgrounds have experienced frustrations in their efforts at socialization and acculturation, these users tend to be wary and untrusting of the actual help that the CAB can offer.

In Chapter 6, "Network of Access Systems in Israel: A Conceptual Analysis," Abraham Doron and Eli Frenkel analyze CABs as one type of system of entry among other access systems. While there is no central coordinating agency in Israel comparable to the British Community Information Project (CIP), the authors suggest a conceptual model of access systems which includes a broad range of different types and levels of access services. Selected entry systems are analyzed according to the availability of the access systems to the total population, such as public health services, and the availability of services to selected population groups, such as the aged. The types of information services may also vary, depending on whether they operate within a specific jurisdiction, such as the Jerusalem Municipal Information Office, or whether the CAB system is a national network. Services vary from information-giving only to referrals and brokerage services for clientele. Irrespective of the level and type of access service in operation, the authors emphasize the overall need for greater involvement of access agencies in social policy and social action programs. This emphasis on the broader social aspects of access services is in agreement with the views expressed by Easta-brook of the United Kingdom and Smith of New Zealand regarding the capabilities of access systems to serve as vehicles for policy formulation and program innovation.

1

THE BRITISH CITIZENS ADVICE BUREAU
Entry to the Social Services System

ALEX EASTABROOK

Perhaps the best definition of the role a Citizens Advice Bureau should assume in the community is given by Kahn in his description of neighborhood information center:

> The term is here employed for the entry point to the total social services system, whether education, housing, public assistance, recreation, social insurance, consumer guidance, homemakers, or many other specific fields. The centre would have to be a general, unbiased, easily accessible, visible, unstigmatized, universally usable facility. Its basic function would be information, advice, and referral. (Kahn, 1973: 164)

As basic functions, this center would provide simple and complex information, explain the law, advise on how to proceed, refer to specialist agencies by appointment, provide a supportive service, write letters, and mediate as indicated. More complex functions could be added, such as case advocacy, community work, "class" advocacy (the seeking of policy change), "outreach" (the recruitment of clients), and feedback or monitoring.

This is perhaps an ideal world. The reality is that the efficiency, in terms of both service provision and cost, of such an entry point to variously complicated networks of social services is not always recognized by funding agencies or by legislators. There is, however, general agreement for the provision of first-line introductory advice and information service that is given that role and the resources with which to fulfill it.

As early as the 1940s, Beveridge, the architect of the British social security system, recommended that

> there should be in every local Security Office an Advice Bureau to which every person in doubt or difficulty can be referred, and which will be able to tell him not only about the official provision for social security, but about all the other organs—official, semi-official, and voluntary, central or local—which may be able to help him in his difficulty. (Beveridge, 1942)

Thirty-five years later, the National Consumer Council concluded, in a major review of advice agencies, that

> small GP (General Practitioner) advice centres should become the principal constituent of the future service. . . . No other organisation can rival the Citizens Advice Bureaux in organisation and experience. So we see the CABx as providing the basic local general practitioner service that would be the foundation tier of a properly integrated local advice structure. (National Consumer Council, 1977: 64).

The remainder of the chapter will describe the CAB Service, as the entry point to the social services system.

HISTORY

While there were a small number of local advice centers in existence during the 1920s and 1930s, it was the trauma of the 1939-1945 period that gave the CABs their initial impetus. During the 1938-1939 period, as war became more and more likely, the need for local centers, which could act as a focus for giving advice and information to the public likely to be affected by bombing and evacuation, began to be identified. Within a short time after the outbreak of war, over 1,000 such centers were established and the Citizens Advice Bureau service, as a national service, had begun.

The wartime CABs were established through a variety of local mechanisms, usually at the instigation of existing voluntary organizations such as personal service societies and councils of social service. Some bureaus were run by local authorities, and one by the Public Assistance Department. Quite soon, however, a fairly clear organizational pattern emerged for the service, with each bureau being run by an independent, community-based organizing committee, and with the National Council for Social Service providing a central service function, especially in relation to the provision of information material to the bureaus.

The experience of the wartime CABs indicated the need for a continuing advice and information service for the public. During the war, both the local bureaus and the National Council of Social Service were aided by central government funding. Later local bureau funding was withdrawn, although local authorities were both encouraged and given specific powers to fund local CABs—an option that many local authorities at the time accepted.

The service also began to pay closer attention to both constitutional and administrative structure. In 1950 the central Citizens Advice Bureau committee of the National Council of Social Service adopted the name "National Citizens Advice Bureau Committee" and drew up a constitution that recognized the role of the local bureaus and their representatives in the organization as a whole. However, in the same year the government also withdrew its grant to the National Council of Social Service for certain of the central and regional services operated by them. As a result, throughout the 1950s the CAB service was able to maintain only a small central secretariat and an almost non-existent regional support structure at a time when the local bureaus were establishing a new "postwar" role. This meant that while local bureaus were free to develop their services to meet local needs, there was little opportunity for the movement as a whole to identify gaps in the services being offered and to explore new areas of involvement. Essentially this was a period of local consolidation rather than national development.

This situation began to change rapidly in the 1960s and 1970s as growing interest began to develop at the central government level in the working horizons and the potential of the CAB service. This expressed itself in the mid 1960s with renewed grant aid from the central government for central and regional services and encouragement to local authorities to assist any request for help in the expansion of an existing bureau or the provision of a new one. The '60s marked the beginning of continuing government support for the CAB service and its development.

In 1965, the grant for central and area support services from central government was a total of £35,000. Nineteen years later government funds amounted to £6 million, including some direct grants to individual bureaus. The nature in which this financial support was given also proved to be significant for the CAB service. The initial grant was made by the Board of Trade on the recommendation of the Molony Committee on Consumer Protection as a recognition of the part played by the CABs in dealing with consumer problems. The intent was to strengthen the CABs generally. Successive central government support continued to be channelled through the Board of Trade and its successors. However, while support has clearly been for the development of the "generalist" CAB, the pattern of grant aid centrally for bureaus has continued to show a major interest from central government in the specialist consumer protection aspects of CABs work, perhaps at the expense of other, equally important, aspects of the work of the CAB service.

The latter half of the 1960s showed a steady expansion in the number of CABs, a pattern of growth that continued and accelerated during the 1970s. The 1970s and early 1980s have been a period of particularly rapid growth for the bureaus. In 1974, the central government recognized the need for funding the development of the service with a five-year "pump-priming" grant, originally amounting to £900,000. At the end of the five years, that grant totalled almost £3 million, which enabled the establishment of over 100 new bureaus in partnership with local authorities, and over 500 bureaus received some form of grant towards improving their service. The number of bureaus increased from 473 in 1966 to 674 in 1976. By 1980 the number was over 850. Parallel to that development was a rapid increase in the number of inquiries from just over 1 million in 1966 to over 5 million in 1983.

In 1978, the CAB Service became a separate organization in its own right, the National Association of Citizens Advice Bureaus (NACAB). In 1980 central government withdrew its grant from the local Consumer Advice Centers (CACs) and gave a yearly grant to NACAB of approximately £1½ million in recognition of the additional work which would result from the CAC closures. Just under 50 percent of this additional grant was given to bureaus in areas where CACs had closed.

Thus, a considerable and rapid growth in the number of bureaus occurred over a relatively short period—a quantitative development. The qualitative development of the service in terms of standards, depth of advice work, recruitment, training, and methods of provision, tended to take second place until the more recent period. As additional funding has become scarcer, and the CAB Service has had to adapt and respond to development, greater recognition has been given to the need to improve the standard and quality of the work of

CABs. At a policy level the CAB service had to reach a balance between the needs and demands of a rapidly increasing number of clients, and the kind of operation that had been established in the bureaus practice by the bureau organizers and their staff of workers and the local management committees. Some conflict also emerged as a result of the need to introduce a degree of "professionalism" and the inherent reliance on the volunteer "amateur." The major obstacle has been and still is a lack of adequate resources with which to operate a "total service" based on the principles discussed in the following section.

PRINCIPLES

The basic principles of the CAB Service are independence, impartiality and objectivity, and confidentiality of service. The aims of the service are stated as follows:

—to ensure that individuals do not suffer through ignorance of their rights and responsibilities or of the services available, or through an inability to express their needs effectively;
—to exercise a responsible influence on the development of social policies and services, both locally and nationally.

CABs provide a free and impartial service to all individuals consisting of information guidance and support. CABs also provide feedback to local and central government by utilizing the experience gained. In addition to information provision, with the agreement of their inquirers' bureaus can take appropriate action in situations where the clients are unable to take such action effectively themselves. Local bureaus can take their services out to a wider public in whatever way is most suited to their area. It should be noted that the NACAB also shares its information and training services with other agencies. Where a specialist agency that is acceptable to the client is available, it may be more appropriate for that agency to take the necessary action.

CABs recognize the need for a generalist service but also for specialist advice to be accessible to all. Bureau staff is therefore urged to make the best use of the specialist services available, including holding specialist sessions on their premises.

It is accepted that many problems would never occur if individuals were better informed of their rights and responsibilities. Bureau workers are, therefore, encouraged to give talks to local educational institutions and other groups and organizations about the rights and obligations of the individual in society. They also describe a CAB, what to expect from it and how to use it.

The experience of bureaus in handling unsolicited inquiries is used on a national, area or local basis to influence government or other bodies to change the law and administrative practices where these warrant review. The presentation of evidence on the need for change is an essential and natural complement to CAB work in dealing with individual problems.

The three basic tenets of the CAB Service are:

(1) *Independence*. The service provided by CABs is completely independent. Bureaus are therefore able to offer impartial advice to all inquirers and to take up any issue with the appropriate authority on behalf of individuals or groups. The policies and practices of the CAB Service are decided solely by its members. Decisions are made collectively through local management committees, area committees and, on the national level, NACAB's council. No other individual or agency, even one giving financial support or other aid to bureaus, has any right to determine or influence these policies or practices.

(2) *Impartiality and Objectivity*. The service provided by CABs is impartial. It is open to everybody, regardless of race, creed or politics, and advice and help are given on any subject without any preconceived attitude on the part of the organization. Appropriate action is taken on behalf of the inquirer regardless of how unpopular or unpalatable it may be with the community or the bureau itself. The provision of an impartial and objective service demands that bureau staff members must recognize their own prejudices and sometimes take action to control their feelings.

(3) *Confidentiality*. Bureaus offer confidentiality to inquirers. Nothing learned by a bureau from inquirers, including the fact of previous visits, will be passed on to anyone outside the CAB Service without their express permission.

STRUCTURE

The CAB Service is made up of over 900 full- and part-time bureaus throughout the United Kingdom, supported by 25 area offices, including the Northern Ireland Association (NIACAB), the Scottish Association (SACAB), and the Greater London CAB Service (GLCABS).

Each bureau is a local self-governing unit, organized in a community for the citizens of the particular community. Bureaus are governed by a management committee which represents local interests, including voluntary and statutory bodies. These may include community groups and other appropriate voluntary organizations active in the community, together with local authority departments such as Social Services or Trading Standards.

The day-to-day administration of a bureau is the responsibility of the bureau organizer. The number of staff members varies according to local needs and facilities, and staff may be paid or voluntary, full- or part-time. Most bureaus rely heavily on the commitment of volunteers who staff the bureau on a regular sessional basis.

Bureaus are grouped in CAB areas and each area is serviced by an area office, which acts as the link between the bureaus and the central administration. The area officer heads a team which is responsible for servicing the area committee, providing training at all levels in the area, promoting new bureaus and new services within existing bureaus, providing support to management committees, and maintaining standards in accordance with the requirements for membership of the NACAB. The area officers also are responsible for ensuring that the central administration is aware of the needs and problems of bureaus in their respective areas.

Each bureau is represented on an area committee, which, in its turn, elects a representative to the council of the NACAB. The council, together with its executive committee, is responsible for national policy, which may arise from motions at the annual general meeting; motions forwarded from an area committee or from other committees of the council; submissions made by specialist staff; or matters of general concern. Provision of support for bureaus and for staff in the areas is by the administrative and specialist staff in the central office in London. The Scottish and Northern Ireland associations provide complementary services to deal with the different needs of their respective countries.

STANDARDS OF SERVICE

The CAB Service is a voluntary and charitable organization. Maintaining the highest possible standards for maximum effectiveness of the service offered is a major concern of the NACAB. Membership of the NACAB is restricted to the bureaus which have satisfied the following requirements of the Council:

(1) *The Constitution*. All member bureaus must be governed by a constitution that is acceptable to the NACAB and registered with the Charity Commissioners as a charity. Bureaus must produce audited accounts and an annual report.

(2) *Management*. A member bureau must have a management committee, the members of which have a real involvement in the affairs of the bureau. The committee must meet at least three times a year and be responsible for preparing annual estimates of expenditures, presenting audited statements of accounts, and making available for circulation a report on the work of the bureau. The committee should include representatives from appropriate voluntary and statutory organizations.

(3) *Premises*. Interviewing must be in confidence and the interview rooms must reflect this. The bureau must have its own telephone line, receiver, and entry in the telephone directory. Premises should be readily accessible and immediately identifiable.

(4) *Staff*. All staff members must work in the bureau for a sufficient time each week to ensure an adequate and growing experience with the CAB Service. Interviewers need to attend a minimum of one session per week plus attendance for formal training. Appointment and retirement ages are specified.

(5) *Training*. All staff members who interview clients must complete the basic training course and undertake such further training as is required.

(6) *Selection*. The management committee appoints a selection panel, which selects the organizer and the new workers.

(7) *Records*. A daily record must be kept of all inquiries received, and statistical returns made.

(8) *Opening Hours*. The bureau should open at least two hours each day on five days of the week, preferably at the same time each day.

(9) *Publicity*. All available means of publicity should be used to bring the service of the bureau to the notice of the public.

FUNCTIONS

It is not possible to attempt a better description of the actual work carried out by a CAB than that identified by Brooke (1972: 46) as five basic functions:

Information giving implies an essentially passive role on the part of the informer. What the informer is doing is passing on information, giving relevant leaflets or explanatory leaflets, explaining generally about social services, and eligibility. To give adequate information may mean that the worker has to consult reference books, statutes or explanatory leaflets. It means that generally the informer will not probe beyond the presenting problem.

Advising has two aspects. The adviser not only may interpret the information in order to suit it to the needs of the inquirer, but may also offer an opinion about the wisdom of obtaining a solution in one way in contrast to another way. An adviser may find it necessary to go beyond the problem presented, to see if there is a far more serious problem.

Referral is a process that may happen as a result purely of information given and may occur after the inquirer and adviser have discussed the problem. The referral process also covers those situations in which the adviser makes contact with the specific agency, and arranges an appointment.

Action involves doing something on behalf of the inquirer over and above the giving of information and advice. Action may take the form of writing a letter for the inquirer to take to the agency to which he has been referred, or it could entail telephoning or writing the agency directly. In other words this process involves *advocacy* on the part of the worker.

Another function can be carried out by agencies, namely a *feedback* function. This involves the agency in trying to achieve an overall solution, not only a solution for the individual, by reporting back on the experience of the agency. This possible aspect of the information and advice process implies that the agency is seen as critical of a current situation. The feedback function has another aspect, since many problems which people may experience are similar: therefore, these are collective problems as opposed to exclusively individual problems. Any information and advice agency that is consulted can try to help on the strictly individual level or on the collective level, which may in the end lead to a more satisfactory solution.

Information and Advice Provision

The basic functions of a CAB are information, advice, and referral. Only belatedly has the CAB Service been able to pay serious attention to the action/advocacy and feedback functions.

The central information system, prepared for use by every CAB, is the fundamental "tool of the trade." The functions of the central Information Department of NACAB are first, to ensure that all bureaus have readily available to them all of the information they may need to assist members of the public; and second, to provide the machinery whereby the NACAB may call for reforms in social legislation and practices where the experience of its bureaus indicates that such reform is necessary. The department provides information for all bureaus by the regular circulation of information materials and by the operation of a "consultancy" service. The information "pack" is circulated once a month.

The material distributed consists of the following:

(1) *Information Circulars* are items that deal with new legislation as it comes into force, areas of the law on which CAB clients are likely to seek advice, or particular firms or organizations about which inquiries are frequently made.

(2) *Leaflets and Booklets* are provided by government departments and other bodies and serve as a compatible part of the comprehensive information service.

(3) *An "Action List,"* which, in addition to providing a checklist of all the material in each circulation, also updates and amends the material previously circulated.

(4) *A "Noticeboard"* that is designed to complement the items of information and to be read by all bureau staff members immediately upon receipt of their pack. It provides a brief comprehensive summary of changes in the law and current items of immediate interest, and, where appropriate, directs the reader to more detailed information in an enclosed circular.

(5) *Reference Books* are used to supplement the information circulated to bureaus. Bureaus need to hold certain standard reference books, which are provided as part of the information service. In addition, guidance is also given to any bureau wishing to increase its reference works by the provision of a monthly book list containing reviews of relevant publications.

A considerable number of sources are used to collect potential material for NACAB's circulation of information. They include *Hansard* (The House of Commons daily record); the daily list of publications from Her Majesty's Stationery Office; the national daily press; numerous Journals; and press releases issued by government departments. The major sources are Acts of Parliament, Statutory Instruments, White Papers, Green Papers, and so forth. All the material collected is screened and a decision is made as to whether it is of sufficiently common interest to justify distributing it to all bureaus. A draft item is then prepared and sent to the appropriate outside body or bodies to be checked. In the case of new legislation, this will normally involve the civil servants who have been involved in the passage of the legislation through Parliament, trade associations, lawyers known to have an interest in the particular field, and other specialists. It is only after this rigorous checking process that the information is printed and circulated to the bureaus.

The advice CABs give to their clients is based mainly on the stock of information sent out by the central office. To provide this service to bureaus, there is a constant check on relevant new legislation, changes in the provision of services to the public, and the emergence of other helping organizations, so that the facts bureaus have in their files are always kept up to date. The monthly information pack that is sent to all bureaus is the means of updating the information system.

The present filing system for this information was developed to enable bureau workers to keep this wealth of available information in a form that is logical and easy to update. The system is not unlike the reference system in a public library, where books are filed according to broad subject heading and subheadings. In the CAB system, all information is classified under sixteen broad subject headings, which may include such diverse headings as employment and leisure activities.

Each of these sixteen main headings is then subdivided. For example, the "housing, property, and land" category has subdivisions on homelessness, private tenancies, and rates among a total of nine in all. The range and importance of the information service can be judged by the number of current individual circulars held by bureaus stemming from government regulations and legislation.

In addition to the central information service, which covers items applicable nationally, each CAB holds files on items which are locally applicable. Although these vary in extent and scope, there is a local information index of file headings, which ensures some degree of standardization.

Action: Mediation/Advocacy

Most CABs undertake action on behalf of clients in some form or another. The information and advice given will include a wide variety of mediation activities, ranging from telephone calls to drafting letters on behalf of a client right through to acting on a case on behalf of a client. The cases may vary in nature from a debt problem where possible prosecution is pending to a situation that pertains to electricity or gas disconnections because of unpaid bills. This "case-oriented advocacy" is common practice in CABs.

Since the mid-1970s, there has been an obvious thrust to broaden the case-oriented advocacy services, generally limited to a selected clientele, to an explicit policy to develop effective overall services to larger groups of clients. Local bureaus have facilitated this development by encouraging workers to become more extensively involved in claimants' cases and adjusting the agency's working patterns with a stronger emphasis on the wider dissemination of information and training resources to community groups and other social welfare agencies.

The NACAB assists local bureaus to implement this broader policy by training and by adapting its national information to deal with matters such as welfare rights. In particular, workers are encouraged to undertake representation work. A representation service based on existing bureau staffing structure is possible, but a national service based on such a model alone is not practicable. A mixed approach in representation services is actually more practical. The NACAB is currently engaged in the role of an enabler in the process of identifying gaps in representation services, and in helping to fill these deficiencies through staff training and through lay representation available to tribunal agencies that operate outside CAB.

Feedback/Prevention: The "Second Aim"

This second aim is probably the most underdeveloped function in the CAB Service, and yet, paradoxically, it is a major means of relieving the stress on bureaus and the distress of clients. An effective feedback policy which has a *preventive* objective through social policy change, added to an *educative* function in the community could go a long way toward making information and advice agency services unnecessary to many thousands of people.

The first of these, the preventive function of social policy change has been very largely stillborn in the CAB, since this activity has been considered both partial and political, neither of which has been acceptable within the existing policies of the NACAB until recently. The second, that of community education, is also almost totally underdeveloped. The concept of educated self-help is perhaps not a feasible short-term possibility, but it ought to be a long-term objective. To educate a society in the provision of its essential services should be an inherent part of that society. But millions of people either do not know their benefits, or, even if known, do not know how to claim their rights as citizens.

The current feedback system in the CAB permits responses to existing legislation and its effects based on direct bureau experience. The NACAB identifies such "information retrieval" as part of its central work. Its main function is the retrieval of information regarding the bureaus' practical experience of dealing with the inquiries brought to them by the general public. All bureaus maintain a record of their day-to-day work with clients. By analyzing this information, the NACAB finds itself in a position to comment on a vast range of social issues, policy decisions and legislation which affect CAB clients and, by implication, other members of the community.

The NACAB therefore works with bureaus to retrieve this information according to selected specific issues relevant to its interest. Clearly, as a generalist advice service, the range of subjects on which the NACAB may be expected to comment could be as broad as that upon which bureaus workers are asked to advise. In practice, to do so would be impossible, so choices have to be made.

The selection process is particularly important, since the NACAB is committed not only to responding to issues raised from outside but also to initiating debate on problems and concerns identified by bureaus. Informal resolutions from area committees and recommendations from advisory groups all influence the identification of the subjects for review and discourse.

"Specialist" Advice Services

The provision of specialist advice—for example, legal advice or debt counseling—plays an increasingly important part in CAB work. This is when the CAB uses the services of specially trained workers or of professionals to give free sessions or "clinics" on the CAB premises. The direct provision is an extension of the referral service to agencies or professionals outside the CAB, and is recognized as preferable because of the high dropout rate among clients referred elsewhere.

The most developed example of specialist advice is the "legal rota scheme," in which local solicitors attend the CAB on a rota, not only to give free legal diagnostic interviews but also to accept inquiries needing further action at their own offices. The success of this rota scheme—now widespread in CABs in urban areas, less so in rural CABs—has encouraged similar clinics in other areas of CAB work. Housing advice, financial and money advice including budgeting and debt counseling, planning advice, and, increasingly, advice on enti-tlement to state benefits ("welfare rights advice"), are more and more seen in CABs.

A second kind of specialist advice service occurs when a CAB takes its service to a place where generalist and specialist advice is needed but a full CAB is not possible. Examples of this kind of service are hospitals, prisons, courts, factories, old people's clubs, poverty areas, and areas with high unemployment. It has become recognized that CABs need to target their clients in ways such as this and to ensure that the service gets to the client rather than the client to the service. This is particularly important for the areas with a high con-centration of "information poor," where the ability to understand the social services system is the most needed and the least available.

STAFFING

Over 90 percent of the 1,200 people working in bureaus are volun-teers. Some have specific skills such as administrative experience, legal or financial knowledge, and social work, but all are selected for their maturity, understanding and sympathy. Staff members are ex-pected to be impartial and flexible. Bureau work calls for interper-sonal skills, deliberate commitment, and a professional attitude. Each bureau worker is on duty at least once a week except during holidays or illness. All bureau workers are expected to attend regular workers' meetings and local and regional training courses as they become familiar with the information resources in the local bureau and the working of the filing and indexing system.

From the very outset, the CAB Service has been essentially "volunteer" in nature. It was the volunteer who provided the initial enthusiasm and drive that established the service during the wartime years, and who maintained the CABs during the lean years of the 1950s. The volunteer in the 1970s was also at the forefront in dealing not only with the vast increase in the number of inquiries but the growing complexity of the inquiries themselves. As the influence of legislation on the relationship between the individual and society gained greater prominence, and as government information increas-ingly pointed the public toward the CAB Service for advice, the demands being made on the volunteer rapidly increased.

Increasingly it was recognized that a paid corps of staff was necessary for the efficient administration of a bureau, and in 1974, at the annual general meeting, the NACAB called upon central government to recognize the need for paid bureau organizers and staff. The pivotal role in the CAB Service is that of the organizer of the bureau. This is increasingly the case as the pressures of work on bureaus mount and inquiries become increasingly complex. Yet in the last survey in 1980 only 150 organizers in over 750 main bureaus were both full-time and paid. The job specification for a CAB organizer makes quite clear the importance of the organizer's responsibilities.

The bureau organizer is responsible to the management committee for the following:

   (i) Requirements for membership
  (ii) Staffing
 (iii) Administration
 (iv) Liaison and public relations
  (v) Finance
 (vi) Development
 (vii) Membership
(viii) Area Committee Representation

Recruitment and Selection

There is a standard procedure for the recruitment of new workers to CAB that is generally followed, with some variations, in most CABs. It is designed to provide a systematic means of ensuring that the best possible applicants are recruited into the service and that all potential workers are given the opportunity to decide whether they wish to commit themselves to the work.

Recruitment. The most commonly used method of recruiting is by publicity in the local press. An advertisement can be inserted asking for volunteers, or it may be possible to arrange for a feature article on the bureau, highlighting its work and explaining that more workers are needed. Local radio is increasingly being used in the same way. Posters and leafleting campaigns in the neighborhood, involving other organizations as well as the general public, may also be useful. Members of the bureau staff also find that giving talks to other local groups may bring in volunteers.

When a new bureau is to be opened and a number of new workers are needed, other methods are also available. It is common to call a public meeting, advertising its purpose extensively, as a means of alerting as many people as possible to the promotion. At the same time it may be helpful to arrange with a local continuing education college a course of general interest to people considering voluntary work, with an offer of selection for CAB work for suitable candidates.

Many bureaus find that workers can also be recruited by personal recommendation of another worker or by a member of the bureau management committee. In the best circumstances this can be very successful—a volunteer recruited by an experienced bureau worker is often well informed as to the nature of the work and the commitment needed. It is essential in these cases, however, that all those involved should understand that the selection procedure is a rigorous one and that there is no commitment to take on even a locally eminent applicant unless he or she is suited to the work.

Whatever method of recruitment is used, it is always made clear from the outset the type of person sought for position and the commitment that the bureau expects in terms of time, training and reliability.

Selection. After recruitment, the first step in the selection procedure is normally an informal interview with the bureau organizer. Here applicants see the bureau at work and have an opportunity to discuss the duties of a CAB worker and the terms on which they may be accepted. This first interview is vital in establishing a common view of the work and setting out the expectations both of applicants and the bureau organizer. It is made clear that acceptance for full-scale bureau work will depend on the results of the ensuing selection and training process.

The organizer in this first interview pays particular attention to applicants' motivation to undertake the work, their willingness to spend the necessary time in training and attending the bureau, and their ability to fit in with the existing team of workers. It is also necessary to establish applicants' suitability for the training required. A genuine acceptance of the need to train, regardless of previous experience or age, and the capacity to benefit intellectually and personally from the training are equally important.

If the organizer feels that the applicants are suitable for CAB work, they normally are asked to complete a standard application form for the information of the selection panel. The point is made that the application does not imply any obligation to either party. References are also taken up at this stage. If the organizer has a poor impression of the applicants, they are rejected at this point.

At some stage in the newcomer's training it is essential that the candidates be interviewed by a committee, made up of one or two members of the management committee and the area officer. The organizer's participation in this interview is a matter of choice. The selection committee has an important role to play in maintaining the quality of the CAB Service, and members are chosen and briefed carefully. Trainees are not allowed to see themselves, or to be seen by others, as CAB interviewers until they are formally accepted following a satisfactory probationary period.

Unsatisfactory applicants are informed verbally at the time of the interview or by letter, and, if appropriate, suggestions are made as to other forms of voluntary work for which they may be suited. Whether or not the second interview is held at this stage, the applicants who have been accepted for training are now expected to attend the bureau regularly, and the organizer arranges attendance at the next basic training course.

During the basic course, the training officer and the tutors will gather a good deal of useful information about the trainees. At the end of the course, an assessment is given to the organizer, at the very least on such matters as the regularity of attendance, punctuality, and return and quality of homework papers. This, and the organizer's own collected views on the suitability of the trainee, form the basis of a report by the organizer to the bureau management committee.

If applicants are selected for training by the selection committee, it is likely that they will have completed the course successfully, and, subject to a satisfactory report to the management committee, acceptance as bureau workers are a matter for formal confirmation at the end of a probationary period consisting of a minimum of 50 hours spread over three months. If accepted, the trainees are allowed to interview and continue in-service training as members of the team of interviewers until the probationary period is satisfactorily completed.

If the probationary period is successful, a formal letter is sent from the chair of the management committee accepting the trainees as bureau workers.

Training

Once selected for training, all bureau workers undertake the constituent parts of basic training; pre-training, the in-bureau training program provided by the organizer or tutor, the external basic training course, and any further training that may be considered appropriate. It is the combination of these elements that offers the full program of skills and knowledge which the new worker will need. The external course, therefore, has to be seen in the context of other formal and individual training, and as a vital element of the complete program. Because of the increased recognition of the importance of in-bureau training, many organizers have been led to delegate this task to a bureau tutor, who supervises the progress of trainees, arranges visits for observation, and generally provides opportunities for training at all levels for the bureau.

The "pre-training pack" provided by the central training department is designed as a briefing for the newly recruited trainees on the scope, style and implications of CAB work. The pack is divided into units, and the organizer or bureau tutor will normally decide whether to give the whole pack to the trainee at once or one or two units at a time. In either case it is essential that the trainee has the opporunity to discuss the content with the organizer or tutor so that questions can be answered, the trainee's understanding assured, and misconceptions averted.

In-bureau training introduces the trainees to CAB work in detail. Informal methods of training, involving reading, case discussion, practice exercises, and units of the in-bureau training pack, are used to develop the skills of mediation, interviewing, case recording, and the use of reference material. At the same time the trainees acquire the ethos of the CAB Service and begin to examine their attitudes in relation to those of the bureau.

The ex-bureau basic training course is normally provided at an area level for trainees from a cluster of neighboring bureaus. The course is practical in approach, and aims to equip the trainee with the skills and knowledge to deal with the simpler and more commonly ocurring problems relatively unaided.

Another crucial ingredient of the course is the further examination of the values and attitudes implicit in CAB work. It is considered that the service has an obligation to make its objectives and operating principles as clear as possible to recruits, and to give them the opportunity to see how the work will accord with their own values. This approach is central to the course, and every occasion is used to discuss any issues that might raise strong personal feelings within the context of the subject material. Thus, the social security session could include discussion of the right of the individual to receive help from the state, and the family and matrimonial session brings up questions on the role of the family and breakdown of marriage.

It is acknowledged that the trainees may need further training after the end of the ex-bureau course. Even the fuller training program in effect cannot leave the new workers fully prepared for practice as soon as the course is over. According to the needs and abilities of the individual trainees, they may be offered further self-study material, continued instruction within the bureau, or suitable courses as they are available.

TABLE 1.1   Inquiry Levels to CABs, 1974-1982

Inquiry Type: Selected Categories	1974-1975 ('000)	1981-1982 ('000)	Percentage of Change
(1) Family/personal	471	607	29
(2) Housing	453	684	51
(3) Consumer	399	790	98
(4) Employment	142	467	229
(5) Social security	118	595	404
Total all inquiries	2304	4515	96
Number of CABs	619	914	48

Clientele

It is recognized that many potential users do not find their way to organized services, since as Kahn says,

"Access requires mobility, information, and initiative . . . many people who need help suffer considerable buffeting until they reach a proper source of help, if indeed they ever do . . . many citizens never learn about rights, benefits or entitlements that would ease their lives . . . consumers may fail to find adequate means of redress." (Kahn, 1973: 162)

Although NACAB does not identify who its clients are, case records are filed that include age, sex, socioeconomic grouping, occupation, and other inquirer details. A recent survey establishing some CAB user characteristics found that numbers of male and female clients were approximately equal; that 40 percent of clients were aged over 50; that over half of the clients were married; that 74 percent had left school at the age of 16 years or earlier; and that 60 percent of all clients were in manual occupations. From this the CAB user could be described as older, undereducated and nonprofessional.

Some examples of the types of problems faced by clients of CABs were detailed anonymously in an application to central government for additional funding to enable the bureaus to cope with the increases in workload resulting from the effects of the economic recession over the period 1979-1981. These gave a dramatic picture of the type of multifaceted problems increasingly being brought by clients to CABs.

From an analysis of inquiries by selected categories to CABs over an eight-year period, 1974-1982, consumer inquiries almost doubled, increasing by 98 percent; employment inquiries increased by 229 percent; and social security inquiries increased by 404 percent (see Table 1.1). Total inquiries for these five categories increased by 96 percent, while total number of CABs increased by only 48 percent.

What is striking for a generalist agency such as CAB is the fact that in 1981-1982, 4½ million people out of a total population of approximately 55 million used a CAB, or twelve percent of the population.

Funding

The policy of the NACAB is that there should be a funding partnership between central and local government to fund the CAB Service. The existing partnership is recognized by central government, which places the responsibility for funding for local CABs firmly on local government, while providing grant aid for the central and area offices for support services, such as the information pack and the training program. In addition, central government provides over £1 million for grants to local bureaus, mostly to compensate for the additional work CABs have had to undertake following the closure of the specialist Consumer Advice Centers (CACs) in 1980.

In the main, however, virtually all CABs are funded locally, but not in any kind of systematic way. The basic elements of expenditure incurred by a bureau are for staff and staff training; for rent, heating, lighting and cleaning; for telephones and stationery; and for publicity. There may also be capital items of expenditure—for example, for premises improvements, alterations and equipment.

It can be safely concluded that the quality of service offered by a CAB is dependent on the resources available to it. The recognition by central government that the service needs a higher level of funding can be seen from Table 1.2, which shows marked increases in the numbers of inquiries and in the number of CABs, to which the central government has responded through generous increase funding over the last ten years.

The level of funding for individual bureaus from their local authorities, (the district councils, county councils, the metropolitan councils, and the London boroughs), which represents the other half of the "partnership," is not as encouraging. With the exception of some authorities, mainly in the high population areas, the levels of funding are very low.

A recent survey into the funding of CABs reveals that in over 60 percent of CABs, total annual expenditure was less than £5,000 (at

TABLE 1.2   Number of CABs Inquiry Levels
            and Central Government Income, 1971-1982

Year*	Number of CABs	Total Inquiries ('000)	Total Income from Central Government (£'000)
1972-1973	566	1881	110
1973-1974	614	1910	113
1974-1975	619	2304	397
1975-1976	674	2695	762
1976-1977	710	2890	1152
1977-1978	756	3100	1435
1978-1979	818	3295	1271
1979-1980	859	3485	1821
1980-1981	879	3929	4018
1981-1982	914	4337	4936

NOTE: The additional grant in respect of CAC closures was made available from 1980-1981 onward.
*The years of the Development Grant were 1974-1975 to 1978-1979.

1979-1980 prices). At today's prices, that figure could approximate £8,500. That is approximately the cost of one full-time salary. Examination of the earlier description of the work of an organizer, together with dramatic increases in inquiry levels to CABs, point to the need for funding for at least one full-time paid organizer in addition to operating costs in the smallest bureau, and for higher numbers of full-time paid staff plus operating costs in larger bureaus. This is in addition to the volunteers who make up over 90 percent of the workers in bureaus.

In 1977-1978, a development plan for funding the CAB Service was presented to the government. This plan identified the costs of a potential national network of some 1,400 CABs, compared with the figure at that stage of 756 main and extension bureaus. The plan assumed that well over 5 million inquiries would go to a national network of 1,400 CABs. With hindsight, it can be stated that this was an underestimation of the potential inquiry volume that the service could undertake in England, Wales, Scotland and Northern Ireland with a network of that size.

The broad total cost of that plan (at 1977-1978 prices) would have been approximately £20 million per annum had it been fully implemented. It was suggested that the plan should be a rolling program of build-up rather than a five-year fixed plan as in 1974-1979. However, the case made for a network of generalist advice centers with proper central and field support stood independently of consideration of how it should be implemented. It is of more than passing interest that the resource issues identified in that plan for resolution still form a part of the agenda for the CAB Service over coming years.

A second funding application in 1980 was made in the light of the effects of the economic recession in the CAB Service, having examined the future workload projections, both in terms of internal resources and internal and external indicators of future demand upon the CAB Service. The application included proposals to meet the extra workload, both current and envisaged, and sought (unsuccessfully) additional funds for: increasing public access, by longer opening hours, improving facilities in existing locations, and moving premises to better locations or opening extension or main bureaus in the catchment area served; more paid and volunteer generalist workers in CABs; and paid specialist workers in welfare rights/money advice work in individual CABs where there is at present no alternative source of necessary skills and the local circumstances indicate a need.

There is no doubt that additional funding is now the major priority for the CAB Service, particularly realistic funding at local levels so as to be able to meet existing and future demands for services. It is to the local authorities, in addition to central government, that the CAB Service will now need to look.

Networking/Linkage

In CAB operations, there is extensive liaison and linkage with voluntary and statutory organizations and with local and central government departments, at local, area and national levels.

Local and Area Linkage

At the local level, the CAB has client-based contact with professionals and specialists, such as solicitors. The bureau aims to have close client-based links with specialist advice centers, such as consumer centers, law and legal centers, and housing advice centers, and other more issue-based agencies, such as welfare rights agencies. These centers are mainly in urban areas. In addition to specialists and specialist advice centers, a local CAB will need to have close client-based links with statutory agencies at the local level, as, for example, Health and Social Security, Environment, Housing, and Employment departments.

Extensive contacts also need to be maintained with the local district councils and councillors over the level of the bureau grant aid and the state of the premises. It is advisable that the statutory departments, local advice centers, and the district council be represented on the CAB management committee, which has the responsibility for funding and staffing the bureau.

Given the extremely wide and varied contacts and informal links the CAB has at local level, it is surprising that the major formal linkage is to the referral system. In only a few areas is there formal interagency linking. There may be informal meetings and arrangements dealing with clients, but only seldom is a coordinating committee developed with responsibility for planning of local services. There are some advantages in the flexibility of the informal ad hoc linkage relationships which exist now, in that it is probably providing a better service for those clients who manage to get to the agency in the first place. Formal arrangements may tend to restrict agency intake. However, there are major disadvantages in that a lack of planning and coordination results in the problems of access described by Kahn:

> For lack of adequate access machinery and channeling provision, social services involve tremendous wastage. People in need of advice or service go from place to place, sometimes never getting to the right place, sometimes getting to the right place after inordinate expenditure of 'steering time' by personnel in a series of agencies, sometimes getting good service but using personnel where more "parsimonious" provision is possible.

> Since people in need of services will seek them wherever possible, a social services system without adequate channeling provision tends to provide a biased access. Each agency to which a person comes by chance or recommendation to ask for help has a stake in the outcome. Some want more cases; some do not want any; some want particular types of cases. More formal access machinery, while not free of stereotypes and subject to the perceptual and prescriptive biases of the system it serves, is less likely to be tied to the stakes and limited perspectives of given agencies, their characteristic vantage points, and the unique assessment about the superiority of their service modes—which are normal for agencies. (Kahn, 1973: 163)

National Linkage

The NACAB has formal links with other national agencies, with central government departments, and with individual experts, through their representation on the committees and advisory groups. There are in addition constant informal links between individuals. It is at the more formally structured level that discussions over policy and planning take place, not at the level of the local bureau.

A list of the organizations represented on the committees and groups is the easiest way to demonstrate the breadth of the formal links.

The "Legal Services Group" has representation from CABs, and from the Legal Action Group, The Law Society, the Lord Chancellor's Department, the Senate of the Bar, the Child Poverty Action Group, the National Consumer Council, and the London School of Economics;

The 'Welfare Rights Group' has representatives from CABs, and from the British Association of Social Workers, the Department of Health and Social Security, the Child Poverty Action Group, the London School of Economics, the Trades Union Congress, and the Department of Employment.

The "New Technology Group" has representatives from CABs, and from the Department of Trade, the Department of Industry, the Department of Health and Social Security, the Local Authority Management Services and Computer Committee, the Open University, the National Consumer Council, the Social Security Advisory Commission, and the Legal Technology Group.

The NACAB therefore is in a good position to contribute to developments in services in terms of specialist service provision. Where the NACAB is relatively inactive is in the field of overall planning of advice services, including the provision of bureaus, and the levels and standards of a nationally available service. The National Consumer Council (NCC) has begun the analysis of the overall provision of advice services with four publications, and a planning document. The four publications are "The Fourth Right of Citizenship" (1977), "The Right to Know" (1978), "Advice Agencies—What They Do and Who Uses Them" (1982), and "Information and Advice Services In The United Kingdom" (1983).

The NCC planning document describes a national policy for local information and advice services in terms of location, funding, staffing, client need, specialist/generalist, independence and interagency cooperation.

The debate is now beginning, and will become urgent because of the increasing need for information and advice. Interagency linkage at a national level is relatively well developed, and the CAB Service, together with other national agencies, is well placed to take a major part in that debate. However, at the local level the debate is almost nonexistent, overall national planning is probably anathema, and interagency linkage could therefore remain minimal.

FUTURE DIRECTIONS

Almost all the emphasis over the past ten growth years in CAB has been on quantitative needs, on more bureaus, on filling gaps, on funding levels, on meeting client demand. Latterly there has been an attempt at assessing qualitative performance and at improving the levels and extent of advice given. All this has been a relatively ad hoc development. Nowhere in this major growth period has there been a planned approach to meeting client need. This is not a criticism; it is a fact. There has been neither the time nor the resources available. A review of the ways in which the national and area structure meet bureau needs has now been undertaken. No review of the NACAB's work and needs in terms of the *potential client* demand has yet been considered.

It is legitimate to ask whether the policy objectives that stem from these aims satisfy the demands inherent in the aims. It could be argued that at this stage in the development of the CAB advice service network they do not. The future directions of the CAB Service will need to set specific policy objectives. The following is a possible list of such objectives which could guide the Service into the next ten years, in accordance with previously stated aims of the CAB Service.

(i) First-Line "General Practitioner"—It is recommended that the role of the *first-line general practitioner* be reorganized by local and central government as the entry point to the social service system. Add-on specializations and planned linkage with other agencies need to be acknowledged.

(ii) Funding—A stable funding partnership needs to be established in central and local government in accordance with the anticipated local demands for services based on selected and specific variables, such as population trends and type of catchment area.

(iii) Deficiencies—In the operation of existing CABs and the establishment of new CABs, the identification of current deficiencies and needs is important in assessing CAB operations relative to potential inquiry rates, clientele, funding patterns, staffing levels, and organizational planning on a national basis.

(iv) Clients' Needs—Maximizing the service to clients in terms of the client need implies identifying client types/needs at the local level, and gearing CABs to meet those needs.

(v) Interagency Networking—Developing links with other voluntary and statutory agencies to provide the best possible local service can avoid duplication. Availability of CAB Services (information, training) to other agencies, and affiliation with other agencies, in accordance with standards of service can promote effective networking.

(vi) Education and Prevention—By improving channels to central government and maintaining a feedback system at local, area and national levels, CABs can more rigorously influence social legislation both prior to and post-enactment. Client education at a local level can promote prevention and enhance quality of life.

(vii) Standards—To ensure the highest possible standards of service by every CAB, the standards to which all CABs conform require continuous refinement.

(viii) Service Delivery—Identification of new methods of service delivery and feasibility studies to test out these methods in relation to CAB programs can help to meet current and potential service needs, which will improve the ability of CABs to fulfill their client potential.

The major recommendations of the "Review of the National Association of Citizens Advice Bureaus," published in February 1984, are that the CAB Service should give priority to the basic functions of information and advice provision over those functions which involve taking action on behalf of clients; that feedback and evidence should be based clearly on bureau experience, avoiding a campaigning style; that the principles of impartiality, confidentiality, and independence should be maintained; that bureau management committees recognize their financial responsibilities and take an active part in monitoring the operation of the bureaus; that there should be more rigorous analysis of bureau statistics; that training for bureau workers should be more standardized and centrally coordinated; that the NACAB's strategic planning needs to be more realistic; that the management structure of the servicing staff of NACAB needed reorganization; and that central government should increase its funding to bureau through NACAB while preserving the principle of local authority funding for bureaus.

Essentially, the proposals amount to a streamlining of existing practice. The NACAB is asked to formulate its objectives for the future in more realistic terms. In the light of the current pressures on local authority funds, and the restrictions on public expenditure generally, the likelihood is that the short-term future will lead to bureau closures and to a period of contraction in the service generally. It is to be hoped that the projected economic recovery will allow for the national CAB coverage previously envisaged over the longer term. Otherwise, it will be increasingly difficult for the CAB service to implement its stated aims.

REFERENCES

Beveridge, Sir William (1942). *Social insurance and allied services* (para 397). Her Majesty's Stationery Office, Cmnd. 6404.

Borrie, G. (1982). *Advice agencies–What they do and who uses them.* National Consumer Council.

Brooke, R. (1972). *Information and advice services.* London School of Economics Occasional Papers on Social Administration, No. 46.

Kahn, A. (1973). *Social policy and social services.* New York: Random House.

National Consumer Council (1977). *The fourth right of citizenship. Review of the National Association of Citizens Advice Bureaus.* (1984). Her Majesty's Stationery Office, Cmnd. 9139.

2

THE COMMUNITY INFORMATION PROJECT
A British Resource Center

GRAINNE MORBY

The Community Information Project was conceived as a conventional information center to provide assistance to researchers and practitioners concerned with community information. From that beginning it has developed into a major national resource center that has contributed significantly to the development of information and advice provision.

The project was established in November 1977 by the British Library Research and Development Department as part of its emerging program of research into community information. The British Library provided the funds for the first 4½ years of the project's life, and in this way helped it to become firmly established. As this initial period of funding came to an end, it became obvious to everyone associated with the project that the work should continue, and so, in April 1982, the Community Information Project Ltd. was established to act as the national resource center for the information and advice movement.

The reconstituted project is now operating successfully and is continuing to meet the movement's needs by

(1) Working with individual information and advice centers
(2) Working with national associations and networks
(3) Undertaking specific pieces of research

This chapter attempts to describe the development of the project during its first five years and to record the contribution which the project has made. The needs the project is meeting now are even more pressing than they were back in 1977. The number and scope of information and advice centers continues to grow, and as new forms of service are developed there is continuing need for objective evaluation, informed assistance, and thorough research. The Community Information Project Ltd. aims to provide all of these.

THE ORIGINS OF THE COMMUNITY INFORMATION PROJECT

Organized community information services really began in the United Kingdom during World War II with the creation of a network of Citizens Advice Bureaus, set up to provide basic information and guidance about how to survive in war-time conditions. Over 1000 of these Citizens Advice Bureaus were established during the War, and many have continued until this day. There was, however, a marked reduction in their number immediately after the war, and it is only within the last few years that the number has approached the 1000 mark again.

Other forms of advice centers are of more recent origin. The first consumers advice center was established by the Consumers' Association in Kentish Town in 1969 and the first law center was founded in North Kensington in 1970. Since that time there has been a dramatic increase in the number of advice centers and in the range of specialist subjects covered. Isolating the precise cause for this rapid growth is difficult.

In the *The Fourth Right of Citizenship,* published by the National Consumer Council, (NCC) in 1977, it is noted that

> Advice is a growth industry. During the past few years there has been an unprecedented increase in the number and variety of information centres to which the ordinary person can turn for assistance. Society has become so complex that the experience of friends and neighbours is no longer enough. Specialist knowledge and skills are needed to cope with an increasingly forbidding bureaucratic apparatus.

This NCC monograph provided the first clear evidence of the need for information and advice services and graphically illustrated the provision of such services, noting the large areas of unmet need. The book did much to stimulate discussion about advice provision and provided the stimulus for accelerated growth. The years that have followed have seen the establishment of several more law centers, a large number of independent advice centers, housing advice centers, consumer advice centers and other service centers dealing with specialist topics such as money advice.

New forms of service have developed, using mobile advice centers, telephone advice services, village contacts and local radio. Public libraries and rural community councils are among the official bodies which have become involved, and the pace of development continues to accelerate.

One result of this growing interest in information and advice was that the British Library Research and Development Department began to receive a number of applications for research grants into community information. The British Library Research and Development Department exists to award such grants, but until that time it concentrated on information work in science, technology, and the social sciences. It was clear that the interest in community information research originated from a number of disciplines, including geography, planning, social psychology, and systems science, as well as from librarianship and information science.

Consequently, in November 1976, the British Library convened a meeting at which research workers and others with a knowledge or interest in community information and advice agencies could exchange experience and ideas. One of the main recommendations was that there should be "a permanent facility for the collection and dissemination of information."

The British Library subsequently agreed to develop a community information research program and to begin by funding a research officer to report on the current state of development. The Library Association was invited to house the project, and with the appointment of Elaine Kempson as Research Officer for Community Information Services, the Community Information Project was initiated.

It was originally intended that the research officer would spend the first three years of the project building up a collection of information, after which an information officer was to take over to run it as an information service. However, by May 1978, when Grainne Morby joined the project as the research assistant, it became apparent that what had begun as an information gathering process was developing into something that had far-reaching ramifications.

Project Initiation

It soon became apparent that very little information about local information and advice provision is available in print. Either practitioners are too busy developing a service to write up their experience or they do not recognize the general applicability of a particular project. It was therefore necessary to collect available information by letter, telephone, or personal visit. This was a major factor in determining the form of the information collection.

It was also clear that if the project was to succeed it should be fulfilling a need that could not be met by any of the existing networks or national bodies. Further, because of the wide range of organizations to be covered, it was essential that the work should be carried out in cooperation with the networks and national bodies wherever possible. Consequently, much of the first six months of the project was spent in establishing a close working relationship with all the relevant organizations.

From the outset the project adhered to three working principles

(1) To work closely with other bodies, research workers, and practitioners in order to avoid duplicating research work, services, or publications.
(2) To foster and encourage interagency cooperation.
(3) To provide services and publish materials only when the need for them has been identified by practitioners or when there is a clearly expressed demand.

Guided by these principles, the project assembled a very large information collection relating to all aspects of information and advice work in the United Kingdom and in a number of other countries. It was recognized that simple descriptive information was only of limited value and therefore every attempt was made to evaluate the services in relation both to the community served and to other schemes in the country. It has been possible in many instances to build on the work of other researchers who have willingly assisted the project in evaluating specific aspects of local community information provision.

While the information collection covers all aspects of information and advice work, the emphasis is on unusual developments and initiatives, particularly concerning the delivery of service. This focus has helped to identify good practice and to stimulate new developments elsewhere.

Disseminating the Information

From the outset the project tried to avoid the academic approach to the dissemination of research findings, which places a heavy emphasis on the printed word, particularly with reference to journal articles and research reports. Such an approach would have hindered the work of the project, only because there were no journals dealing specifically with information and advice work that could possibly be read avidly by busy practitioners. The possibility of a newsletter was considered and rejected because information and advice workers already receive a plethora of written material, and there was a good chance that any newsletter produced by the project would simply join the ever-increasing pile of material for which there is usually no time to read. More significantly, it soon became apparent that practitioners in the information and advice field preferred a more immediate and more personalized consultancy and advisory service at the time when they are planning the development of a new or improved service. This approach also suited the project's need to generate its own information by personal discussions, telephone conversations, and visits.

The project workers have found it necessary to spend much of their time on personalized consultancy work with service providers. This usually involves having detailed discussions with agency staff and working through their ideas by discussing alternatives and options based on the project worker's knowledge of similar work elsewhere. Agency staff could also be referred to other individuals, agencies, or research projects as deemed appropriate by project consultants. In this way the project has served as a continuing source of assistance as well as a repository of significant information. By maintaining contact with inquiring providers of services, the project has been able to benefit from the corresponding two-way flow of information that has produced interesting spinoffs. This mutual exchange has strengthened the project, which is now in the fortunate position of receiving information on national as well as local level developments unsolicited.

Since such a personalized consultancy service is very labor-intensive, it has been necessary to explore other channels for communicating the information. One method that has been used quite successfully has been to present papers at conferences and participate in seminars, courses, and workshops.

In the early years of the project, conferences were held at the Library Association, a location that attracted many requests of interested persons to speak at conferences. After a very successful interagency conference organized by the public library service in Hertfordshire and attended by citizens advice bureaus workers and others concerned with information and advice work, it was decided to restrict conference papers to national conferences, and regional conferences were restricted to those involving workers from more than one type of agency. This proved to be a wise decision, as it not only rationed the number of conferences but also encouraged different agencies to explore the possibility of joint events.

The location at the Library Association led to an involvement in the development of a set of guidelines for librarians who wished to become involved with community information provision. The project workers were invited to contribute to a working group of practicing librarians, and were able to provide information about a variety of initiatives. The result of this working group was the publication *Community Information: What Libraries Can Do* (Library Association, 1980). This document did not set out to provide a blueprint of the ideal service, but instead put forward a series of options and alternatives based on practical experience gained in different parts of the country. The members of the working group then took part in a series of workshops around the country to promote the book.

The involvement with libraries was followed up by contributing to the *Library Association Record* details of new initiatives that evolved from the application of some of the ideas suggested in the guidelines. The *Record* is delivered to all practicing librarians, and it was therefore possible to tailor the information to the needs of a clearly defined audience, a targeted approach that has not proved possible with other journals. Instead of looking for specialist journals, the project tended to rely more on generalist publications to help create a wider awareness of information and advice provision, and has contributed feature articles to publications such as the *Radio Times* and the *Guardian*.

As well as contributing to publications produced by other organizations, the project has produced a number of its own books. The most successful has been *Know How: a guide to information training and campaigning materials for information and advice workers,* which is now in its second edition. Other publications include *On the road: a guide to setting up and running a mobile advice centre, Computer benefits? Guidelines for local information and advice centres,* and *Village Contacts: Setting Up a Village Based Advice Service.*

In addition to the priced publications the project has produced a number of background papers to meet the specific need of practitioners. These have included a pack for youth advice workers bringing together examples of publicity and providing details of a number of youth advice centers with which the project had been in contact; a similar paper on telephone-based advice services; a paper on information sources suitable for a resource library for community groups, and a paper on the potential of library support for other advice and information services. This last paper was produced for the Advice Services Alliance, and was later adopted as policy by the Association of County Councils.

All of the publications produced by the project have been written in response to an expressed demand by practitioners, and reflect the basic principles on which the project operates.

The project has helped a number of other individuals and organizations with their publications in response to some expressed need. In some instances this has gone beyond simple assistance. For example, as a result of numerous visits from overseas individuals and organizations, the project identified a need for a good international overview of community information provision. The project developed an outline for such an international review and helped the Library Association Books Editor to arrange a contract with Allan Bunch, an Information Librarian in Cambridgeshire, for a book. This has now been published as *Community Information Services, their origin, scope, and development* (Bingley, 1982).

The project acknowledged that the mass media are the most powerful channels for communicating information in modern society and accordingly has built up contacts with a number of the more relevant groups within the broadcasting organizations. Practical assistance has been given on a number of occasions to the British Broadcasting Company (BBC) *Grapevine* unit, and through this a useful exchange has been established with the BBC TV's Community Programmes Unit. The project also was closely involved with the support provision for the BBC programs *Roadshow* and *Speak for yourself*. Project staff members also broadcast on radio's *You and Yours* and on a number of local radio programs.

Fostering Interagency Cooperation

The need to encourage cooperation among groups and agencies which have a tradition of independence, if not insularity, has conditioned the way in which the project has elected to operate. The organizations in which the project is involved have not in the past willingly cooperated with one another. They have a tradition of autonomy and self-sufficiency based on lack of knowledge of each other's services plus a degree of professional rivalry and competition for funding. Genuine differences in style of service, work philosophy, and action priorities have impeded interagency cooperation. It has been necessary to be sensitive to these factors, to establish credibility with the different networks, and to develop a genuine position of "honest broker." This stance was helped by the fact that the project was originally located at the Library Association. Since libraries are perceived by most groups as being neutral, the project was thus not automatically allied to any single agency. The mixed background of the two original staff members—in libraries and citizens advice bureaus—also helped to establish credibility with both of these service networks. When these two project workers undertook voluntary work in independent advice centers, a similar confidence was built up within the independent advice centers. This climate of trust helped the project to provide objective advice, since the workers are regarded as supporters of the overall improvement of services rather than involved with the particular needs of any individual interest group.

Working with the National Networks

As well as encouraging cooperation at the local level, the project has assisted the development of cooperative approaches among the national networks. This kind of close working relationship, which can only exist when an outside agency is providing services of real value to other organizations, signified the project's relationship to networks such as the National Association of Citizens Advice Bureaus, the Association of Housing Aid, and the Law Centers Federation. There was, however, one important sector that was not covered by a national network. This was the independent neighborhood advice sector. It has been estimated that over 300 individual centers make up this group and in 1977 they had no means of presenting a unified voice. However, the project, in cooperation with the National Consumer Council, has assisted with the planning and operation of four national conferences for this council and has helped to set up and extend services to the National Coordinating Group, which now administers the Federation of Independent Advice Centers (FIAC). The project has tried hard to develop this severely underfunded network and has made a number of practical contributions to help this effort along. The involvement of the project in FIAC has consequently had benefits for the project and has also helped FIAC to provide contact with many of the centers most in need of the services of the Community Information Project, particularly as they have few other sources of help. This experience with FIAC has helped the project workers to understand better the needs and problems of part-time, volunteer-run advice sessions that exist without the benefits of the information, training and back-up resources which can be provided by a securely financed national body.

One other network has developed during the first five years of the project. This the Disabled Information and Advice Line (DIAL) groups' network. There are now about 50 local DIAL groups, and they have proved to be one of the fastest-growing networks. Their small national office, DIAL UK, staffed by a single development worker, has been under considerable pressure to maintain and develop its services in response to increasing demands. The project has tried to provide some assistance and advice, particularly in the areas of presenting information materials, fundraising and on the potential of computers for the network.

In 1979, the National Consumer Council (NCC) convened the Advice Services in a Crisis Working Party in response to a potential funding crisis for advice and information services in the voluntary sector. The Working Party brought together for the first time representatives of all the information and advice networks and marked an important step in the development of interagency cooperation. The project was especially pleased when one of its staff members was asked to chair the Working Party for the first year of its existence. As the immediate funding crisis receded into a longer-term funding problem, the Working Party developed into a more stable forum for advice services. This change was reflected in a change of name to the Advice Services Alliance.[1] The project's participation in the program of the alliance has provided invaluable opportunities to disseminate information through the national networks, and to identify new needs for information or research work. The project has worked closely with the NCC, a member of the alliance, and has produced background and policy papers at their request. The project has also been closely involved with the development of a national policy for advice provision and is now working with the alliance and the NCC on the development of standards for information and advice services.

Conducting Specific Research Projects

It has often been the case that needs identified by the project required more than the collection of information or the exchange of experience. In such instances the project has undertaken specific areas of research, sometimes from their own resources, more usually with outside financial assistance. The number of projects undertaken, as described in the subsequent section, is continuously increasing. The willingness to undertake this type of research does, however, reflect the fact that meeting the needs which existed requires more than a conventional information service. It has involved a dynamic approach to information and consultancy work, meeting needs in a very practical way and being prepared to go out to find the information when none existed in the files. This type of dynamic, flexible style of work has been, and continues to be the hallmark of the Community Information Project.

PROJECT ACHIEVEMENTS (1977-1982)

A great deal has been achieved since 1977. Much of the lasting benefit has come from the day-to-day assistance provided in response to specific inquiries. The project receives between fifteen and twenty inquiries each day and this constant exchange of information must have helped to shape many of the developments that have taken place in the provision of information and advice services. The following section documents some of the more obvious achievements of the last five years. Like the visible part of an iceberg, however, these accomplishments are supported by a much larger mass of achievements which though not obvious are no less real.

Work with Individual Information and Advice Centers

The three examples cited below are indicative of the type of direct assistance that is given to local groups, but do not reflect the volume of services provided by the project.

Westminister Libraries

The public library staff in the London Borough of Westminster formed a working party to identify the role it should be playing in developing community information services. Initial contact was made (when the staff asked the project) for information about community profiling. Subsequent discussion made it clear that the library service needed to consider wider options and more practical initiatives than merely attempting a profile of the area. The working party accordingly produced an interim report, which was sent to the project for comment. A meeting was then arranged with members of the working party at which it was possible to explore in greater detail their potential role and to suggest that they make contact with local advice agencies known to the project.

In offering further assistance, the project sent additional information on ways of assessing the need for community information services on community profiling and included detailed plans for information dissemination that were being considered at that time by a neighborhood advice center in the south of the Borough. The project also discussed the possibility of co-opting one of the librarians onto an information subgroup of the management committee of one of the local advice centers.

Assistance to Cambridgeshire Community Council

The project was at one time involved with Cambridgeshire Community Council relevant to its research efforts, which pertained to the National Consumer Council's review of information and advice services in the county. Closer involvement occurred in 1980, when the Community Council appointed a Rural Information Officer to implement the findings of the review and to develop rural information services. The officer visited the project before starting work to obtain detailed background information about rural information needs and services.

Since that first meeting the project has been in regular contact with the officer and has benefited from a two-way flow of information. The project has provided information on village contact schemes, mobile information services, working with libraries, educational programs in schools, classification schemes for community information materials, printing and publishing community newspapers, the use of computers in social welfare information, training courses in information work, directory compilation, and the use of local radio for advice giving. One of the project workers has attended meetings in Cambridgeshire about rural information and provided a paper setting out possible options for services.

Assistance to Citizens Advice Bureaus in East Anglia

The project staff has centered its services around two main projects—the development of rural employment advice and the use of computers. The first area of assistance was delineating needs that exist for employment advice and arriving at ways to meet these needs in East Anglia.

In response to a telephone discussion with a NACAB Area Officer on using microcomputers as a source of information in rural areas, the project was able to supply detailed information about other relevant computer systems, as well as advice about the use of computers generally and the problems of getting suitable programs written. The project was able to put the Area Office in touch with a research worker in Cambridge who was working on the development of a self-assessment computer system for welfare benefit claimants. This has provided the CAB staff with a source of valuable technical information, and, as a result, an arrangement was made whereby CAB inquirers could test the welfare benefits program. In providing further follow-up, the project introduced a second computer programmer who was interested in writing a computer program on tax assessment.

Other kinds of assistance given by the project staff to East Anglian CABs has included encouraging and assisting linkages with the county library services. Guidance in the use of the local radio for advice-giving has also proved helpful.

Assistance to Research Workers

During the first five years of the project, direct assistance was given to over 70 research workers. This assistance included initial literature searches, discussion of research approaches and techniques, and the provision of other informational services.

The project was fortunate in being involved in a workshop for community information researchers organized by the National Consumer Council in 1978. One of the workers was invited to chair the workshop, and this provided an invaluable chance to identify all the research that was taking place and to establish a personal contact with each of the researchers. The initial contact was maintained, and in many instances it has aided the dissemination of the research results. The project staff has been called upon to give advice on a number of aspects, including the indexing of reports and publications, the design of questionnaires and research methodology, the identification of useful contacts, and the evaluation and dissemination of the findings. In return, the researchers contributed to the evaluation of various initiatives and services.

The project is called upon to help students on librarianship and to participate in information and community work courses with research leading to M.Sc. or Ph.D. degrees. The project concentrates its attention on those areas of research that are likely to be of benefit to practitioners and areas that are identified as having a high priority. Generally, it has been found that the students welcomed the opportunity to do research that is related to practical benefit, and a number of these small-scale projects have proven extremely valuable.

One example of this type of research was a project carried out by a M.Sc. information science student to investigate the extent to which the NACAB information service was used by advice centers other than CABs. With the help of a research worker at NACAB and the project staff, the student developed a detailed postal questionnaire which achieved the exceptionally high response rate of 95 percent. The project provided some assistance with the analysis of the information collected and helped to interpret the data in the light of other research findings. The final results provided valuable insights into the patterns of the uses of information in advice and information centers and offered grounds for discussion within the NACAB and the Advice Services Alliance about the possibilities of greater access to the information.

The South Molton Project

The project also has helped with major research programs dealing with community information, and has often been involved throughout the duration of the research effort. This was the case with the South Molton Project, which attempted to establish the feasibility of developing a multiagency advice center in a small market town. The project was funded by the British Library and involved the participation of Devon Library Service, the Devon and Cornwall Citizens Advice Bureaus Area Office, and the Devon Community Council.

One of the project staff members attended a meeting before the study began and helped to formulate the idea and the plans for a multiagency center involving the use of spare accommodation in the library at South Molton. Project staff also assisted with the development of the research proposal and the application for the research grant from the British Library, which entailed background information on other relevant initiatives and included a description of the detailed research methodology.

From the very outset of this study, a project representative was invited to attend the steering committee for the research at South Molton. Project staff continued to be closely involved in all stages of the research, offered detailed comments on the draft report, and

assisted with the dissemination of the research findings at a subsequent conference.

Research at NACAB

During the five-year period from 1977-1982, the project contributed to at least three research projects at the National Association of
Citizens Advice Bureaus; namely, the classification research project,
the research relevant to the potential of mini-packs of information,
and the research undertaken for the joint NACAB/Commission for
Racial Equality publication on Asian-language information materials.
The classification research project discussed below best demonstrates what was achieved.

The research project began by helping the NACAB information
department identify research objectives beyond the immediate needs
of NACAB, and to look at what was required by other types of
information and advice services. Having established the objectives of
the research, the project helped to draw up a research proposal and
apply to the British Library for research funds. During the course of
this research, the project kept the study team informed of other
relevant developments, provided them with contacts outside the
CAB service who were interested in becoming involved, and advised
on methodology. Thereby, the project staff was involved in the research continuously, and has been consulted regularly by the research
workers. The project staff also has attempted to promote research
among other agencies and networks by addressing meetings of the
Advice Services Alliance and the National Coordinating Group of
the Federation of Independent Advice Centers.

This close involvement during all research stages has helped the
project to develop a clear understanding of the process and the problems faced by researchers. Consequently, much-needed moral support and access to source material have yielded research findings that
might otherwise not be exposed.

General Development Work

As was noted previously, the general development work of the
project has tried to foster an interagency approach to the solution of
problems. It has also attempted to meet and, where possible, anticipate practitioners' needs. The inquiries received by the project have
provided a useful means of monitoring topical issues and identifying

emerging problems. A pressing need for the acquisition and identification of information materials became clearly apparent. This led to the production of *Know How*, the project's most successful book.

Know How

From the outset the project began to build a collection of information sources that would be of assistance to advice centers in answering inquiries for the purposes of staff training and public relations. This collection includes over 600 items ranging from established legal textbooks to locally produced leaflets. Based on this collection the project published an evaluative bibliography entitled *Know How*, which received a great deal of media attention. It sold over 3000 copies and eventually went out of print in September 1980, only nine months after it had been published. It was awarded the 1979 Besterman Medal by the Library Association for the most outstanding bibliography or guide to the literature. A completely revised, updated, and expanded edition has now been published jointly by Pluto Press and the Library Association.

Know How has stimulated considerable interest in printed information sources and has led to the production of specialist mini-guides such as the Lambeth Umbrella Group's *Basic Information Guide*, *Roof's* specialist housing bibliography, and the British Library-funded *Help for Health*, a bibliogrphy on health materials produced by the project.

On the Road

In June 1979 a conference of mobile CAB organizers in the West Midlands identified a need for a publication which would provide a practical guide for establishing mobile advice services. The project broadened the task to include non-CAB mobiles. Every mobile advice center that was "on the road" was visited and the experiences gained were documented. Before publishing the results of the research it was agreed that a deeper understanding of the issues could be gained from discussions of the draft report. Accordingly, a "mobile meet" was arranged and mobile advice centers traveled from various parts of the country to attend the meeting and participate in workshops on staffing, funding, conversions, and other technical aspects. This opportunity for detailed discussions was found by the participants to be valuable and helped to overcome feelings of isolation. It also helped to ensure that the final publication—*On the road: a guide to setting up and running a mobile advice center* (Community Information Project, 1981), which contained all the practical information—is required by anyone interested in mobile advice. The mobile meet and the book have stimulated many local community information agencies to consider the use of mobiles for extending their work in both rural and urban areas. The project also stimulated a great deal of interest in the mass media, including the press, television, and local and national radio.

Computer Benefits

The project always has been closely involved with applications of new information technology to information and advice work. Project workers attended both the Public Information Providers Group and the Social Information Providers Group meetings to discuss the implications of Prestel, and they also took part in the National Council for the Voluntary Organization's New Technology Group.

More recently, the rapid development of the use of microcomputers has added a new dimension to information and advice work. For the first time computer technology is available at a price a large number of advice centers can afford. More importantly, the technology is in a form which allows the advice workers considerable control over the content and structure of the system. Consequently, when the project was approached by the Department on Health and Social Services (DHSS) for advice on computerizing a welfare benefits system, a concerted effort was made to consider the information and research needs of practitioners.

The National Consumer Council promoted this effort by commissioning the project to undertake review of the use of computers for local social welfare information systems. Fortunately, the project was able to obtain the necessary technical input from a psychology student at Cambridge who was at that time employed on a research project to develop the DHSS's own pilot welfare benefits self-assessment program. Based on an evaluation of nearly twenty applications, a manual was produced on the use of computers. This manual was subsequently published by the National Consumer Council in 1982 as *Computer benefits? guidelines for local information and advice services.*

The CIP staff has assisted with workshops and conferences and has contributed to the efforts of the National Consumer Council. The project also has provided consultation on computer applications to governmental authorities as well as to other service organizations.

Village Contacts

The project always has been aware of the pressing need for information and advice services in rural areas to overcome the disadvantages of possible isolation and inadequate provision of basic services. Evidence based on the project's study of mobile advice centers, coupled with experience gained from participation in various research projects such as the South Molton Information Center, led the project to produce a manual on how to establish village contact schemes. The manual suggests that one or more persons in a village should provide information and advice and act as a link through which inquiries can be referred to appropriate advice centers. A number of these schemes are currently in operation and have been compiled in a book, *Village contacts: a guide to providing information and advice in remote villages,* published by the Community Information Project in 1982. The publication of the book coincided with the major Rural Advice and Information Conference, which took place in December 1982.

The Public Library Contribution

The establishment of the project coincided with the growing interest on the part of the public libraries in the provision of community information services. When the project workers were asked to act as consultants to the Library Association's working party on community information, the project staff contributed by sharing information from different sources and by providing linkages to other agencies working in this field, thereby promoting a cooperative approach. The final report is the basis of the monograph entitled *Community Information: What Libraries can do*. This book, published by the Library Association in 1980, is based on the involvement of the project in library-based access systems.

Local Radio and Advice Work

From the outset of the project, close working links were maintained with the Volunteer Center and in particular with the center's Media Project. When the question of the use of local radio for advice and information work arose, it was agreed that the project could

contribute significantly to public relations effort. It was decided that
as the Media Project was more familiar with research techniques for
assessing broadcast programs, it should take the lead, with information being channeled by the project, particularly in relation to the
needs in rural communities and the type of research that would most
benefit information and advice workers. Advice was given on the
methodology as well as on the selection of the locations to carry on
the research, the findings of which appear in the project's final report.

Community Resource Centers

Since it has not been possible for the project to take on everything
that has appeared necessary, it has been essential to assign priorities
and to find alternative ways to accomplish goals. For example, at the
time that the project began to receive many inquiries on community
libraries and community resource centers, the project staff was fully
committed to other tasks and not able to follow things up as
thoroughly as desired. Fortunately, British Library funds were made
available for a small-scale project to produce an information guide to
establishing a service in a community library or a resource center. The
project produced a final report, entitled *Community Resource Centers* (Flat Publication, 1981).

Another area of interest arising from an inquiry was the use of
telephones for advice work. The inquiry originated from the Scottish
Consumer Council, which was involved with the development of an
experimental "Highlands Freephone" service. The information
gathered to answer the inquiry appeared to have general relevance
and broad application. A brief report was produced by the project and
eventually over 100 copies of the report were distributed upon request. The content of the report served as a basis for a seminar,
convened by the Mutual Aid Center, which explored the potential for
telephone-based information and advice services.

Developing National Networks

The work of the project in helping establish national networks
for advice agencies has been described previously. Very significant
benefits can result from the actions taken by a vigorous national network. Not only can the network help to create the environment for
greater success in fund-raising by local centers, it can also offer very
practical assistance by providing an information service, staff training

programs, and explorations of potential benefits of computerization. Therefore, the project always has tried to work with existing networks and encourage the formation of new ones where required. The work with the Federation of Independent Advice Centers and the Disabled Information and Advice Line, UK, has perhaps been one of the project's most important achievements. By making a very direct contribution to the operation of FIAC and DIAL-UK, the project has been able to help, indirectly, many local centers.

Advice Services Alliance (ASA)

Another major contribution of the project has been its support and assistance to the Advice Services Alliance. At a time when all public services are under threat, advice services, many of which are financed through discretionary local authority grants, are especially vulnerable. Through the ASA, the project is able to stimulate a continued awareness of the importance of information and advice services in modern society.

The ASA represents a unique collaboration of advice services that might otherwise be competing with each other in the relentless struggle for adequate resources. The Community Information Project is committed to preserve and strengthen the spirit of cooperation that marks the Alliance and promotes the long-term benefit of information and advice provision in the UK.

THE FUTURE

In March 1982 the initial funding from the British Library Research and Development Department ended. In April 1982 the Community Information Project Ltd. was established as an independent organization and new staff appointments were made to carry on the work of the project. The project is now supported by a management committee composed of people who were also closely involved with the developments during the first five years of the project. In addition to participation on this management committee, the ASA also has agreed to act as an overall advisory committee to help with matters of policy.

The project currently is funded by grants, subscriptions, and contracts for specific pieces of research. In some instances the research is carried out by the full-time staff members, but where the project is beyond the resources of the full-time staff, the project can engage a number of freelance researchers who have agreed to be directly associated with the project and participate in the work of the program. The project has also planfully set up a book distribution service to sell Community Information Project publications and other relevant materials which has proved of interest to information and advice workers.[2]

The project, which began as an information center in response to apparent needs, has developed into a national resource center. It is likely that CIP will continue to serve as a vital center in promoting the development of information and advice services based on the following aims:

(1) To collect information on research, practice, and development in response to expressed or identified need.
(2) To provide a personalized advisory and consultancy service to researchers and practitioners.
(3) To stimulate or carry out research in promoting innovation and avoiding duplication.
(4) To participate in national and local development work to develop and publicize community information services.
(5) To promote cooperation between networks of advice and information agencies by sharing knowledge within the field and helping to develop new networks where a need is identified by the practitioners.

The record of achievements established by the Community Information Project, Ltd., since 1977 suggests a promising future as CIP continues to meet the needs of the information and advice movement.

NOTES

1. The Advice Services Alliance is the national forum that brings together representatives from the National Association of Citizens Advice Bureaus, the Federation of Independent Advice Centers, the Law Centers Federation, the Association of Housing Aid, DIAL UK, the Institute of Consumer Advisers, the Library Association, the National Association of Young Peoples Counseling and Advisory Services, and other bodies concerned with the development of information and advice service provision to the public.

2. To obtain the *Publications Catalogue of the Community Information Project,* direct inquiries to CIP at Bethnal Green Library, Cambridge Heath Road, London E2, U.K.

3

THE DEVELOPMENT OF
CITIZENS ADVICE BUREAUS IN
NEW ZEALAND

NEIL SMITH

AN ISLAND NATION

New Zealand is an island nation of the South Pacific, situated 1,600 kilometers east of the continent of Australia in the temperate zone. The total land area is almost 270,000 square kilometers (slightly larger than Great Britain), with a population of just over three million, giving a population density of less than 12 people per square kilometer.

The indigenous people, the Maori, Polynesian voyagers, occupied the country in virtual isolation from about the tenth century until European penetration of the South Pacific in the Eighteenth Century. Their descendants are now about nine percent of the population, while almost 90 percent of the population are of European descent. Most of the remaining 2 percent have come from other Pacific Islands, largely since World War II.

The economy is based mainly on the export of pastoral products, along with manufacturing, tourism, forestry products, coal and natural gas. Levels of prosperity are, therefore, closely dependent on the state of world trade. The three major urban centers of Auckland, Wellington, and Christchurch have populations of 750,000, 330,000 and 297,000 respectively.

Politically and socially New Zealand is a parliamentary democracy on the Westminster model, with extensive government intervention in economic and social welfare policy generally accepted and expected. From the late 1930s welfare state policies have developed a social security system with benefits covering medical care (in part), family allowances, universal superannuation, unemployment, widowhood, and other domestic circumstances that prevent people supporting themselves and their dependents. Provision of welfare services is seen generally as a responsibility of central government, either directly or in the form of subsidies to independent agencies, many of them reliant on voluntary workers. The main organization which has arisen to help people get more effective access to these human services is the network of Citizens advice bureaus now operating throughout the country.

1. HISTORICAL DEVELOPMENT OF CITIZENS ADVICE BUREAUS

In New Zealand the first CAB was established in October 1970 in Ponsonby, an old-established inner city area in Auckland then going through the stress of the first wave of urban renewal in the country. The concept of a "citizens advice (an information and referral) service" was borrowed from Britain, where such services had developed during World War II in response to a dramatic dislocation of community life. In the postwar years the increasing complexity and pressures of everyday living have been linked with high population mobility. The informal and often invisible networks of support, which were an integral part of more stable communities, crumbled. Those that were left, such as church and "old boy" networks, have served to support only a minority of citizens. More and more people find themselves living in comparative isolation, with no feeling of belonging to a community, and unsure of their rights and responsibilities. Frequently, either people are unaware of the information and help which could be available to them or they find the approach to large statutory agencies formidable. Citizens advice bureaus have been established as local communities have organized themselves to share with each other their experiences of their citizens' specific needs. They have tried to respond to these needs.

By 1973, twelve bureaus were in existence. Over the previous three years bureaus in Christchurch, Wellington, and Auckland had been conferring and developing a common understandng of the basic aims and desirable standards for a national CAB service. In September 1973, the New Zealand Association of Citizens Advice Bureaus was formally constituted as an incorporated society. The reasons for setting up a national body were twofold. The first was to ensure the highest standards of service to inquiries by setting up a self-imposed monitor on those providing the service. The other objectives was to set up a national structure so that it would be possible to speak on behalf of CABs with one voice—especially to central government and other national organizations. It was felt that such a national structure would best serve the future growth and development of CABs by providing a way of sharing experiences at the community level and the opportunity for mutual support. The New Zealand Association has always recognized that bureaus can and will develop differently in different areas but with a unifying basic philosophy and common standards.

By 1976, 34 bureaus were handling over 100,000 inquiries and by 1978 52 bureaus dealt with over 150,000 inquiries. In 1982, in addition to the 64 established bureaus, 14 other groups throughout the country were in various stages of establishing the service in their local communities. By 1983 the 2,000 rostered workers in the bureaus handled a total of 200,530 inquiries.

In order to cope with this phenomenal growth, the N.Z. Association, which is basically a voluntary organization, has developed regional structures to coordinate the work of bureaus in geographical regions. By 1982 the South Region, covering most of the South Island, had 10 bureaus; the Central Region 16; the Waikato-Bay of Plenty Region 8; and the North Region (which contains New Zealand's major metropolitan area: Auckland) had 30.

2. THE SERVICE COMPONENTS: WHAT THE BUREAUS DO

The N.Z. Association of Citizens Advice Bureaus has adopted the two principal aims of the British service: First, to ensure that individuals do not suffer through ignorance of their rights and responsibilities or of the services available, or through an inability to express their needs effectively; and second, to exert a responsible influence on the development of social policies and services both locally and nationally. The service therefore aims to offer freely to all individuals an impartial service of information, guidance, and support, and to make responsible use of the experience so gained.

To help bureaus fulfill these aims more effectively, the national association has published a comprehensive handbook of principles and practice, recently revised for the third time in eight years, in response to changing demands and experience. Much of the content of this present account of the service derives from the Handbook (N.Z. Association of CAB, 1981).

A citizens advice bureau is a local community service where trained volunteer workers offer any person a wide range of free, confidential, and impartial information or other help on any matter. A bureau worker's task may be to provide information on some relatively straightforward matter, or to listen at length to find out what the main problem is and assist in gaining access to whichever service will provide the most appropriate help and ensure that there is nothing that will hinder the person in making this contact. This may mean anything from strengthening the confidence of the person who needs to approach an agency to finding help, if necessary, with transport to get them where they need to go to on occasions making an approach on their behalf.

Although the service has adopted the term "advice" bureau from the British model, the policy is to resist giving advice, and the training of bureau workers stresses the importance of giving accurate information and helping the inquirer to look at the pros and cons of possible courses of action, rather than advising him or her what to do.

Bureau premises are usually located near some focal point in the community: in a shopping center or alongside a community center, library, child health center, or kindergarten. The premises consist of a main office/interview room and a waiting room, with one or more further interview rooms, and kitchen, storage, and toilet facilities. A small-scale, informal, comfortable, *homey* style of accommodation and furnishing is preferred.

In most areas, well over half the inquiries are by telephone rather than by personal visits.

The association has developed guidelines for information storage and retrieval systems, and each bureau adapts these to meet local needs and management styles. A record of each inquiry is kept for statistical and possible future reference purposes. But workers are encouraged to limit written recording to the bare essential minimum. For filing and statistical purposes, a standard national category system has been adopted by most bureaus, though some have preferred to retain a local but compatible system. Under this national category system inquiries are classified into 14 groups:

(1) Travel, communication
(2) Education, training
(3) Employment/unemployment
(4) Local information, services
(5) Personal, family
(6) Government Departments, services

(7) Community support, welfare groups
(8) Accidents
(9) Health, medical
(10) Housing, tenancy
(11) Housing: property, land

(12) Consumer complaints
(13) Financial, budgeting

(14) Legal (not covered elsewhere)

A citizens advice bureau hears daily about how life is for people and therefore is in a prime position to be a window on the community, giving a picture upon which reflection can take place regarding our society and the way it either enhances or severely limits the rights and life styles of various groups of people.

Bureaus will identify gaps in existing services and explore possibilities of filling these or ensuring easier access to services for those who have a right to them. This may mean pressing for removal of anomalies in regulations or alteration of criteria of entitlement to benefits or services. It may involve bureau workers acting as advocates, intervening with service administrators on behalf of people who have failed to get access to necessary services. In some cases it may involve joint action by several bureaus or the N.Z. Association of CAB to advocate some desirable change in social service policy in the interests of, for example, social justice, people's statutory rights in terms of cash benefits, housing or legal services.

Bureaus may act to stimulate innovation in or new methods of delivering existing services. This may be, for instance, a matter of involving the local community in decision-making about decentralization: bringing the agency to the people, opening local offices of the Department of Social Welfare, having an officer of the Housing Corporation come to the bureau on a weekly basis to see tenants, or setting up a family planning clinic in an adjacent office. This sort of arrangement helps an agency worker in discussing varied needs of a client so that it is easier for the person to go on to other appropriate neighboring services, such as child care or family budgeting.

Bureaus may be associated with the establishment of community-based projects such as halfway houses catering to particular accommodation needs, the running of a local food co-op, the setting up of care and craft centers (day activity centers), a learning exchange promoting extended skills and knowledge, or an attempt to secure individual access to, and use of, legal services. The range of information and help given will be discussed further in Sections 4 and 7.

3. STAFFING

Citizens advice bureaus are staffed by selected and trained volunteer workers serving on a roster system. The center may also have the full-time or part-time services of a paid professional community social worker, usually employed by the local authority in whose area the bureau is situated.

The centers are usually open each day, Monday to Friday, generally between 10 a.m. to 4 p.m. Most are open also at least one evening a week or on Saturday mornings for representatives of some specialist service to be available. Bureau workers commit themselves to at least one half-day of duty every two weeks, and a reasonably busy bureau can usefully involve a team of about 40 workers. In 1981 bureau staff members ranged from a total of 71 in one center to 8 in another.

The success or failure of any bureau depends on the quality of the volunteer workers, and the association continually stresses the importance of careful selection and training. From the start, much thought and sensitive commitment has been devoted to establishing and applying appropriate criteria so that high standards will be maintained while ensuring that workers in a bureau represent as wide a cross section of the population as possible.

> The workers usually belong to the local community (though) in some inner-city areas there has often been a significant proportion (from outside), and represent a wide range of ages (from 17 to 70), occupations, experience and knowledge and the ability to relate it to the needs of those seeking help. (*Consumer Review*, 1974)

It is worth noting that although senior citizens are considered invaluable because of their knowledge, experience, and availability, their alertness and ability to relate to people over a wide range of age and value systems may need to be particularly carefully checked out. Specific religious or political beliefs or lack of them on the part of applicants are considered worth checking only where there seems either an unhealthy emphasis on proselytizing or a prejudice against another group.

Accepted applicants undergo an initial course of training, usually 12 two-hour sessions over a period of six weeks. The detailed content and style of training is under constant evaluation and revision in light of the practical experience of trainers, supervisors, and bureau workers, all of whom are represented in planning of future programs. Typically, courses have included

- listening and communication skills, with emphasis on telephone and basic interview techniques,
- the history, function, and role of CABs and the N.Z. association,

- a knowledge and understanding of available, relevant community resources, including local and national social services, and how to locate and use them,

- some awareness of the factors involved in human behavior and relationships, personal values, and coping with new experience, including relating with people from differing cultural backgrounds, and

- some basic analysis of the nature of communities and contemporary society, and of the social structures that assist or hinder the life of individuals, families, and groups in the community.

Stress is laid on the code of ethics for bureau workers that the association has adopted. This emphasizes the inquirers' right to be accepted as the people they are, and to choose. It stresses the need for the worker to aim to be impartial and aware of his or her own values and prejudices, to avoid emotional involvement (in the sense of distorting judgment), and to maintain good working relations with others. Above all, it stresses the importance of strict confidentiality. To reinforce this trainees are asked to sign a declaration of confidentiality.

After successfully completing the course and a three-month probationary period of service in the bureau, applicants are accepted for ongoing duty. This stage usually is confirmed by presentation of a certificate of proficiency, and this ceremony is often used as an occasion for public recognition of the contribution the bureau is making in the life of the community, with representatives of community groups, politicians, and interested citizens invited to join in the function.

In the case of applicants whose assessment indicates that their talents are not those required for work in the bureau, care is taken to suggest and discuss alternative forms of community service whenever possible.

Ongoing support, supervision, and training is provided on an individual and group basis. Each bureau is responsible for initial and ongoing training and usually maintains a program of monthly workers' meetings, often incorporating case discussion, updated information on community resources, and consideration of current items of bureau management. Some bureaus will have separate meetings for each of these functions. Groups of neighboring bureaus sometimes combine for training courses to make more effective use of valuable resources of people, time, and space. These programs are supplemented by periodic regional and national seminars, culminating in the annual general meeting and national conference of the N.Z. association, which is increasingly becoming an occasion for searching

study and discussion of some important social issue that has currently
made an impact on the work of the bureaus: for example, the crisis in
access to adequate housing for low-income families, or the short- and
long-term effects of unemployment and the future of work.

Naturally, as in all human organizations, the daily reality is not the
same as the ideal. Standards of selection, training, and service vary
from place to place and time to time; also, members of each community will have limitations in resources, including blind spots in their
social awareness. Hence, some workers and bureaus will at time fail
to maintain a desirable standard of work and commitment. But in my
view, after ten years' experience with the bureaus locally and nationally, the movement has shown a remarkable and largely justified faith
in the talent of a very wide cross section of the people—often people
whom some of the established agencies would never have considered
as acceptable workers in the community. Bureau work has enabled
them to demonstrate that, given the opportunity and resources, their
life experience, common sense, and commitment are the key to
developing the citizens advice bureau (like some other community
action projects) as a neighborhood mutual help network.

In this process, although there is the tension that always exists
where members of the community work as volunteers alongside paid
community workers, the movement has constantly worked through
this to achieve a rewarding harmony through which each has learned a
great deal from the other and the distinctive contribution of each is
valued.

Bureau workers are frequently reminded that they are not counselors but referral agents. This is a necessary warning to give to new
and inexperienced trainees. It is the official policy of the association,
and it is true in the sense that they are not involved in the long-term
dynamic process using the complex techniques derived from psycho-
therapeutic theory. But the training principles are basically parallel to
those of client-centered counseling. In emergency situations at the
bureau, many of the more experienced workers are, in effect, engaging in crisis counseling that is providing more practical help than the
inadequate attention their clients would often receive if referred to
some of the overworked, undertrained social workers, especially in
some of the large statutory agencies.

This is not to coin an *Animal Farm* slogan: "All bureau workers
good, all social workers bad!" Many social workers are well trained,
deeply committed to the interests of their clients and the health of
their society, and do magnificent work. And it is often essential to call
on the resources at their disposal in the interest of a client. But it is a

major dilemma in social policy in the contemporary welfare state that, too often, social workers in big agencies are, through no conscious fault of their own, severely limited by pressure of case loads and the red tape of bureaucratic procedures. The model developed by volunteer workers in groups (like the CAB) growing out of the community may provide useful clues to corrective action. Hence, the effective bureau workers deserve more credit when they have so worked on behalf of inquirers, or so boosted their confidence, that they are enabled to confront those who obstruct them, and obtain their rights. And other bureau workers can learn from this that inquirers may be caused extra unnecessary delay and distress by being referred on prematurely or inappropriately when the bureau worker may, in fact, be the person with the time to give the most effective help.

As with the "client groups" in community houses noted by Megan Lawrence (1977) in her argument for the demystifying of counseling, the experiences of bureau workers "have often enabled them, with support and adequate training, to become highly efficient counsellors themselves, thus spreading a network of care, concern and practical help even further into the community at large."

4. THE CLIENTELE: WHO GETS HELP AND WHAT IMPACT DOES THE SERVICE MAKE?

Citizens advice bureaus offer information—and offer it free to anyone on any question. And everyone needs information sometime. So *anyone* is likely to call on the CAB for help at some time or other.

Consistently each year, both nationally and regionally, inquiries for information about local services, facilities and events are the predominant category, comprising between 30 percent and 40 percent of all inquiries. These calls appear to come from people right across the social spectrum.

Many people with family and other personal difficulties seek help from the CAB (11 percent to 14 percent, the second-highest category). These inquiries include marital and health problems, related legal matters, and how to handle domestic violence.

Especially in the urban areas of the North Island, housing problems relating to rental tenancies are the next significant group (8 percent to 12 percent), reflecting a housing crisis that particularly affects lower income families with dependent children. The combined effects of a period of rising inflation, higher unemployment, changing patterns of marriage and family life, and a decline in the building of public rental housing have meant that an increasing number of these families are deprived of access to adequate housing at a cost appropriate to their income. Unsatisfactory housing conditions are a major factor leading to serious family stress, and in the absence of radical changes in social or economic policies, it will often be hard for the worker to see any way these situations will be resolved.

"Local information" queries usually can be met factually and quickly, and personal, domestic, and legal problems may be talked through and, if necessary, often referred on to other specialist services with some confidence. But when the worker is faced, as in the case of homelessness, with a series of human situations that seem to offer no hope, the effect can be traumatic. Some workers will put up the shutters; others will reach a new awareness of the limitations of the bureau and other service agencies in the face of the realities of economic and social forces, and may feel impelled to take a fresh look at the factors involved in such social issues as the housing crisis. If the issue is significant enough and has made an impact on enough bureau workers it will eventually surface as one of the regional or national concerns of the association.

Thus, in 1981 in fact, the association conducted a limited general survey on housing and homelessness, which was then studied at the national conference. Summarizing workshop discussion a delegate recorded:

> The (questions) appear endless and the solutions very few by comparison, but very thought-provoking. It may make us realize that the housing shortage is in many cases due to ourselves. How many of us have adult children who have gone "flatting?" How many of us are in broken marital situations where instead of one family home there now needs to be two? How many of us stay in houses too large for our personal needs?

The workshop also noted a number of commercial and political factors contributing to the crisis, listed the disastrous human consequences, and concluded with suggestions for a more constructive housing policy. The 1982 conference resolved that the association should "continue to urge the Government to provide enough rental accommodation to ensure that all citizens, especially those families on lower incomes, have access to adequate housing at a cost appropriate to their income."

Apart from the practical day-to-day service the bureaus provide in the community, one of the chief benefits of the work over the years has been its impact on the workers themselves, and, through them, on their whole circle of family, friends, and acquaintances. The bureau training and service have opened up a whole new world of experience for most workers, bringing them in contact with a far wider range of people and circumstances than they would otherwise have met, and often giving them a deeper appreciation of the difficulties others have to face, the gaps that there are in social services, and the realities of conflict and power in society. Although the details of bureau work are confidential, changes in views and attitudes cannot help being reflected in the workers' daily conversation and discussion and, therefore, make some contribution to changing public opinion on matters of social policy.

One major aspect of this is the fact that for many women bureau work has been a first significant step toward personal independence and confidence outside the home. It has given them confidence to launch into activities, and at a level of responsibility they would not previously have considered, and many have gone on to other more varied fields of voluntary service, taken up advanced courses of study, or gone into full- or part-time paid positions.

5. BUDGET COSTS AND FUNDING SOURCES

The cost of a citizens advice bureau can vary. Obviously the cost of the building is the most variable factor. If existing premises can be used rent free then the cost may be limited to essential renovations and maintenance. Otherwise the cost will be that of renting, buying, or building new premises.

Some bureaus identify the need for salaried staff for administration and supportive supervision. The salary will depend on the hours the person is employed and the job specification. The salary scale may be related to local authority or public service social work scales. In practice it is unlikely that a bureau will have salaried staff unless it is being financed by the local authority. Full-time community social workers could expect to spend at least one-third of their time on supervising a bureau. A share of the workers' transport and administrative costs must also be allowed for.

Establishment costs include furniture and other equipment for two interview rooms, a waiting room, and associated facilities. In practice, furniture can often be donated or acquired second hand. In any case, estimates have to include such items as floor coverings, heaters, curtains, desks, chairs, filing cabinet, phone, signs, stationery and printing. Ongoing costs will include rent, salary, training, telephone, power, stationery and printing, publicity, cleaning, coffee, tea or other refreshments, and kitchen-running costs.

Advice bureaus usually exist on a shoestring budget. Those that are sponsored and financed by a local authority have the advantage that workers and management committee are relieved of the responsibility of fundraising and can concentrate on providing and administering the service. Once having decided to sponsor a bureau, the local authority usually will provide a building, insurance coverage, employment of a community worker, and at least part of the running costs. Some authorities fund the operation fully apart from the central government grant.

Independent bureaus, administered by a local community group, have the advantage of independence but generally have to expend continual effort in fund-raising, locally and by applying to charitable trusts, to supplement the annual government grant.

From 1975 the government gave a basic annual grant of $NZ15,000 through the national association, later supplemented by varying grants from national lottery funds. From 1980 the association was assured of ongoing government financial help from the Department of Social Welfare. The funding is being done on a three-tier basis. For the year 1982-1983, for instance, $NZ34,000 is being allocated to the general committee of the association for administration; $NZ18,000 is shared among the four regions to finance training and coordination; and a further $NZ32,000 is shared among 64 individual bureaus, giving a grant of $NZ500 to each. This makes a total of $NZ84,000 for the year.

6. AUSPICES OF THE SERVICE: WHO RUNS THE BUREAU?

At present, bureaus may be administered either by a local authority or as an independent organization, an autonomous community group.

It is important for a CAB to be sponsored by the local authority: It helps to make clear that the CAB is a local community service available to *all* citizens and has official recognition. Local authority commitment helps to guarantee long-term continuity as against a purely voluntary support group, which may lose impetus or even cease to function if key people withdraw. The local authority can give valuable practical help, which may include finance, provision of a building, and, where appropriate, employment of a community social worker with responsibility for integrating the CAB into an overall community development program.

At the same time, if the CAB is to be available to all citizens it must pursue an independent, impartial policy with no discrimination as to religion, politics, race, or sex. It is, therefore, essential that the CAB is seen to retain an impartial position in relation to any political authority, central or local. If citizens seek help from the CAB in a matter in which they are having problems dealing with "the council," for instance, they must feel confident that the CAB is not just another arm of council authority and that they will receive impartial information or other help from the worker.

Once established, a CAB supported by a local authority should have an independent management committee, including a majority of bureau workers along with, if desirable, other representatives. This committee is responsible for the policy and day-to-day work of the bureau within the policy of the national association. The title "Citizens Advice Bureau" and its symbol are registered with the Registrar of Incorporated Societies and may be used only by member bureaus affiliated with the national association.

The majority of the bureaus are now sponsored and fully financed by their local authority, especially in the metropolitan areas of the North region. Most of the remainder receive *some* funding from their local authority.

In practice, there seems little indication that local authorities have seriously threatened the effective independence of bureaus in the conducting of their community service. Although some authorities at first have strongly resisted taking on the responsibility of sponsoring a bureau, once it is established they are usually quickly impressed by its contribution to the community and happy to accept the credit for this.

On occasions misunderstandings have arisen, or a dominant individual has attempted to take over and distort the function of a bureau in the interests of a particular person, group, or ideology, and this may happen in either a sponsored or an independent bureau. Usually the mature common sense of some other concerned citizens, sometimes with the help of mediation by representatives of the national association, has been sufficient to resolve the situation and achieve a better understanding of the role and function of a CAB in their community.

7. NETWORKING WITH OTHER SERVICES

As already indicated in Section 2, a bureau helps serve the important function of locating a social service where it is needed and using the community's own resources to meet the need, so it is not in a remote central city area but in the place where the people are. This is particularly important in New Zealand, where the majority of metropolitan populations tend to be living in very spread-out suburbs rather than in central city apartment blocks. Some agencies are willing to have their specialists come and use a spare interview room in a bureau for perhaps one session a week to help people with such services as housing, marriage counseling, family financial budgeting, and so on. One such service that has so obviously met such a need that it is now associated with nearly every bureau is the free legal advice service: the local District Law Society provides a rostered panel of volunteer lawyers available on one or two evenings a week, or Saturday mornings, to give free advice on legal matters and, if the inquirer wishes, to refer him or her to an appropriate lawyer for further action. The legal service has now provided the new edition of the association's handbook (1981) with a 56-page legal supplement for the guidance of bureau workers.

Further steps in the struggle to enable disadvantaged people to get easier and more effective access to the law have been the setting up of Small Claims Tribunals, and the establishment of the pilot Grey Lynn Neighborhood Law Office in inner-city Auckland, as the start of a network of such offices undertaking legal representation for those otherwise unlikely to get satisfaction for their needs: many of the members of minority ethnic groups, the poor, and the illiterate, for instance. The association and local members have been active in promoting both these developments.

The advice bureaus are actively involved in assisting inquirers with consumer problems as an integral part of the service, and the association has developed a close working relationship with the Consumer's Institute of New Zealand. Under this arrangement the Institute provides bureau workers with basic training in handling consumer inquiries and complaints, together with a detailed reference manual for each participating bureau. Bureaus in turn supply the institute with statistical returns on this work.

In this way, the bureaus have supplemented the work of the institute's Complaints Advisory Service operating in the main urban centers and enabled it to be extended to many more contact points beyond the scope of the Institute's present budget.

At the 1982 annual conference of the association a quick survey of 40 of the bureaus revealed a wide range of other linked services. These included Plunket Society (infant care) service; a community mutual-help family health project for Pacific Island and Maori women; tenants protection association; emergency housing service; women's center, including rape crisis, battered women's support group and short-term crisis accommodation; job assistance center and youth unemployed support group; reporting center for probation service; mental health support group, including follow-up for out-patients of the psychiatric hospital; food coop; learning exchange, including adult literacy project; family day-care project; and emergency home help service.

Many bureaus have cooperated with their local authority Community Development Department or local Council of Social Services to compile, publish, and update comprehensive directories of local social services, sometimes including recreational and other leisure activities, which have proved invaluable to the general public as well as agency personnel.

Some have cooperated with other community action groups in periodic publications, reporting new local developments or discussing current social issues.

The Auckland Region coordinator helped to set up publication of a community action newsletter, *Community Forum,* and its spin-off, *Opportunities For Change* (1980 on), a series of collected papers on community action, with four volumes now published.

In fulfilling its second aim of exercising a responsible influence on the development of national social policy the association has working parties periodically making submissions to parliamentary Select Committees on legislation coming before the House. Recent examples have been amendments to the Children's and Young Person's Act, and the Law Practitioners' Bill. Besides this, there have been submissions to particular departments, such as a report to the Justice Department on access to the law.

8. FUTURE DIRECTIONS

Individual bureaus in New Zealand have retained a considerable amount of autonomy and flexibility within the unifying structure of the national association. A major factor in this has been the strength of local bureau worker participation in the management of the bureau as well as in delivery of the service. This shows no sign of diminishing, so bureaus are likely to keep on modifying their functions and practice in response to changes in local and national conditions, though this will vary, depending on the extent to which the management and workers of any particular bureau really reflect the vital concerns of the neighborhood community. Whatever the changes, the basic need for a generalist information and help service in a complex society will remain.

It is not hard to predict that the pace of technological and, hence, social change will continue if not intensify, and that laws and regulations, and the resulting official pamphlets and forms, will become more numerous and complicated. In these circumstances, the bureaus will continue to be among the catalysts stimulating the setting up of further special-purpose crisis help centers and other community action projects which in themselves are beyond the scope of a citizens advice bureau. In fact, the tactics of some of them may well conflict with the basic views and commitment of many bureau workers, especially if conditions deteriorate for significant groups of people and the conflicts of interest in our society show up more clearly and brutally. Other bureau workers may wish to get more formal recognition for the personal advocacy work they are doing already, for instance, on behalf of welfare beneficiaries or tenants, along the lines of the Welfare Rights Workers Group in the CAB in Britain.

Regionally and nationally there is an increasing concern to respond to the need for more thorough and effective training and supervision. As funds permit, this will lead to the provision of more resources both in personnel and in detailed training material.

The main concerns are to harness and maintain the initial enthusiasm of the volunteer workers: first, to establish and use the best methods to enable them to learn how to interview inquirers most effectively, so that the people really get the service of information and help that is what the bureau is there for; and second, to overcome the difficulties there are in keeping up the standards of the work by setting up a style of ongoing training and supervision that the workers will be strongly motivated to take part in, and evaluate their own performance with far more commitment than has often been the case in practice.

A progressive step has already been taken in the production and circulation of two valuable, clearly expressed position papers entitled *Worker Selection* and *Preparation of Training Syllabus*.

There is also a drive for more comprehensive and sophisticated systems of information storage and retrieval to enable workers to have a wider range of accurate, up-to-date information in a readily accessible form. Seminars are being held already to prepare workers for this.

At present the whole national administration is served by a very capable part-time secretary operating from home. But the suggested developments will obviously make far heavier administrative demands, requiring the establishment of a national secretariat with adequate premises.

The pace of these developments will depend on what happens in New Zealand's social, economic, and political future. An economic downturn under a conservative government may lead to a demand for cuts in welfare funding, while at the same time increasing the need for welfare services. Increased prosperity might lead to complacency and some slackening of overt demand for crisis services. But more fundamental trends (assuming we avoid world economic collapse and World War III) may be ongoing high rates of unemployment, along with an increasing public acceptance of the concept of expanding the opportunities for paid service in the fields of recreation, leisure, and community welfare, to take up the slack in the more traditional forms of employment. This climate could be favorable to the type of development associated with citizens advice bureaus.

REFERENCES

The C.A.B. a community signpost. (1974). *Consumer Review 4* (November). Wellington: Consumers Institute of New Zealand.

Haigh, D. et al (Ed.). (1979-1984). Opportunities for change. *Community Forum, 1-4.* Auckland, New Zealand.

Lawrence, M. (1977). The need for counselling training for voluntary workers. *Community Forum* (June). Auckland, New Zealand.

New Zealand Association of Citizens Advice Bureaus (1981). *Handbook on the Administration of a Citizens Advice Bureau.* Auckland, New Zealand.

4

IMPLEMENTING A CAB SYSTEM IN CYPRUS
Prospects and Problems

ELENI WILTCHER

The experiences of the author over many years as a Greek Cypriot led to the realization of the almost total absence of any advice-giving centers on the island. Consequently, citizens either went without service or sought legal advice at great expense. Because of the author's training and experience in the United Kingdom in a London Local Authority, the idea that people are extremely capable of seeking appropriate solutions to their own problems provided they are given unrestricted access to advice and information was reinforced.

THE PLANNING PHASE: THE PROPOSAL

Based on a decision to return to Cyprus for a year, the idea of developing an advice agency in Cyprus became attractive and plans for its development began six months prior to departure for Cyprus.

In order to gain some expertise, the author carried through the following program:

(a) Initial discussions with representatives of the National Association of Citizens Advice Bureaus. Contact with a worker at NACAB offices specializing in assisting the development of CAB-type services abroad was helpful although the association could offer no financial support.

(b) Attendance in a CAB Organizers Course. NACAB arranged for participation in an organizers course which included knowledge of the following:
Finance
Staffing
Accommodation
Type of problems brought to CABs
Training
Advertising
Liaison with official and voluntary agencies
Advocacy

(c) A period of part-time placement in a local CAB, which provided experience of the day-to-day pressures facing CAB workers in terms of the complexity of their task and in terms of organizational structures and limitations.

The Project Proposal

From the above-mentioned experience, a document was written entitled "Proposals for the Setting Up of a Citizens' Advice Bureau Service in Cyprus." The first part of the report described the origins and development in CABs in the United Kingdom, the range of information, areas covered, and the aims of the bureau. Key points stressed the rights of individuals to *know,* to be *impartially advised,* and thus to be in a better position to articulate their needs.

In addition, this document emphasized the role of CABs in social policy development at both national and local levels. The notion of information and advice for a citizen being too important to be left to chance was stressed, as was the recognition accorded to CABs via central and local government funding.

The second part of the report focused on Cyprus and the effects of the war of 1974; the problem of the massive number of refugees; and the difficulties of ordinary people both in locating basic sources of information, advice, and advocacy and also in being able to afford the costs of any such service then provided by solicitors. It was also suggested that the development of a *free, impartial* and *confidential* advice-giving agency in Cyprus was a current and very urgent social need and that its establishment would be based on the United Kingdom model and principles.

The third part described the project and detailed the proposal for the initiation and implementation of a CAB:

(a) "to establish . . . in the South of Cyprus a Project aiming to develop an advice-giving agency based on the United Kingdom model and to also evaluate the need for possible expansion of the service at the end of the Project."

(b) Financing was recommended as being by International Bodies concerned with the provision of this type of service in developing countries. Funding and involvement by the Cypriot Government was seen more viable at the post-evaluation stage rather than at the initial stage. The reasoning behind this was twofold: the need to establish the independence of the advice-giving agency, and the belief that because of the uniqueness of the project, government support would be more likely once the project had begun, proved itself, and undergone evaluation.

(c) Due to the Project Leader's limited time available on the island, the length of the project was limited to one year (9/79-9/80). The time projected was as follows:

   (i) 3 months —developing contacts
              —publicizing the agency
              —setting up the agency
   (ii) 6 months —operation
   (iii) 3 months —evaluation and report.

(d) The venue was favored as being either: (i) at the natural center of a town and hence accessible by transport from villages, refugee camps; or (ii) at the center of an area of obvious needs, e.g. a refugee camp. The ideal was seen to be a central town office in conjunction with a part-time agency in an area of acute need.

(e) Accommodation, as a minimum, would consist of a waiting room and separate interviewing room together with basic furnishings, typewriter, telephone, stationery, and so forth.

(f) Staffing was proposed as follows:
   (i) One full-time paid leader.
   (ii) One part-time typist/receptionist.
   (iii) Volunteer workers recruited locally to assist the project leader. Training of volunteers was to be undertaken by the project leader.

(g) Financing was calculated after discussion with the United Kingdom NACAB staff and proposed at £10,000.

(h) Having proved its value, the project's future operation could be financed by a combination of funding from the Cypriot government and local Cypriot organizations. Future staffing development was foreseen as being provided by suitably trained people.

Following the circulation of the above report with NACAB staff, the report was circulated to various relevant United Kingdom agencies, professional workers, and academicians with knowledge of Cyprus. Letters of interest and support were received and all were sent to United Kingdom organizations for potential financial support.

However, all organizations contacted noted that it was outside the scope of their interest.

THE INITIATION PHASE: CORE GROUPS

Since the earlier, exploratory phase had not yielded financial support for the project, it was clear that the projected time frame for the program would have to be altered. Upon arrival in Cyprus, I met with several individuals who had contacts in the United Kingdom or the United States and were highly respected in Cypriot society.

After these meetings, the report was translated into Greek, an introductory cover letter was attached, and both were sent to individuals, groups, and organizations known for their interest in similar developments on the island. It should be noted here that the emphasis on Greek is because of the separation of the peoples of Cyprus into two military divided areas. The project certainly would have encompassed the Turkish community had its members been in the south of the island or had the island not been divided. As it stands at present, the north of Cyprus is closed to Greek Cypriots. A list of select contacts was then prepared by the "Cypriot co-worker," who also undertook to assist the author with the report's translation, its circulation, the financial costs involved, and general promotion. At the same time, the report was sent to the national press requesting consideration for publication, a request that was received very favorably.

Within a short time after the report's circulation and publication, a steady stream of letters arrived from numerous sources representing a broad cross-section of groups, including heads of churches, associations of social workers, political associations, and representatives of trade unions, banks, business, and government, as well as voluntary clubs and associations. Generally these responses were supportive, included some offers of financial assistance for publicizing such a project, volunteer support to operate the project, and practical advice. Given the overall encouraging reponse, a core group of significant community leaders was identified and invited to a meeting.

This main core group included the mayors of Limassol and Nicosia (the two largest urban areas on the island), the bishops of Limassol and Larnaca, the area social services manager for Limassol, the president of the Supreme Court, the director of the Bank of Cyprus and, of course, the co-worker in Cyprus.

It is worth noting here that in a small country such as Cyprus, and particularly among people such as the Cypriots, who are informal in virtually all matters, it is perfectly feasible, given sufficient reason, to contact senior figures and heads of organizations. The value of this cannot be underestimated, particularly given the earlier setbacks and lack of substantial support. Instead of dealing indirectly with impersonal organizations, it is important to be able to meet decision makers themselves.

The Core Group

This group, chaired by the mayor of Nicosia, met to consider the feasibility of the project.

The following was agreed:

(a) That such a project would fill an existing gap in services to the public by offering free, independent, impartial and confidential services to all citizens.

(b) That the project, as a center of information, would assist all other governmental and voluntary organizations by virtue of referring the inquiry to the correct source. This was recognized as improving the efficiency of such organizations, plus greatly reducing difficulties to the public.

(c) That the project could develop as an information and advice resource for service needs not currently covered by existing agencies (e.g., marital work and difficulties with young people) and would thus have a developmental focus.

(d) That the project had a clear advocacy role in enabling citizens to claim and secure their rights.

(e) Finally, that the project would act as a necessary reminder to all public service agencies of their primary function in serving the needs of the citizens (e.g., its social policy development role).

It was further agreed that the project, referred to as a "Pancyprian Pilot Scheme," would run from September 1980 to August 1981. In July a statistical report would be prepared and a project evaluation made with a view to considering its extension from the town of Limassol to all other major Cypriot towns. All core group members agreed to support the project, to become its representatives in their own town and to investigate local funding sources and support. It was also projected that local core groups would be established to implement the operation of local CABs. Details of these explorations and relevant fundings were to be sent to the author, who acted as the coordinator of activities.

In addition, it was agreed that a constitution would be prepared and attempts made to secure links with Paphos in the west of Cyprus, which was unrepresented at the meeting. Furthermore, a leaflet giving details of the project would be compiled and distributed across the south of the island.

Finally, members of the core group shared all above tasks as outlined and agreed to meet again in September 1980 to report back on developments and to consider a starting date if funding sources were secured. It was noted that premises would not present problems, since both the church and Town Hall in Limassol were in a position to make rooms available for the project's operation.

Publicity

The key issues now were publicity and organization. A leaflet was compiled, set out in the following manner;

(a) What is a CAB and what is its purpose?
(b) How does a CAB differ from other agencies?
(c) Who will fund the CAB?
(d) Who will operate the CAB?
(e) Who should be contacted for further inquiries?

In general, the leaflet emphasized the unique aspects of the project that set it apart from other agencies: Its service would be free, universal, centralized, open to all, and focused on problem-solving for the citizens, as well as concerned with seeking changes in other agencies that could lead to improvements in services to citizens. Moreover, it would be the first island service that was client based and not related to political, religious, or governmental influence. The service would also offer a strong advocacy policy on behalf of those who lack the necessary means to achieve a resolution of their problems.

The leaflet further emphasized the need to secure funding sources that will enable these tasks to be undertaken. Donations were requested from anyone wishing to support the project. It was noted that while the pilot scheme would be based in Limassol, the agency would be open to all inquiries from any part of Cyprus. Guided by a trained and experienced professional, staffing proposals would be reviewed. It was agreed that the language in use would be Greek initially, but that Turkish-speaking workers would be sought. Finally, the leaflet listed the names and addresses of all members of the core group for further inquiry and made a clear statement to the effect that "*you* can become a supporter of this progressive project."

The aim of the leaflet was to arouse interest and stimulate concern for the establishment of the project. Its intention was to strike a chord with people who would respond by saying, "Of course, we should have something like this in Cyprus." It was assumed that if the notion of a system of CABs would be accepted, the rest would simply follow subsequently. Copies of this leaflet were sent to all members of the core group for circulation in each major city.

Funding

In addition to the role of coordinator, the author had to explore funding possibilities in Limassol. In conjunction with several others, a list of possible contributors was prepared and each individual personally approached these potential contributors, who included heads of voluntary associations and churches, presidents of local professional associations, trade union and political leaders, and selected individuals in athletic clubs, banks, insurance companies, and refugee associations.

In order to make this rather enormous task possible, efforts were begun in Limassol. Of those contacted, most individuals were very willing to offer a monthly donation of £5.10 during the first year of the project. Most organizations and associations offered a lump sum of between £200 and £1,000. Having established a general *willingness* by the people of Limassol to financially contribute, the local core group met again to discuss ways of implementing these contributions and to prepare the relevant documentations.

It was agreed that:

(a) A committee composed of representatives of local voluntary, community, and statutory groups should be formed to manage the affairs of the CAB.

(b) Accessible premises should be secured with all the necessary equipment.

(c) A paid organizer should be appointed who will have responsibility for the day-to-day running of the bureau and for the training of volunteer workers.

(d) A bank account should be established so that contributions can begin to be deposited.

(e) Volunteers should be organized to collect monthly contributions.

These decisions were presented to the main core group at its next meeting in September 1980. The local core group was to be represented at this meeting by the author, who also undertook to prepare the relevant materials for a vigorous public relations campaign.

THE IMPLEMENTATION PHASE:
PROBLEMS AND CONSTRAINTS

The implementation phase began with a second meeting of the main core group. At this meeting, some difficulties arose because several members of the core group were absent, the project was already delayed, and the personal pressures on the author to return to the United Kingdom added to the existing problems.

Bearing these points in mind, the meeting proceeded to consider the following:

(a) The leaflets were distributed but the responses were limited.
(b) Apart from the list of contributors in the Limassol area, no other lists were prepared nor were any names for representations for Paphos proposed.
(c) While the church was able to reconfirm its offer of premises, there was no confirmation from the town hall.
(d) The preparation of the CAB constitution was delayed.

In view of these problems, the attendees at the meeting openly acknowledged that the work and tasks had not been effectively tackled. A number of explanations for this were discussed which merit further consideration. There had been difficulty in finding appropriate people to commit themselves to representing each town. While the concept of the project was received enthusiastically, many expressed a wish to await its functioning before committing themselves to active participation. Yet many would-be contributors in other towns than Limassol were reluctant to do so, since the project was to serve mainly citizens of another town.

Since it was acknowledged that the imminent departure of the author would further complicate the situation, a fresh proposal was drawn up by the Women's Voluntary Association in Nicosia. This proposal, which was received from the president of the association, attempted to proceed with the project in the following manner. Two paid part-time organizers (one for Nicosia and one for Limassol) would be appointed. Premises were available at the town hall in Nicosia and in the church in Limassol. Their salaries would be paid through offers of contributions from each town. Thus each town could meet its own costs. Volunteers assigned to two paid organizers could be trained by the author, who was due to return to Cyprus for this purpose for a short period. It was agreed to consider these proposals and to consult further with the initiator of the project (the author).

Before leaving Cyprus the author had several discussions with the president of this association and was advised that the plans were to:

(a) Prepare a constitution.
(b) Form an association.
(c) Elect a committee.
(d) Find volunteers and paid organizers.
(e) Set dates for training.

Since the author's departure in October 1981, a number of attempts have been made to complete these tasks but, to date, little progress has apparently occurred.

CONCLUSION

The attempt to establish a CAB in Cyprus was the outcome of an individual initiative that arose from the author's personal background and early experiences in Cyprus and professional education and training in the United Kingdom. While the project was initially well received in Cyprus and appeared to have a good chance for implementation, lack of sufficient time, resources, and involvement with community organizations contributed to the failure of this effort to establish an access system in Cyprus.

5

CITIZENS ADVICE BUREAUS IN A CHANGING SOCIETY
An Israeli Report

YEMINA BARNEIS
OFRA FISHER

Since its founding in 1948, Israeli society has experienced long periods of rapid social and economic change. It has also absorbed a large number of immigrants from nearly 100 countries. Today these immigrants make up 50 percent of the country's Jewish population of 3 million. The challenge of the last 35 years has been the absorption of these immigrants with their very different social and cultural backgrounds into Israel's constantly changing society.

This chapter is intended to discuss how Israel's Citizen's Advice Bureau Service attempts to provide an advice and information service within the above context. The paper shows how the CAB service attempts to maintain a flexible bureaucratic structure for the purpose of adapting its resources to local needs.

HISTORY AND DEVELOPMENT

The growth and development of CABs in Israel has paralleled the three stages of development that Israel has experienced as a nation. The first stage extends from 1948 to 1970, from the establishment of the state to the end of the War of Attrition. The second stage dates from 1970 to 1977, from the end of the War of Attrition to the election

AUTHORS' NOTE: *We would like to thank Dr. Reuven Barneis and Dr. Ron Meier for their invaluable assistance in the completion of this chapter.*

of the Likud Party to form the government. The third stage extends from 1977 to the present.

1948-1970: This period after Israel's independence was characterized by social and economic instability. Externally, defense considerations absorbed most of the country's limited resources. Internally, the country was faced with problems of absorbing large numbers of North African and Asian immigrants of diverse linguistic, social, and cultural backgrounds, most of whom were poor. Concurrently, survivors of the Nazi Holocaust also arrived in significantly high numbers.

The main response to this great influx of immigrants was the establishment of a centralized social welfare system. Designed to provide a universal system of social benefits and services, the system tended to foster a paternalistic dependency among the citizens seeking help:

> Israel, being a rather centralized welfare state, has an elaborate administrative structure. The ordinary citizen cannot avoid permanent contact with a complex array of bureaucratic institutions. The immigrants are even more dependent on contact with bureaucracies. The organization of the whole process of immigration and responsibility for the primary absorption of immigrants is the concern of the State and other public agencies. From their very first days in the country, the immigrants are dependent on the official arrangement, hence they have to cope with bureaucracy. This high level of organization has undoubtedly its positive aspects as no immigrant is left helpless and uncared for in this new and strange situation. People are housed, clothed and fed, work is provided, children are sent to school, and the sick are hospitalized, and nevertheless the situation has its desocializing effects. . . . The danger of this situation lies in the apathy and tendency to self-segregation, caused by the cutting of channels of communication and the diminished contacts with the surrounding social groups. (Rivka Bar Yoseph, 1981, pp. 25—27)

For an extended period of time immigrants were dependent on the social welfare system to facilitate their absorption into Israeli life. Because of the centrality of these services and the limits imposed on local autonomy in adjusting national benefits and services to local needs, the system fostered dependency upon citizens while others "fell between the chairs."

Another response was the establishment of a local CAB office in Haifa in 1948, followed by similar offices in other cities and towns. The local offices, operated by volunteers and geared to local needs, were not bureaucratically accountable to a centralized service. The first CAB offices provided a limited information and advisory service, which was different in nature than the national services. These early offices provided information and advice, encouraged "self-help" skills, and helped citizens maximize their rights and in turn their independence.

In comparison to the national network of social services, the CAB offices were only marginally influential in changing the social welfare system. They adapted to local needs by remaining independent of the national welfare system, but at the same time were unable to expand because of budgetary limitations.

1970-1977: The second period in CAB's development began during Israel's rapid economic expansion following the Six-Day War and the War of Attrition. Until the 1973 Yom Kippur War, the country experienced a period of economic expansion and relative peace on its borders, which, from a social point of view, encouraged the public expression of social tensions that had been previously sublimated to the needs of national defense. An example of this is the Israel Black Panthers:

> In January 1971, the Israeli public was shocked to discover that the Black Panthers had arrived on the Israeli scene. A society preoccupied for many years with external tensions, wars, and relations with Arabs in occupied territories was made rudely aware of the existence of serious unrest in its midst. A group of Oriental Jews from Jerusalem, mostly of Moroccan origin, proclaimed themselves "Panterim Shchorim" (Black Panthers) and put forward a series of peremptory demands. They asked the government to immediately stop all alleged discriminatory practices against Oriental Jews and root out poverty. (Erik Cohen, 1981, p. 147)

Because of relative peace on the country's borders, the social issues raised by the Black Panthers and similar protest groups were accepted by the press and government as legitimate topics for national concern. For the first time systematic public attention was given to the socioeconomic gap between the different classes and ethnic groups that made up the different waves of immigration that occurred. In order to bridge this socioeconomic gap, additional funds were allocated to social services on the national and local levels.

This attention to social issues and reallocation of public funds encouraged the rapid growth of CAB offices. The minister of welfare at the time initiated a program for a national system of CAB offices, which called for (1) an increase in the number of local CAB offices as part of a national information and advisory service, and (2) the financing of the program through a special ministerial fund earmarked for experimental projects. This was done in order to ascertain the visability of a national information and advisory system and retain the CAB's local focus and flexibility.

The Yom Kippur War did not abort the program. The economy continued to expand to provide both "guns and butter," and the program initiated by the minister of welfare was put into practice in 1974. Using a modified British CAB model, 70 CAB offices were established by 1978 in over 40 towns and cities. At the same time, experimental projects were initiated for the purpose of reaching wider populations. Examples of these projects include the opening of a CAB office in a factory and a general and psychiatric hospital, and the funding of a mobile office to provide CAB services to residents of small development towns, primarily in the southern region of the country.

1977-1983: The year 1977 was a turning point in Israel's political history. The 1977 elections found the Labor Party at its lowest level of popularity. As the main coalition party in every previous government, the Labor Party had been held responsible for the post Yom Kippur War, corruption, high inflation and taxation, the drop in immigration, and the rise in emigration. In protest, the Likud Party headed by Menachem Begin replaced Labor as the country's largest political party and formed the first non-Labor coalition government (Frankel, 1980, p. 11-12). One of the major aims of government policy was to increase governmental efficiency. In the field of welfare and labor, one of the first acts initiated was the amalgamation of the welfare and labor ministries under one umbrella ministry. As part of a coalition agreement, the portfolio of this ministry was given to the "Democratic Party for Change," and the minister to whom this portfolio was assigned was Israel Katz, a social worker and former head of the National Insurance Institute. This was the first time a non-Labor, secular party was responsible for the operation of Israel's social welfare system.

During Israel Katz's tenure as minister, several decisions were made that affected the CAB service. First, the responsibility of determining who is eligible for insurance benefits and income maintenance was transferred from the local welfare offices to the National Insurance Institute. In effect, the local social worker's discretion in determining eligibility was replaced by law, thus legalizing the provision of financial assistance to people in need. As a result, welfare benefits became a citizen's right, and not a privilege, by being based on clear rules of eligibility. Clearly, eligibility for benefits was dependent upon the citizen's knowledge as to how to apply. CAB offices, as well as other service organizations, assumed responsibility to provide this information. Second, the CAB's status as an experimental project ended when it was absorbed into the ministry as an "established" service. Third, the CAB was combined with two other services, the ombudsmen service and the appeals committee, and formed one umbrella organization called the "Service for Citizens' Rights."

In the beginning of the 1980s, in response to rapid inflation and the growing national debt, governmental funding of the ministry's services was cut back. Some CAB offices were closed, dropping from a total of 70 offices to a low of 40 offices that are currently functioning. All special projects were "frozen." In addition, TV and radio advertisements designed to acquaint the public with CAB services were cut back or cancelled.

In 1982, the service received 60,000 requests for assistance, which indicates that the general public perceives the CAB as a reliable and trustworthy problem-solving agency. On the other hand, this number represents a growing demand on CAB resources, specifically the service's front-line workers. In order for the service to offer a high level of assistance, it has placed increasing importance on the competency of its volunteers, the availability of all-inclusive up-to-date information, and the maintenance of open channels of communication.

IDEOLOGY OF THE CAB SERVICE

The CAB service in Israel has not developed a clear ideological statement of its purposes. Though the objectives that have evolved remain "uncodified," they provide the "glue" that holds the service together and allows it to adapt to economic and social changes at the local and national level. (This point is discussed in more detail in the section on "Bureaucratic Structure.")

The five main objectives shared by both volunteer and paid workers in CAB services are:

(1) To provide information to citizens about their rights.
(2) To maximize citizens' self-help skills in dealing with problems.
(3) To advocate for individuals and groups with problems, as indicated.

(4) To provide services by means of an impartial system of peer counseling (i.e., volunteers).
(5) To conduct its work with confidentiality.

To put these objectives into operation is admittedly not simple in a society experiencing rapid social and economic changes. During times of instability, when personal and social problems are exacerbated and solutions are less readily available, the Israel social services tend to foster a paternalistic dependency among welfare clients. This dependency, labeled the "Magiya Lee" ("Give Me") syndrome, accentuates the passivity of a person seeking help as he transfers responsibility for his circumstances from himself to the service involved. Although the "Magiya Lee" approach to problem-solving helps a person cope with his primary anxiety over lacking solutions to his problems, it tends to foster long-term dependency.

The aim of CAB service to provide assistance is very different from the approach described above. The service tries to provide information and counseling focused on a particular issue and not on a person's total situation. The CAB service attempts to help a person exercise his rights and utilize self-help skills that may be applied to other problem-solving areas in the person's total life adjustment. The fact that the service provided by peers (volunteers) is intended to prevent to some extent the development of paternalistic dependency.

The application of these methods has proved difficult for two main reasons. First, except for a relatively short period between 1967 and 1973, Israel has experienced rapid social and economic change. At a time when social problems for citizens have become most acute, the services of the CAB have been cut back. Second, citizens advice bureaus do not function in a vacuum. Many of the people approaching the CAB for assistance are already socialized to the frustrations in seeking help and therefore tend to be reluctant and not absolutely trusting.

BUREAUCRATIC STRUCTURE

The CAB Service is similar to other ministerial social services in that it is divided into different strata of responsibility, authority, and accountability. The service is divided into four hierarchical levels: (1) the national office, consisting of a director, information officer, and supportive staff; (2) regional offices, staffed by regional supervisors; (3) local offices, comprised of area coordinators; and (4) individual

CAB offices staffed by volunteers working directly with those seeking assistance. These strata interlink "organically" (Burns and Stalker, 1961) in most matters of mutual concern. Individual offices have the necessary autonomy to adapt to local circumstances and situations. The exception is in the realm of yearly budgeting and staffing, for which decisions are made generally on the national level with minimum consultation with the regional or local offices.

In carrying out its program of services, communication between the CAB offices is primarily advisory and not directive. Interlevel communication does not follow a hierarchical order but rather a horizontal pattern, as workers from one office are permitted to consult with workers from another. For example, a local coordinator is permitted to consult the national information officer in resolving a particular problem and only report the interaction post hoc to the immediate supervisor at the regional office. In other words, interaction and communication between service workers is primarily involved in problem-solving and is not bureaucratically oriented.

The following two examples are illustrative of the points discussed above. In the first instance, the setting up of a new office is discussed in terms of how its place in the hierarchy permits it to adapt service ideals to local circumstances and situations. In the second instance, front-line work in a CAB office is discussed in terms of how the service's ideals are implemented in direct work with clients.

Setting Up a New Office

In 1982, after being closed for some time, an office in a suburb of one of the country's largest cities was reopened following a decision reached as the result of a series of meetings between service representatives and local community leaders. The contacts with local leaders fell into two categories: (1) the contact made by the national office with community leaders and officials for the purpose of offering CAB services; and (2) the longer period of negotiation between the parties in order to determine whether a CAB office is actually needed and whether it is feasible.

In order to open a CAB office, three criteria must be met: (1) a population is identified that needs and can make use of a CAB office, (2) the local community is willing and able to provide the physical premises for the office, and (3) there are no other organizations in the community that are currently offering a similar service.

The latter two criteria are relatively easy to determine. The first criterion, however, is problematic, particularly since the concept of need becomes even more complex during times of economic and social stability. A CAB official negotiating with local community leaders should be able to determine what the community's main problems are and whether a CAB office can fit into the community and offer a viable service. Although admittedly this is an idealistic prescription of what should be done, the gap between the ideal and practice is narrowed because the negotiating official is given a considerable amount of autonomy in the negotiating process. Usually a regional staff member or local coordinator together with a regional supervisor conduct the negotiations. Thus, regional and front-line CAB workers determine how service policy is implemented, whether a CAB office can provide viable service to a particular community, and how it will function in response to local situations and circumstances.

After a decision is made to open an office, a salaried person is hired to coordinate its daily operation. In the example mentioned above of the reopened office, the national supervisor may temporarily assume responsibilities of a local coordinator supplemental to other responsibilities in order to facilitate the rapid opening of the office. This reflects the service's flexibility, inasmuch as the national information officer is not tied down to a job title but is also free to take on appropriate tasks that promote the ideals of the service.

A second example of staff flexibility is the possibility that a local coordinator may assume responsibilities usually delegated to volunteers because no volunteers may be found in the community. This shows how CAB workers identify with CAB ideals beyond their particular job description. And since workers identify primarily with these service ideals, their job descriptions are adapted to local conditions and circumstances. This permits the CAB to adapt services to local needs, rather than adapting the local needs to prescribed service patterns.

Front Line Work in CAB Offices

Two factors contribute to gaining satisfaction and high status in front-line work. First, volunteers are usually elderly persons who have retired from successful careers, albeit different from CAB work. As a result, interactions around work issues between salaried and volunteer staff tend to be conducted as between equals sharing similar goals. Second, a significant amount of time and energy are invested in the collecting, updating, and disseminating information, which is considered high-status activity. As a result, this front-line work by a direct service agent is considered high-status work.

The following sections examine three aspects of front-line work: (1) the relationship between the salaried and volunteer staff; (2) the volunteers, who they are and how they are screened; and (3) front-line work with individuals seeking assistance. These procedures may not be clearly defined, but are functional in the light of the CAB's attempts to maintain an "organic" structure in providing information and advisory services.

The Relationship Between Salaried and Volunteer Staff

CAB is described by service workers as a "professionally planned, volunteer service agency." This relationship between salaried and volunteer staff can be problematical. The balance in decision making is usually weighed in favor of the salaried staff, which is always responsible for decisions concerning the opening and staffing of an office. This could create tensions on the part of volunteers who perceive the salaried staff as using their powers to divide work into "professional" work, which they take on themselves, and mundane, "dirty" work, which is allocated to the volunteers.

However, this has not happened in the CAB service. For the reasons noted above, front-line work is considered high-status work. This permits a generally accepted division of work responsibilities between the two groups, albeit with some overlapping. As a rule, salaried workers are responsible for administrative matters on all levels of the CAB Service strata except in the local offices. This includes participation in national policy-making, training and supervision of volunteers, and building ties with relevant institutions and community groups. Provision of direct services in day-by-day operation are the joint responsibility of volunteers and the local coordinators.

Who are the volunteers, and how are they screened? As previously mentioned, volunteers tend to be elderly persons who have completed successful careers of their own. Although this profile of a volunteer has its exceptions, the service has discovered through experience that the most successful volunteers tend to come from this population group. At present, the service continues to recruit the senior citizen but will accept and screen other candidates.

Once volunteer candidates are identified, a two-way screening procedure is carried out, the dual purpose of which is to help the candidates decide, on the basis of first-hand observation of office activities, if they want to join the CAB. At the same time the suitability of the candidates is considered by the local coordinator.

As an integral part of the first meeting with the candidates, the coordinator emphasizes that volunteering is very demanding and includes extensive responsibilities. This message is important, as it communicates to the candidates the high regard that volunteer work is accorded. This attitude is in contrast to the relative low status of volunteer work in many other community settings. If the candidates agree to continue contact, a program of observation is arranged in which they observe the workings of a CAB office first-hand over a six-week period and not less than one day a week for four hours.

At the end of this period the coordinator meets again with the candidates at a formal, scheduled meeting. (They meet informally during the six-week period in chance encounters when the coordinator visits the office, or at scheduled meetings for the purpose of answering specific questions the candidates might have about office activities.) The purpose of this final meeting at the completion of the training period is to decide on the candidates' interest and suitability in becoming CAB volunteers.

Rarely are these meetings used to "screen out" candidates. The observation-screening procedure tends to self-select volunteers, since most candidates who find that they do not "fit" as volunteers drop out before the end of the six-week period. Rather, these meetings serve as initiation ceremonies in which the candidates' status is acknowledged as that of a CAB volunteer.

A volunteer's job description includes the following: initial work commitment of no less than one day per week (four hours or more) on a regular basis, which at a later date increases to two days a week; attendance at monthly volunteer training sessions and other regular volunteer meetings; receiving people seeking assistance during office hours; and keeping written records of services provided. In addition, the volunteer is required to schedule his personal holidays during the month of August when the CAB offices are closed and accept supervision from the local coordinator. In other words, the work demands of the volunteer is strikingly similar to the job descriptions of salaried workers at other CAB levels, and extends well beyond the usual expectations of the "volunteer." This contributes to the view of the volunteer as front-line activity that commands a high regard.

Front-Line Work

A definition of front-line work is the cutting edge or the point where the service comes into contact with the population seeking its assistance. The focus of these contacts is problem-solving through advice-giving or the provision of information.

In order for the CAB office to function successfully contact between volunteers and clients must include three elements: (1) a pool of updated information or a readily available source of information that can be enlisted in the solution of a particular problem; (2) a system of communication between the different levels of the CAB in order to facilitate the quick dissemination of information; and (3) trust between the volunteer and client. Each of these elements is discussed below.

(1) Sources of Information. The quality of service offered in front-line work is dependent on the quality of information available to the volunteer. This requires knowledge of a wide range of information, including relevant laws regarding services available in the community. This information is acquired in four ways.

(a) The volunteer is encouraged to read newspapers and relevant periodicals regularly.
(b) The volunteer is encouraged to make use of the CAB's sources of information. One of the most important of these sources is the national information officer, who, located at the national office, is responsible for collecting data on civil rights and services offered by national, regional, local, and voluntary agencies. Periodically updated information is disseminated through the CAB offices in the form of an information sheet, which is kept on file in each CAB office.
(c) Volunteers are encouraged to use the information file of any office and contribute to its updating. Over a period of time, a local file system of a particular office will reflect the needs of the community.
(d) When beset by a particular problem, volunteers are encouraged to consult with local coordinators, regional supervisors, or the national information officer.

(2) Dissemination of Information Through the Different Levels of the Service. In addition to the information sheet, volunteers are encouraged to participate in monthly training sessions, the purpose of which is to provide current information about a particular issue. Topics of past sessions include labor laws, presented by a legal advisor from the Ministry of Labor and Social Affairs; new national insurance regulations presented by an official from the National Insurance Institute; the rights of citizens to use the small claims court and how to file a claim presented by a judge; housing laws, as issued by a representative of Israel's public housing corporation (Amidar);

also, special problems of and facilities for battered women as presented by the director of a shelter for battered women.

Information is also disseminated throughout the service via bimonthly two-day in-service training sessions for all salaried staff. These meetings have two purposes. First, they provide opportunity for workers to discuss their experiences and problems on a national level, contacts which are essential in deepening their understanding of social issues on the local level. If a common problem cannot be solved locally, these meetings serve as a forum through which this information is brought to the national level. On several occasions, issues discussed at in-service training sessions have become government bills presented to the Knesset (Israeli parliament) with the assistance of the CAB national director.

Second, these meetings provide an opportunity for workers to become acquainted with current social problems on a national level. Structured around discussions led by outside lecturers, some of the topics include the following: new services for women, the role and function of shelters for battered wives, and "burnout" among workers in public service. Local coordinators are expected to discuss the content of these meetings with CAB volunteers.

(3) Development of Trust Between Volunteer and Client. As in the relationship between salaried and volunteer staff, the relationship between volunteer and client has a built-in difference in status. This difference in status, however, only marginally affects volunteer-client relationships, and an atmosphere of trust generally characterizes most meetings between the two parties.

The full reasons for this are complex and too numerous to discuss in full within the context of this paper, but it can be said that the main reasons are the following:

    (1) Volunteers, as noted earlier, are usually elderly persons who have successfully completed a career. Older volunteers often project confidence and reassurance in a tension-free manner, and so the individual is willing to trust them.

    (2) The client is promised confidentiality. Case files are not opened in local or national offices. Names of clients are used. only if the service takes on an advocacy role and use of the name is necessary in correspondence with outside agencies, and when one volunteer communicates to a second volunteer or local coordinator relevant information about a case, which is written in the office's daily diary. The diary is not used for any other purpose.

(3) Probably the most important reason is the confidence inspired by the success of the CAB offices in solving problems on the local level.

CONCLUSION

It is the intention of this chapter to show how Israel's citizen advice bureaus provide a valuable service to citizens in a country that has and continues to undergo rapid social and economic change. The chapter has also shown how the service strives to maintain an "organic" organizational structure for the purpose of providing an information and advisory service that is responsive to individual and local needs.

REFERENCES

Bar Yoseph, Rivka (1981). Desocializing and resocializing: The adjustment process of immigrants. In *Studies of Israeli society: Migration, ethnicity, and community.* Ernest Krausz, (Ed.), Transaction Books, New Brunswick, NJ: Transaction.

Burns, T., & G. M. Stalker (1961). *Management and innovation.* New York: Barnes and Noble.

Cohen, Erik (1981). The Black Panthers and Israeli Society," In Ernest Krausz (Ed.), *Studies of Israeli society: Migration, ethnicity, and community* (vol. 2). New Brunswick, NJ: Transaction Books.

Frankel, William (1980). *Israel observed: An anatomy of the state.* Thames and Hudson.

Sherkensky, Arey (n.d.). Public administration in Israel: A criticism (in Hebrew), *Iyunim, 34.* (A Government publication of Israel's Internal Auditing Office.)

6

NETWORKS OF ACCESS SYSTEMS IN ISRAEL
A Conceptual Analysis

ABRAHAM DORON
ELI FRENKEL

The welfare state is at present the target of serious attacks by its opponents as well as its supporters. There are many factors involved in the creation of this critical attitude towards the welfare state which are beyond the scope of this chapter. Our concern here is to deal with the particular set of relationships between the individual and the welfare state institutions at the point of access and the actual utilization of available benefits and services. In the ongoing debate over the welfare state, the increased specialization and bureaucratization of public services in general and of the social services in particular have made the problems of access and the use of existing networks of services a critical issue. The central questions are these: To what extent can these barriers to access be overcome, and can a properly organized network of information and advice services make a significant contribution to solving some of these problems of access and use. The important issue is whether such a range of services can enhance the well-being of the individual by enabling the person to use the services that are available and helpful. It is also important to consider whether improved access facilities can change the existing critical attitude toward the welfare state.

It is generally accepted that the increased bureaucratization and specialization of social welfare services have created barriers of access between people in need of services and the available resources. Furthermore, it has been argued that the most vulnerable population groups, which are in greatest need of these services, are faced with the greatest difficulties in gaining access (Kahn, 1973). The barriers of access to social welfare services are twofold. First, people have only a vague idea of their rights to a particular service benefit. It is very difficult for most people to find their way in the complexity of policies and social service programs. Second, even when people are aware of their rights to a particular service they may not know how to qualify for available benefits. The difficulties of access may be due either to bureaucratic requirements at the entrance level or to difficulties in actually linking up with the appropriate services (Perlman 1975).

One of the efforts to overcome these barriers to access has been the development of information and advice services. The adaptation of the British citizens advice bureau has served as a major model in the development of differential access systems in Israel. A major objective of this chapter is to report on these various access systems and to suggest a conceptual model of operative access systems that are designed to link the inquirer to the needed resource.

NETWORKS OF ACCESS SYSTEMS

Israel has three main networks of information and advice services: a network operated by the central government, a local authority network, and a network maintained by a number of specialized agencies to serve their specific clientele.

The Central Government Network: CABs

A national network of citizens advice bureaus, patterned after the CAB in Britain, was established in 1974 by what was then the Ministry of Social Welfare, which has since been combined into the Ministry of Labor and Social Affairs. This is a governmental network of information and advice services that operates in various cities and towns (usually one CAB per locality), and generally in jurisdictions that are not capable of maintaining such a service on their own.

The network was established in the mid-1970s with the clear intention to progressively cover the entire country with its bureaus. The changing political and economic circumstances made it difficult, however, for these goals to be realized. Since the late 1970s the service has been seriously affected by cuts in public expenditure for social welfare activities. Instead of expanding its activities the number of bureaus has been reduced from 71 in 1979 to 46 in 1982. Sixty-three

CABs served about 55,000 citizens in 1980 and 50 CABs served about 49,000 citizens in 1981, a reduction of 20.6 percent in the number of bureaus but only 10.9 percent in the population served. On the average, 980 citizens were served in a bureau in 1981 compared to 873 citizens in 1980. The comparative date indicate a stable demand for these services, notwithstanding the reduction of total CABs.

The Local Information Bureaus (LIBs)

Independent networks of local information and advice services were developed mainly in the country's two biggest cities, Jerusalem and Tel-Aviv. At first these were established as part of various social service sectors, and only later became a free standing municipal network of services. The local municipal information and advice services in these cities are located mostly in poor neighborhoods and in newly established parts of the cities, which are populated largely by new immigrants. The inhabitants of these neighborhoods usually face serious difficulties in finding their way in the elaborate maze of existing social services. The aim of the local information services, therefore, has been to help these population groups in facilitating their access and utilization of available services. Although there were some informal and nonsystematic attempts to exchange experiences and knowledge among information services in the two cities, the network in each city has continued to operate independently, and the nature and range of their activities are determined by the local municipality.

In view of decreasing resources and the budgetary cuts, the scope of LIB programs has been drastically reduced. The information services in Tel-Aviv were practically eliminated, and only Jerusalem has retained its network of LIBs. But even in Jerusalem, there was a substantial growth of about 20 percent in the city's population in recent years, from 346,000 people in 1974 to 415,000 in 1981, and the network of information and advice services has hardly kept pace. There were nine LIBs in Jerusalem in 1974. Since then three LIBs have been closed, one of them replaced by a governmental CAB, and two new LIBs have been opened, one in a new section of the city and another in an Arab neighborhood in East Jerusalem. Although CABs have replaced to some extent the local information services of the municipalities, especially in Tel-Aviv, there has been a significant decline in the coverage in these services, as related to population growth. The seriousness of the decline can be understood by the fact that most of the population growth in Jerusalem represents the influx of new immigrants, who constitute the main target population of information and advice services network.

The reduced resources allocated to information services in the last few years has not only resulted in the reduction of the number of CABs and LIBs, but has also severely limited the duration of time that bureaus are open to the public. Very few CABs and LIBs are open five days a week (the working week in Israel is six days). Most of the LIBs operate four days a week and only for four and a half hours a day. Some of the CABs are open only once a week, some two to four days a week and some for periods as brief as two to three hours a day.

As will be more fully discussed later, many of the workers in these services are very enthusiastic and dedicated to their job, but the limited hours of operation significantly reduces the accessibility and effectiveness of these services to potential users.

Specialized Agencies

In addition to the central government and local authority network, which are independent networks of information, advice, and referral services, there exists in Israel a third network of information services, which operates as either a formal or an informal part of the activities of various specialized agencies. Some of these provide information regarding the specialized services of their own agencies such as the public health clinics. Other agencies provide a broader range of information that is more generic in the scope of information available, such as local information bureaus. The effective operation of all access systems, however, is dependent upon two significant factors: the accessibility of the agency to the public and the quality of its personnel.

CONCEPTUAL MODEL

An information and advice bureau has to be well publicized, centrally located, and must maintain an open-door policy. Every person who comes to the bureau needs to be served promptly, efficiently, and without any undue demands. It is especially important for the personnel of these services to be well acquainted with the legal provisions of the programs and resources available in the community, and the up-to-date procedures, regulations, and various entitlements that are available. Of special significance are the worker's skills in

TABLE 6.1 Services by Client Population

Clientele	General Services	Specific Services
Total population	1	3
Selected groups	2	4

transmitting this information and making referrals to other sources as may be required.

The major content of this section will deal with the application of a conceptual model of access systems that relate four major types of services to four levels of operational services, as illustrated by differential access systems. This empirical study of various operating information and advice services is based on information received from the Ministry of Labor and Social Affairs on the CABs network. Data are also based on a series of structured interviews that were conducted with workers in all the municipal LIBs in Jerusalem, and on a study of a sample of information and advice bureaus that represent specialized agencies (including two well baby clinics, the Advice Service for the Aged in the National Insurance Institute, the Emergency Health Care Service (Magen David Adom), and the Police Information Center.)

Types of Services

Information and advice services can be classified on two dimensions: The population or clientele served and the services about which information is provided as seen in Table 6.1

Type 1 information services are of a general nature and usually provide simple information on location of streets or institutions, public transportation, and so forth.

At the other extreme are type 4 services, which are very specific and serve a selected population. For the most part these are information bureaus operating within a specific service that may be involved in referring particular clients to specialized kinds of services.

The most common information and advice services are of type 2. These are services for selected groups in the population that provide information on all or most of the services available in the locality or within a wider geographical area. The selection of the population groups may also be based on defined categories of clientele (e.g., the elderly, veterans, and the like).

Type 3 information services are usually an integral part of a particular service sector and are designed to provide information and advice to a total population. An example of this type of service is the Magen David Adom (the Israeli Emergency Health Care Service), which provides information on health care services to all inquirers.

Levels of Services

An examination of access systems has revealed differential levels of services that suggest a continuum from information only to brokerage and referral to community-oriented tasks and social action.

Level A: Information Only

Providing simple and complex information, offering advice on how to proceed, steering the inquirer to a service able to help, providing personal support, and helping to establish entitlement to a particular service all constitute activities on Level A.

Level B: Client Referral/Brokerage

Level B client services may entail the role of the broker between people and various specific services, including referrals, follow-up, case-integration, and case advocacy.

Level C: Community-Oriented Tasks

Serving as a change agent in the community on Level C entails initiating activities in the Community, including reach out. Community education is also vital where inquiries reveal widespread need of information and community organization to meet human needs.

Level D: Social Action/Policy Role

A social action role with the aim of influencing existing social policies, including feedback to policymakers to promote advocacy and changes in policy and programs is assigned to Level D.

The remainder of the chapter will illustrate how the service types are related to the levels of services provided by a variety of access systems that may serve total or selection population groups. It should be noted that the delineation of service types and service levels are not discrete categories, but rather suggest differentiation, as illustrated by the seven access systems discussed below.

DISCUSSION: DIFFERENTIAL ACCESS SYSTEMS

Type 1: General Services for the Total Population

The Jerusalem Municipal Information Office

This office, one of a kind in the city, is an independent unit not linked to the network of LIBs in this city. The main purpose of the office is to serve tourists visiting the city, but as a municipal service, it is also open to all who request its services. The office is located in the center of the city in a storefront. It has one large room at its disposal, in a corner of which there is a small waiting area containing informative literature about the city, the current entertainment and cultural events, and the various municipal services. The office is open throughout regular working hours during the weekdays, excluding Saturday and official holidays. Those who come to the office in person, call, or write receive service that is provided free of charge and with no precondition. Except for a sign in front of the office, the Municipal Information Office is not advertised.

The office employs three nonprofessional workers who speak a number of languages. Sources of information used are maps of the city, telephone directories, and the publications distributed by the municipality and the Ministry of Tourism, mostly on cultural events and entertainment scheduled to take place in the city. Workers may take the initiative to contact various agencies and organizations for information generally not available through its usual sources.

This service operates on Level A, responding to people's inquiries. It provides mainly simple information: location of streets of institutions, transportation, events in the city, and general information on municipal services. It does not provide more complex information on laws, programs, rights, and so forth. If the client requests such information, he or she is referred to the proper municipal department that can answer his inquiry. In most cases the information involves "steering," which means directing the client to a resource for further follow-up by the client and not the worker.

The Police

The Israeli police, a national service, provides information on the local level through its emergency telephone line when the line is not busy with police emergency calls. This service operates in practically every locality seven days a week, 24 hours a day, and is especially useful for nighttime and weekend service, when other helping resources are not available. All callers receive a response, without restrictions or preconditions. The information provided tends to deal with location of sites or emergency services. When the police cannot answer the inquiry presented by the caller, a referral may be made to another information service, preferably in the location. The police also offer advice to callers on mishaps in cars or homes that may pertain to locked doors, gas leaks, and the like. Such advice is given over the telephone, but in emergency situations a mobile police unit can be sent to the aid of the caller.

Type 1 information services are very general. They serve the whole population, but their activities are limited to providing simple information and "steering" only.

Type 2: General Services for Selected Groups

The Citizens Advice Bureaus (CAB) Network

As already mentioned, the CABs network represents a governmental service and operates in collaboration with the local authorities. The cost of maintaining these bureaus is shared by both sponsors. The Ministry of Social Affairs is responsible for the workers' salaries and their training, and for publicizing the service. The local authority provides the physical location and other required amenities.

The CAB network covers most cities and larger towns in the country. In most places there is one CAB bureau covering the needs of the area. Only in the large cities are there more than one CAB. The population groups served by these bureaus are determined on a geographical basis. The bureaus are located on the site of other municipal or public services and are usually well advertised. There are signs in different sections of the locality which refer citizens to the CAB office. Most of the bureaus are open two to that hours a day, some in the morning, some in the afternoon. The service is free of charge and without any condition. Each bureau is managed by one part-time paid worker who is helped by volunteers of the locality served by the bureau. There are occasional in-service training programs, mainly to update information.

The CAB network operates on a more complex level of activities of Level B; it provides complex information on laws, services, and rights. The Level B activities, which essentially attempt to link clients and the service, include advising, diagnosing and referring, and serving a brokerage function between the person in need and the appropriate service. Level B activities include case integration and case advocacy. Occasionally a CAB worker may become involved in a case and perform the duties of other services. For example, a new immigrant has found a job in one town and an apartment has been offered to him in another town. A CAB worker, after many contacts with the housing authorities, will try to work out a satisfactory solution. Or, to cite another example, a family has problems with a new refrigerator. A CAB worker may contact the company that manufactured the refrigerator and press for replacement. Although the results in both cases may be satisfactory, the amount of time spent by the workers on these activities may be considerable, and divert the worker from other duties of the service that deals with more general information functions.

Local Information Bureaus (LIB), Jerusalem

These bureaus comprise a municipal network of information and referral services, which are loosely linked to each other through the network coordinator as well as through informal contacts of workers of the various bureaus in the course of their formal service delivery. In principle, each bureau is intended to serve the residents of the geographical area in which it is located, but in practice no one is refused service, even if the inquirer resides outside the designated area. Three of the bureaus are located on the premises of recently created "Local Service Centers," which include most of the municipal services in new sections of the city; one is in a Well Baby Clinic; and four others are in community centers or other municipal welfare services. Each bureau has one room at its disposal for reception and arrangements for waiting. Not one of the bureaus is directly accessible from the street level. However, there are signs on the street that publicize the location of the bureau. Six of the bureaus are open five days a week, four and half hours a day, mostly in the afternoon. One bureau, in a new neighborhood, is open all day four days a week, and another, also in a new neighborhood, is open officially five days a week throughout the day. The days when the bureaus are officially closed are often reserved for worker activities whose client case loads may require action beyond the scope or capabilities of the particular bureau.

Publications distributed in mailboxes publicize the location, working hours, and activities of the local bureau within the area. Many of the people who use the service also become aware of its existence through word of mouth.

In most of the bureaus there is one nonprofessional paid worker. Only in those bureaus located in the new sections of the city are there more than one worker. Sources of information available to the workers include staff meetings and information that is shared by the network coordinator. Personal experience and exposure to agency contacts are vital to the worker's background. There are no formal or systematic methods of updating information. When a worker is presented with an inquiry to which he or she has no answer, an appropriate source to obtain the information is sought. Some of the workers claim that more organized and comprehensive sources of information are needed to promote effectiveness and efficiency. Although there is a standard formal organizational pattern for all the bureaus, the nature of the work of the individual bureau and its range and scope of activities are largely dictated by the personality, initiative, and experience of the administrator in charge of the program. The efficacy of the program is dependent upon the extent to which effective personal relationships can be created between the worker and the client. Unfortunately, the less skilled worker may exceed his or her authority, interfere in family relationships, or exacerbate conflicts between neighbors in the area. While the cases do not occur often, they do regrettably occur, more often due to the lack of professional expertise on the part of the service agent.

Though the bureaus are defined as information services, workers tend to see their task mainly as providing a Level B type of service; that is, linking residents to various local services, including those provided by the municipality. Most of the workers note that they rarely deal with provision of simple information (such as location of streets) or even complex information (such as law and programs). Workers acknowledge that they often do not have the essential data to respond to information inquiries. Most of the applications are about concrete problems of the residents, which require an interventive service and not information only. When residents turns to the bureau for help they are referred by the worker to the agency, and often to a specific employee of the agency who deals with the particular problem. The workers do not offer case work as such, but they do try to relate to the covert as well as overt problems if that becomes apparent in the course of the client interview. Usually the service includes the provision of supporting relationships. Any individual who needs to talk to someone will not be turned away, even if he or she does not raise a specific problem.

So far the Jerusalem LIB activities of Level A, responding to clients, were described. Most of the work in the bureau is, however, on Level B, linking the client and the appropriate services. The workers are not content with referrals only but make contacts be-

tween the client and the agency by arranging appointments via telephone, letter, or in person. Moreover, their activities are not limited to
the bureau alone. They pursue their work outside the bureau in the
process of arranging matters for clients and accompany clients in
need of escort services, often including aged clients. Often two work
days a week are set aside for these out-of-office activities.

The workers use minimal entry forms to briefly report the content
of each inquiry and documentation of the service delivered. This type
of case-by-case recording does not permit aggregate reporting by
consistent categories possible. Follow-ups are carried out in some
instances, either through personal attention by the worker or when
the client returns to the bureau after the referral. In certain cases,
although not systematically, the worker tries to coordinate the services pertaining to his or her client. Usually this is done by bringing to
the attention of each of the services the fact that the client is being
taken care of by more than one agency. Occasionally the worker will
initiate a conference meeting of persons from the various agencies
related to the client situation for the purpose of case integration.
Activities of case advocacy are occasional and not systematic, and
are usually carried out at the personal discretion of the workers
themselves. In advocating for the client, workers usually try to "per-
suade" the official who is handling their client's case to respond in a
positive way, if possible.

It should be noted that specifically designed pro-activated
community-oriented tasks and social action activities are rarely undertaken by the access agency. More often, it may occur as a personal
initiative of the worker. Some of the workers are involved in outreach
activities through home visits. Most of the workers are in contact with
neighborhood committees but they do not initiate community activities. In emergency situations the bureau is open 24 hours a day
and, when asked to do so, the workers help in community organization activities.

When workers are presented with an inquiry to which no answer is
available, they report to the network coordinator. There is no formal
of regular way of reporting unserviced or pending cases.

Well-Baby Clinics

These clinics are part of public health services and operate
throughout the country. In addition to providing the main function of
preventive health care services to mothers and their young children,
the clinics also provide information and advice to people in need,
though not as a formal part of their service agenda. Information and

referral services are provided free of charge, and, for the other health-related services, small fees are charged based on the client's income.

The clinics are operated mainly by public health nurses who have no specific training for providing information services. Sources of general information are the personal experience of the nurses, their acquaintance with the existing network of services in the community, and published health information in materials that reach the clinic. No systematic method operates to disseminate current, updated materials.

Information, simple and complex, is provided in all areas, but principally on subjects related to family and community services, since most of the inquiries concern these subjects. The client is usually referred to the agency that deals with the assessed problem. In matters related to family health, the nurse makes an appointment for the client with the appropriate health care agency. Sometimes a nurse may help a client write a letter to a certain agency and may even add her own recommendation. No registration or follow-up is done in these cases.

The work of the clinic as a provider of information may overlap to a certain extent with the work of other information services, although it is of a more limited nature. There is an apparent need for closer contact between the health clinic and other information services located within the same community.

Type 3: Specific Services for the Total Population

It is primarily in the health area that specific services are provided for the total population. The universality of health concerns and the seriousness of health emergencies account for these urgently needed access services as illustrated by emergency health care programs.

Emergency Health Care

It is likely that the most frequently used Type 3 service is involved in emergency health care to the total population. This is a telephone service that provides information on health services, hospitals on call, location of health services, and so forth, as well as advice concerning medical matters, by a doctor on duty at the station. In emergencies an ambulance is sent to the client. The service operates 24 hours a day, seven days a week. The service is universal and not conditional in any way. The service is well publicized and is generally handled by calling an easily remembered number in most parts of the country.

This is a public service. One-third of its budget is supplied by the government, and the other two-thirds by donations.

Type 4: Specific Services for Selected Groups

The following illustration of a specific access service refers to a program of specific services for the aged especially designed for the aged population and delivered for the most part by the elderly.

While social action and policymaking may, by implication, occur or result as an unanticipated consequence, deliberate efforts at policy formulation and social action activities are almost totally lacking.

The Advice for the Aged and Pensioners of the National Insurance Institute

This service was established in 1972 by the National Insurance Institute, which is the state agency operating the country's social security programs. The service started with two bureaus in 1972, in Jerusalem and Ramat Gan, and has been extended to a network of eleven bureaus at present scattered all over the country. This is essentially an "aged to aged" service and is carried out primarily by volunteers. There are at present about 1400 volunteers working in the network. In each bureau there are two salaried workers, usually professional workers, who serve as coordinators. The volunteers are all elderly retired professionals who use their knowledge and experience to help their peers in need of services. The client population is comprised of elderly people, males 65 years and over, females 60 years and over, and other persons included in the pensioners category.

The bureaus are located in the local or regional offices of the National Insurance Institute and usually have one or more rooms reserved as a reception room and an interviewing room. The service is provided free of charge and is not conditional in any way.

Requests may pertain to a broad range of information and is not limited to information concerning national insurance benefits. The information provided is usually of a complex nature, concerning laws, rights, programs, and so forth. Simple information, such as location of addresses or transportation, is also given when requested, but responses to apparent simple inquiries may reveal some significant problems as well. Where specific problems are identified, the aged person is referred to the appropriate service and contact is made by the workers if indicated. Inquiries are registered and follow-ups are made until the case is closed. When the need arises, efforts toward case integration are made through conference meetings at which representatives of different agencies participate. Most of the activities take place within the bureau itself, but when necessary outside work is involved in making home visits or establishing other agencies making arrangements for the aged in various agencies. Most bureaus of this type are not involved in reach-out or other activities in the community.

Sources of information are past experience and updated information passed onto the workers by the supervisor. Most of the volunteers undergo a training program before they begin to work in the bureau, and occasionally there are in-service training courses. For the most part, however, workers rely on their own personal experiences and consult with their supervisors on updated information.

The service is publicized in newspapers and occasionally on television. Many know about the existence of the service as reported by utilizers of the service. There are no linkages between this service and other information services. This is regrettable, since it appears that this is the only information service in Israel that has plans to extend its program of services in the near future.

DISCUSSION/IMPLICATIONS

A network of information, advice, and referral services was developed in Israel in the 1970s, first in big cities under the auspices of municipalities and then a national network was established by the Ministry of Labor and Social Affairs, formed in accordance with the CAB model in Britain. Although there is a demand for these services by the population, its development has largely been brought to a halt in recent years due to cutbacks in public expenditure.

Some of the CABs maintained by the central government were closed. As a result of economic difficulties presently facing Israel, the prospects do not appear promising for further development of CABs in the near future. Actually, there may even be a decrease in the number of operating CABs. Moreover, many of the existing bureaus are open to the public for limited number of days and hours, which reduces their accessibility and thus the effectiveness of the service.

The findings confirm the conclusion of Doron and Frenkel (1977) that there is a relationship between the type of service and level of service. Type 1 and 3 services operate on Level A, responding to clients' inquiries, while type 2 services operate mostly on Level B, linking client and appropriate service. This relationship has some clear implications: Not all information services actually deal with the same information. Type 1 services have to obtain extensive simple information, mostly location of places. Workers in type 2 services have to be familiar with the bureaucratic demands of services and have diagnostic and interpersonal communication skills.

Since not all types of services carry the same tasks in providing information and advice, differential training programs have to be planned for workers in the different types of services.

The organization of an information, advice, and referral network has to take into consideration the balance and relationships between the different types of services. It is suggested that a few type 1 services, which provide mostly simple information to the total population, and a denser network of type 2 services, which serve selected groups in the population, are needed. Type 2 services can be helped by type 1 services, when simple information is needed, and/or by type 3 services when more expert or complex information on a specific service is needed.

Activities of the information, advice, and referral services described in this study are either on level A, responding to clients' inquiries, or on level B, linkage between clients and services. There are generally few activities on level C, community-oriented tasks, and practically none on level D, social action activities, except for possible self-help services for the elderly. Workers in information services meet people in need at a very crucial point in time, their "point of entry" (Hall 1974). The potential contribution of these workers to effectively make changes in the social service system, through feedback to policymakers, is vast.

It seems that the reason for the lack of social action activities in the information services network is threefold. First, there are no systematic or formal channels to pass on of feedback to policymakers. Second, the workers in the information bureaus are not aware of their potential in influencing the operation of social welfare services. And third, there is a feeling of powerlessness in this area of social change shared by workers in the different information service networks. By creating systematic feedback channels and training workers to be sensitive to deficiencies in social services, as well as by using these channels of feedback effectively, this very useful source of information can be utilized by planners and policymakers, who try to improve the social service system and eventually influence the welfare state.

REFERENCES

Doron, A., Frenkel, E. (1977). Information and advisory Services in Jerusalem. *Social Security, 14-15* (November), 103-115.
Hall, A. S. (1974). *The point of entry.* London: Allen and Unwin.
Kahn, A. J. (1973). *Social policy and social services.* New York: Random House.
Perlman, R. (1975). *Consumers and social services.* New York: John Wiley.

II

INFORMATION AND REFERRAL SERVICES SYSTEMS: I&R MODEL

The four chapters included in Part II identify both common elements of I&R provision in North America and describe up-to-date service delivery technologies, organizational structure, and staffing patterns. While they may represent "ideal" or model systems, they are sufficiently representative of common problems, and implicitly provide prescriptions for improved service delivery, and consequently would appear to be of utility to a diversity of information and referral (I&R) providers.

The two chapters by the American authors represent amalgams of multiple examples of I&R service delivery synthesized to array, compare, and critique service delivery styles, technologies, auspices, interorganizational networking, and intraorganizational structures that currently exist in North America. They reflect diversity with respect to geographic location, population density, client population, funding levels, and staffing patterns. These two chapters are a synthesis of multiple programs (the seven model sites noted in the chapter by John J. Gargan and James L. Shanahan chapter as well as the six illustrations highlighted in the chapter by William Garrett) that are discussed in detail in the appendixes to these chapters.

On the other hand, the two Canadian chapters (Donald F. Bellamy and Donald G. Forgie on community information and referral in Toronto and Barbara Ann Olsen's chapter on the AID service of Edmonton) represent specific and detailed illustrations of service delivery. Taken together, these reports provide important generalizable issues and point to potential future directions. Despite the

variability and relative sophistication of these North American information and referral services, and in contrast to the preceding
descriptions of Citizen Advice Bureaus (Part I), even the most comprehensive of the North American I and Rs appears to exclude
certain service components and organizational auspices central to the
former model. For example, the provision of legal information and
quite often of legal service is atypical of the North American services.

The authors of the chapter on "Model I&R Systems: Public
Policy Issues in Capacity Building" define an I&R system as comprised of all I&R related activities conducted within a particular
bounded, jurisdictional area. Units of the system include individual
I&R service providers, funding sources, and entities involved in I&R
planning, decision making, data gathering, and related activities.
Linkages describe procedures for contact, information exchange, and
collaboration. Although the selection of model sites for this research
was based upon criteria descriptive of both internal operations of
service providers and external conditions of the environment, it is not
surprising that the authors' general conclusions noted that system
capacity is, to a large extent, contextually determined. These model
systems ranged from entirely private to public/private funding
partnerships. However, the delivery of social services is often con-
strained jurisdictionally, and thus boundedness to system networking
may be externally dictated. Irrespective of funding source, Gargan
and Shanahan observe that quality coverage can be achieved within a
number of organizational structures ranging from highly centralized
to highly decentralized systems.

The authors conclude this chapter by noting that the opportunities
for better planning, more efficiency, coordination and increased productivity are largely contingent upon the support and funding from
federal and state resources. An ironic dilemma, though not unique to
the United States, is that "as traditional I&R services attempt to cope
with the dilemmas of reduced funding, fragmentation, and competition with other providers, challenges to the services are great." While
collaborative networking and systematic efforts are not simple, the
authors conclude that only by adopting such a strategic approach to
building an I&R system can many of these problems be overcome.

The Garrett chapter, "Use of Computers by I&R Services: An
American Report," provides an overview of the development and
current status of computerization in information and referral service.
Although the 1984 directory of the national Alliance of Information
and Referral Systems (AIRS) includes approximately 800 I&R services that met minimum standards, Garrett notes that less than 75 of

these North American services are computerized. Computerization in I&R has, according to the author, developed in a patchwork haphazard, and accidental fashion. Some began by utilizing and sharing computer resources available at universities or corporations, while others began through the development of their own in-house operations. However, it has not been the unavailability or inaccessibility to hardware that has provided barriers to the development or utilization of computerization in I&R, but rather the unavailability of software capable of meeting I&R's needs while also being financially feasible. Another, more generic obstacle, but one of significance in computerization, is the limited standardization of human service classification systems. Equally as important is the development of an information system that not only provides for the collection, revision, and retrieval of human service resoure information, but can be equally well utilized for planning and/or policymaking at a city, county, or state level.

Most I&R services, Garrett notes, begin computerization with the resource file. Computerized resource files may be updated through batch processing or on-line interactive input. In either case the sorting and retrieval of data are vastly enhanced. The second function related to information aggregation and information dissemination is related to the production of a directory. Clearly, computerization increases the capacity to update directories rapidly, as well as to produce specialized ones with limited cost. Aggregation and analysis of computerized data can also be utilized for media releases, input on legislative issues, and the compilation of service statistics or community directories. An on-line system also offers easy retrieval of service vacancies and reservational procedures.

In looking toward future applications of technology within I&R service provision, the linking of computerized human service information with cable television provides enhanced accessibility potentials in the future. Videotex ("interactive television") combines computer and telecommunications technology and offers access to remote banking, shopping at home, and electronic mail, as well as access to computerized human resources data bases. Further growth in this area is predicted by Garrett due to the continual decline of computer hardware prices and the gradual acceptance of centralized resource files and information aggregation concurrent with the decentralization of actual service delivery. Garrett notes that while the computer can obviously be a valuable and efficient tool in the accomplishment of I&R service provision, without well-trained staff and comprehensive information systems, the computer will be of limited use. Interpersonal relations still remain the most important skills in delivering I& R services.

The chapter entitled "AID Service of Edmonton," by Olsen, reports on several unique services that are not always incorporated within I& R programs. In addition to the generic I& R service component that was initiated in 1960, highly specialized services have been developed within AID which include the Distress Line and CORE, Crisis Outreach and Referral Evaluation, which involves outreach referrals and follow-ups to people in suicidal crisis. Yet another specialized and unique component of AID is the Edmonton Suicide Bereavement Program, which reaches out to help individuals and families move through the crisis of suicidal loss.

Organizationally, AID represents the common pattern of blended money for support from the province, the municipality, and the United Way. As a private-sector agency, it is fully autonomous in terms of its ability to plan for and deliver these services. AID represents a relatively sophisticated model with respect to the technology utilized for information collection and aggregation. In addition to the comprehensive statistical program that permits analysis of data for many of the purposes that Garrett describes in Chapter 6, AID also uses automation for scheduling personnel. Furthermore, the data have permitted AID to act as "barometer of social changes" in Edmonton; that is, AID statistics clearly reflect changes in external conditions that help to indicate the need for new or expanded services. According to the author, a Canadian community development grant will allow for the development of a common data base for statistical recording, the identification of geographic areas requiring neighborhood I& R, and the preparation of a strategic marketing proposal for I& R services.

Impressive in this program is the high reliance on well-trained volunteers in all components of service delivery. Interestingly, as noted by the author, most of AID's permanent staff were line volunteers prior to employment with the agency. As is the case for many I& R's in North America, the future clearly seems to include increased roles for I& R and access services simultaneously with possible decreases in traditional sources of funding. AID, however, continues to see itself as a necessary and central part of the Edmonton human service community.

The Bellamy and Forgie chapter, "Community Information and Referral in a Canadian Provincial Context: The Growing Impact of Advanced Technology," deals with developments that represent current service delivery in North America. The Community Information

Center of Metropolitan Toronto (CICMT), initiated in 1952, was part of the early development of a province-wide association. To date the CICMT represents the largest and most firmly established federation of I& R centers. As a federation of 53 community information centers in Ontario, it has established and promoted standards and tried to ensure adequate and stable financial support. Unique to this federation has been the development and utilization of a uniform statistical reporting system that has improved accountability to center boards and funding bodies, and has promoted working relationships between centers through the use of commonly accepted terms and reporting forms.

Common to descriptions in other chapters is the blended funding of these Ontario associations, which rely on United Way as well as local and provincial government funding. The authors note that the impact of computers introduced in 1980 improved quality and expanded the publication program, thus allowing the quick recovery of the computerization costs. The second step was the application of Telidon, a videotex system, that permits interaction with the data base using common carriers such as a telephone network.

The authors conclude their chapter with the note that a critical area in Canada is the potential use of computer/communication technologies to link centers of information into a coherent pattern of nodal centers with personnel trained in both traditional and emerging methods for storing, accessing, verifying, and networking information resources that are essential to the public—a common thread and a common question among all chapters in this section.

7

MODEL I&R SYSTEMS IN THE UNITED STATES
Public Policy Issues in Capacity Building

JOHN J. GARGAN
JAMES L. SHANAHAN

Despite its relatively short history as a public policy, information and referral has achieved a central role in the social services. The rapid growth and diffusion of information and referral activities has created a new set of problems for social service policymakers. In some communities, multiple funding sources, a perceived need for functionally specialized services, and variation in basic professional competencies have resulted in a proliferation of I&R providers, uncoordinated strategies, and ineffective use of limited financial and human resources. According to evaluations undertaken during the 1970s, I&R arrangements designed to overcome social service complexity and fragmentation had themselves become so complex and fragmented as to be counterproductive.

Reported in this article are findings of a project designed to identify, describe and analyze model information and referral systems. Chosen for in-depth study were seven systems.[1] Though operating in markedly different demographic and organizational settings across the United States, each of the systems exhibits outstanding policies and practices.

DEVELOPING SYSTEMS: A CORE PROBLEM OF I&R IN THE 1980s

The Model Systems Project, as reported in this chapter, is not the first to employ a system approach to I&R. Seminal and influential work by Nicholas Long, David Austin, the United Way of America, and other individuals and organizations have addressed I& R as a system or network. However, the central focus and basic unit of analysis of this study differentiate it from earlier works.

System as a Concept

A system is a concept or frame of reference imposed upon reality by a researcher or observer. At the most general level:

> A system is defined as a set of interrelated parts acting together to reach a predetermined objective. . . . A system at its simplest . . . [is] a set of units with relationships among them. While the units are important, it is the linkages or relationships among the units that make it possible to speak of a system.[2]

Any system is composed of identifiable elements or components. Systems have boundaries that delineate the units and relationships to be included. Within a system, inputs are received and processed by some form of conversion mechanism. Produced by this processing are outputs. Since these outputs feed back into the environment of the system, they affect the volume and nature of future inputs. The environment of the system includes all factors not a part of the system itself. Though abstract, the system concept is useful as a basis for gathering and categorizing data in substantive policy analysis.

To date, analysis has been based upon a limited definition of information and referral systems. By and large, the system has consisted of the activities of an independent agency or program unit in a larger organization. Inputs have been viewed as request for information from individuals and human services providers. Conversion mechanisms have been the staff, procedures, and operations of the agency. Outputs were the linkage of consumers to services. That such concerns constitute a limited definition of system is not to criticize the research done. It is simply to note that the system as a unit of analysis has been the specific I& R service.

Information and Referral Systems:
A Broader Perspective

As used here, an I& R system is comprised of all I& R-related activities conducted within a particular area. Boundaries of the system are defined in jurisdictional terms—a city, county, region, or state.

Units of the system are individual I&R service providers, funding sources, and entities involved in I&R planning, decision-making, data gathering, and related activities. Linkages among the units are the formal and informal procedures for contact, information exchange, and consideration of matters of mutual concern. Inputs to the system are all I&R issues arising within the service area: division of responsibilities among providers, funding arrangements, training needs, resource directory maintenance, and so forth. Conversion mechanisms are the structured arrangements for periodic consideration of, and policymaking on, matters of systemwide concern. Outputs of the I&R system are decisions, policies, and services to the population within the system's boundaries.

While some of the terminology may be unfamiliar, the concept of an I&R system, as outlined, is consistent with the experiences of most human services professionals. In any service area, some means of access to I&R specialists is available, some level of funding is chosen, and some form of resource inventory is maintained. In each area, I&R services are delivered by various organizations, decisions are made, and support functions are carried out. It is the sum total of these services, decisions, and functions that form the I&R system. So viewed, the I&R system is more encompassing than the familiar I&R agency.

Thinking in terms of I&R systems rather than individual agencies directs attention to the overall quality of structures and processes involved in the many aspects of I&R delivery. While all systems produce results that are, by definition, system policies, they do not necessarily all do so in any exemplary manner. Presumably what differentiates model I&R systems from less effective systems is the existence of certain performance levels and evidence of capacities to deal with issues and problems.

Minimal Conditions
and Baseline Capacities
of Model I&R Systems

Capacity implies the ability to do. High capacity systems are those that have the ability to do things well; low capacity systems lack such ability. Comparisons of I&R systems and judgments of how well a given system performs need to take into account the effects of context on system capacity. A system with adequate resources, a manageable volume of problems, and high expectations on the part of autonomous I&R agencies, funders, and clients as to the level of performance to be achieved by the system would be judged to have high capacity. But so too might a system that has limited resources, relatively simple problems, and modest expectations on the part of participants as to performance. The first system might be one operating in a poor, central city service area; the second system might be one operating in a reasonably prosperous, agricultural community.

It is the interplay of resources, problems, and expectations that limits the level of capacity achievable by a system. This is not to say that all I&R systems are performing at optimal levels, given the context within which they function. In most cases there is undoubtedly a gap between existing performance and context-defined achievable performance. It is to such shortfalls that I&R capacity-building efforts are typically directed. Moreoever, systems and their contexts are not rigidly fixed. Though the difficulty of change should never be underestimated, conditions may be altered, sometimes very quickly. Invigorated professional or community leadership, dissatisfied with arrangements in an existing I&R system, can call for change and establish a forum for the exchange of ideas and proposals. Such action, in turn, may create a dynamic within the system which raises expectations, increases resource allocations, and facilitates experimentation with new problem solutions. By such system dynamics, capacity is increased and progress is made toward model system behavior and practices.

A fundamental premise of the model system project was that, whatever the context, for an I&R system to be judged model it must exhibit at least three conditions and the capacities necessary for their maintenance. The first essential condition is that quality I&R services be readily available and accessible to all segments of the population in the service area. A second essential condition is the availability of support functions essential to the delivery of quality I&R services. The third condition is the existence of structured relationships that allow for regular communication and a means of building consensus on needed changes in system policies and practices. In Table 1 are listed the conditions and the specific capacities associated with each.

CRITERIA FOR JUDGING MODEL I&R SYSTEMS

Minimal conditions and capacities are necessary for a system to be designated model. The term model is applied to actual functioning systems. Model systems are not necessarily perfect relative to some set of standards or criteria but are exemplary in their performance in comparison to other functioning systems.

Given this perspective, answers to four questions about I&R systems have been addressed:

- From among the many I&R systems in operation, which can be judged to be model?

- What are the critical events in the life histories of systems that led them to become exemplary?

- What are the established and ongoing structural and process arrangements that enable model systems to continue operating in an exemplary manner?

- Based on life histories and established arrangements of model systems, what generalizations can be drawn, and what recommendations derived, that will benefit the performance of other I&R systems?

Answers to these questions depended upon obtaining nominations, selections, and on-site evaluation of model I&R systems. Since the systems to be evaluated were from a population of unknown size, a random sampling procedure could not be employed. Lacking any comprehensive list of I&R systems ranked by universally-agreed-upon quality criteria, it was necessary to rely upon judgments of knowledgeable experts to provide nominations of model I&R systems.

Obtaining nominations of model I&R systems involved two phases: identification of knowledgeable experts and administration of a nomination instrument to those experts. By early 1982, a list of 1,129 potential nominators was generated and a nomination survey was sent to each. The basic survey instrument was organized around the six capacities listed in Table 7.1 The survey was designed to elicit nominations of specific I&R systems and their component agencies and organizations, all of which had demonstrated the ability to perform in a model or exemplary manner.

The initial survey generated a list of I&R systems and individual I&R agencies and organizations within those systems. A second survey was designed to obtain qualitative data from open-ended questions, and, from scaled items, scores on specific capacity-related activities for each nominated system, overall, and for its component units.

After the quantitative data in the responses were examined, qualitative data from the open-ended questionnaires were coded and

**TABLE 7.1   Model I&R Systems: Essential Conditions
                        and Necessary Capacities**

Model System Conditions	Necessary Capacities
Condition 1:n 1: Quality I&R coverage for the service area	The capacity to provide readily available and accessible quality I&R services on a continual basis for all segments of the population in need, anywhere in the service area.
Condition 2: Quality support functions for all I&R services within the system	The capacity to raise sufficient financial, personnel, and material resources necessary for the provision and maintenance of the highest quality I&R services possible.
	The capacity to attract, train, and retain a professionally competent I&R staff.
	The capacity to compile current information on available services and the agencies that provide these services; and to maintain and regularly update this inventory with minimal imposition on human service providers.
Condition 3: In-place and effective policies for dealing with system concerns	The capacity to organize and to maintain an organization structure responsible for the development and implementation of policies for the I&R system.
	The capacity to identify gaps in service, to determine needed changes in allocations and programs in both I&R system and the human services system, and to formulate and transmit recommendations to policymakers.

studied. The quantitative and qualitative data were reanalyzed to determine whether the component agencies and organizations did, indeed, comprise a system and if, as a system, they provided evidence of exemplary practices and qualities. This interactive analysis produced three system categories: adequate, more than adequate, and exemplary.

As a general rule, all model I&R systems were to be chosen from the exemplary category. However, given a need for balance on several dimensions, this general rule was modified. The seven systems finally selected were from the available national cross-section of nominees that demonstrated significant successful efforts in coordinating information and referral activities.

Case studies of the model systems were based upon site visits and examination of available documents. A set of instruments was developed for administration at all sites. The instruments were used to gather information relevant to the following questions:

- How are capacity activities conducted within each model system?
- Who within the system participates, and in what manner, in capacity activities?
- What criteria of success are used to evaluate the efforts of capacity activities on system performance?

FINDINGS

One general conclusion regarding model systems is that they are, to a considerable degree, contextually determined. Thus, the simple realities of service area size and demography—over which system participants have little, if any, control—influence the feasibility of model system forms. Population served by the model systems ranged from 7.5 million in Los Angeles County to a few thousand elderly among the 150,000 in northern California. While only the Humboldt/Del Norte system serves a primarily rural, remote, and elderly population, those in Connecticut and southeastern Virginia do have significant rural constituencies.

More subtle than the constraints of service area size and demographics are those based in the political and social cultures within which model systems function. In Denver, for example, the absence of any meaningful public financing of I&R and a tradition of agency independence all but dictate a grass-roots approach to system development and preclude a state supported or initiated strategy as in Connecticut and Virginia. System practices of long-range planning, management by objective, and active board participation in policy formulation—most evident in the Akron/Summit County case—have contributed to model system designation. Though exemplary mangement routines would increase the effectiveness of all I&R systems, their adoption and use is not automatic. Effective practices in Akron/Summit County are the end result of a local tradition of capable I&R leadership. Systems lacking such a tradition may need to heighten expectations of key participants (funders, providers, users) as to desired performance levels before any major new management initiatives are proposed.

Model system form is also affected by location in particular states. Though often stimulated and supported by federal funds and organized as public-private partnerships, I& R systems must conform to the details of state law. Within most states the delivery of social services is organized at the county or city level; service areas are limited to jurisdictional boundaries. County governments typically administer state programs carried out locally, though under some circumstances both county and city agencies are involved in service delivery, as in Los Angeles and southeastern Virginia. While Title XX has been a major source of funding, I& R system service areas are often coterminus with county boundaries. This is especially true in strong home-rule states like Ohio.

There are exceptions to the general rule of county or city I& R services areas. State governments can choose to organize the delivery of I& R services on a regional or statewide basis and to contract directly with I& R providers. State-level decisions were made in Connecticut and Virginia to use Title XX funds for the provision of I& R services. The state government has a contract with Info Line of Connecticut to deliver I& R throughout the state. Alternatively, the state of Virginia has entered into five essentially uniform but separate contracts with organizations located in each of five planning regions.

In three of the regional systems—Memphis, Denver, and Humboldt/ Del Norte—I& R service areas have been established without any active state government participation. Since system-building actions in the Denver area were initiated by the Mile High United Way I& R Service, system boundaries encompass the four-county area covered by the service and include all public and private I& R related agencies. Funded exclusively by the city of Memphis, LINC delivers I& R services to the greater Memphis area, including neighboring communities in Arkansas and Mississippi. The newly formed Area Agency on Aging (AAA) in northern California has considered Humboldt and Del Norte Counties as a single system and has encouraged the senior centers in each county to cooperate in providing I& R to rural, isolated, and elderly individuals.

"EXPLAINING" MODEL I&R SYSTEM CONDITIONS

Model System Condition 1: Quality I&R
Coverage for the Service Area

The availability and accessibility of quality services on a continual basis is a necessary, but not sufficient, condition of a model I&R system. Given the overriding goal and primary objectives of information and referral as public policy, the importance of this conditions is self-evident. Nonetheless, the condition is not easily achieved. It requires some minimal levels of communication and coordination among units that plan, fund, or provide I&R services within a service area.

Experience in the seven model systems demonstrates that quality coverage can be achieved whether providers, funders, and planners be few or many. Quality coverage is the result of working relationships and agreements developed to address the following questions:

(1) Who provides I&R more than incidentally as an administrative function?
(2) Who plans or funds I&R?
(3) What is the overall quality, quantity, and coverage of I&R in the service area, including generic, specialized, and limited I&R services? Are there evident gaps in service or duplications that are unwarranted or cost inefficient?
(4) What communications and working relationships among I&R funders and providers presently exist and what other arrangements should be implemented?

Answers to these questions have resulted in three types of arrangements for meeting Model System Condition 1: centralized, moderately decentralized, and decentralized. The criterion of arrangement was used to assess the organization and delivery of generic I&R services—those responding to all people with all types of problems.

Centralized I&R Systems

A centralized system typically results when a single agency receives the major funding for I&R services and other public agencies opt to contract with this major agency for the provision of the service rather than providing it in-house. Most requests for I&R service from the community are directed to this single agency. Three of the systems studies have centralized generic I&R in a lead agency: Info Line in Connecticut, LINC in Memphis, and Info Line in Akron/Summit County.

Even among centralized systems there are differences in the extent to which agencies, other than the primary generic provider, deliver specialized I&R services to specific groups, on certain problems, or to geographic subunits. Probably the best example of a centralized I&R system is Akron/Summit County. Within that system several agencies offer a form of I&R in the course of their day-to-day activities. The Red Cross, Arthritis Foundation, a child guidance center, and two community health centers receive requests for help that are beyond the scope of their basic mission. These agencies respond to information requests, though they do not appear to have made any special commitment to the provision of I& R; they do not appear to maintain specific personnel assignments, have defined performance measures, or treat I& R as a separate program. Info-Line is, in effect, the single and dominant generic I& R provider in the system. Aside from Info Line, there are no other organized I& R programs with a clear identity.

Moderately Decentralized I& R Systems

A moderately decentralized system is one in which responsibility for generic I& R is centered within a single I& R service, complemented by other autonomous I& R services designed for specialized/limited needs. Both the Los Angeles and southeastern Virginia I& R systems fall within this category. In Los Angeles, the I& R Federation's Info Line is the major generic I& R provider offering services to all segments of the population. Increasingly, Info Line is recognized as the point of entry—even for access to other I& R programs—for the general population. Of all systems studied, however, Los Angeles has the most numerous and widest array of I& R programs for particular groups with problems, or for portions of the county area. The county and city AAAs fund separate I& R services for the elderly. The use of these specialized/limited I& R services is sufficiently great that, taken as a whole, they are as important as Info Line in providing quality I& R coverage for the entire service area.

Decentralized I& R Systems

A decentralized system is one in which there is no single service providing most generic I& R. Two of the model I& R systems— metropolitan Denver and rural northern California (Humboldt/Del Norte)—have system service areas with two or more generic providers.

Moderately decentralized and decentralized systems do not develop by accident, and they are not entirely the result of federal government policies and piecemeal funding patterns. A decentralized system may be preferred by local human services agencies that possess a strong community identity. These agencies often believe that they are best able to contact hard-to-reach people and are better able to respond to certain citizen groups than a single generic I& R.

As a case in point, metropolitan Denver has a social service system with no public funding of I&R. However, several social service departments provide I&R services and the AAA requires all agencies with which it contracts to provide I&R for the elderly. In addition, a city/county community services commission performs I&R functions by assisting persons in need of emergency assistance. The Mile High United Way I&R Service, a major provider of generic I&R to the four-county area, is the key motivator in developing a long-range plan for the decentralized system to improve its quality of I&R services through informal voluntary networking.

Disaggregating the Delivery of I&R Services

Even in essentially centralized I&R systems it is possible to disaggregate the actual delivery of I&R services by subdividing the area and engaging organizations in each subarea to provide I&R services. This approach is most typically associated with neighborhood I&R services within a larger urban system, as in Los Angeles, where the AAA supports a network of I&R providers in councilmanic districts. On a statewide basis, Info Line of Connecticut has organized the actual delivery of I&R services around a network of five units, each providing I&R within a different region of the state.

Fundamental to this type of I&R system are the relationships between a central policy-directing unit (i.e., United Way of Connecticut's Department of Information and Referral) and individual agencies that deliver I&R services. In the case of Connecticut, individual regional organizations and United Way of Connecticut are able to give each other considerable mutual support. For larger, more populated states and metropolitan areas, a disaggregated approach as in Connecticut may be a viable alternative to a single centralized generic I&R agency.

There are real differences between the structural forms of centralized and decentralized systems. In the systems studied, structural form has been determined by local conditions. It is important to note that the choice of a centralized, decentralized, or disaggregated arrangement has not been due to any diseconomies or inefficiencies of system size. As with any large enterprise, special problems may be encountered in managing an I&R service simply because of the magnitude of the geographic area and/or population included in the service area. To date, system size has not been a factor limiting structure options.[3]

Strong Linkages Among I&R Providers:
A Critical Step Toward
Achieving Quality Coverage

Where it has been determined that the quality and coverage of I&R services is most enhanced by several I&R programs—generic or specialized/limited—it is crucial that working relationships develop among providers.

A number of specialized I&R services operate as autonomous units in the Los Angeles system. In-depth information on available resources and knowledge of techniques for dealing most effectively with particular groups are considered strengths of the system resulting from the presence of multiple I&R providers. Development of Info Line as a source of quality generic services, coupled with existing I&R programs, has reinforced, rather than compromised, the effectiveness of each system element. Generic providers can ensure that basic I&R services avoid gaps in services and can be available with back-up assistance to individual agencies. Conversely, for persons who contact generic providers but require in-depth information or special assistance, referrals can be made to an appropriate specialized I&R service.

The effectiveness of these systems depends on: (1) the quality of the working relationships across I&R providers; and (2) the affordability of maintaining autonomous units. For model decentralized and moderately decentralized systems, strategic actions are required to generate:

(1) Strong referral linkages, so that each I&R provider is aware of the most effective referral for callers it cannot assist.
(2) A visible generic I&R service for all populations anywhere in the service area to assure total coverage, provide back-up to specialized/limited I&R services, and make referrals to other I&Rs when appropriate.
(3) Opportunities for cost-sharing to minimize administrative and operating costs for smaller I&R services.

In the seven model systems such strategic actions have been undertaken. Working relationships among organizations within those systems are outlined in Table 2. In terms of the first condition of model systems—quality coverage of I&R services across the service area—all systems studied have addressed the issue in some respects and only those in Denver and southeastern Virginia have not made it their number-one priority. For these two systems the central issue is to equip all I&R providers with comprehensive human resource information.

Model System Condition 2: Quality Support Functions for All I&R Services Within the System

The second condition for a model I&R system is the provision of support services—from resource data to competent staff—essential to the delivery of quality I&R. The two largest expenditures in providing I&R services are for staff and for developing and maintaining data on available human resources. Access to I&R services can also vary considerably where each service does its own publicity, is limited to its own hours of service and number of telephone lines, and so forth. The costs of high-quality support services can be prohibitive where each I&R service within a system must provide for its own staff training and resource data development. The reality in poorly functioning systems is great variation in the quality of support services across I&R providers in the system's service area.

In working toward more effective use of the overall system's commitment of financial resources, system entities must consider the following:

- Is there adequate provision for attracting, training, and retaining professionally competent I&R workers?

- Are sufficient financial, personnel, and material resources available to support quality I&R services throughout the service area?

- Is there current, accurate information about available services and agencies that is maintained and regularly updated in a way that is cost-efficient and effective for all I&R providers?

These questions are most important for decentralized systems such as those in southeastern Virginia, metropolitan Denver, and rural northern California. The commitment of Virginia's Department of Social Services has been to building regional I&R centers to provide quality data information to the separate I&R programs operated by local departments of social services. Recognizing the wide range of I&R providers in metropolitan Denver, Mile High United Way I&R Service has assumed the lead in developing a computerized human resource data system for all to use. Finally, in northern California, actions taken by the AAA are in part an attempt to have

TABLE 7.2 Exemplary and Developing Working Relationships Among I&R Interests in Each of the Seven Model I&R Systems

Working Relationships Established	*Centralized*			*Moderately Decentralized*		*Decentralized*	
Structure and System	*Akron/ Summit*	*Memphis*	*Connecticut*	*Los Angeles*	*SE Virginia*[3]	*Denver*[3]	*Humboldt/ Del Norte*
I. Among I&R/Related Interests							
a. Provision of Generic I&R Services							
1. A single I&R service covers all groups and geography	Info[1] line	LINC[1]	Info Line of Connecticut[5]	Info line			
2. Several generic I&R services covering all or parts of the system's area					H.R.I.C. is only regionwide I&R	United Way I&R is leader	N/A
b. Provision of Specialized/Limited I&R Services	No[4]	Yes	Yes, but not emphasized and varies among regional I&R providers	Yes[2]	Yes	Some referrals referrals developing Sharing information	Yes
c. Related Services 1. Crisis intervension 2. Emergency assistance 3. Information services	Yes	Yes	Yes	Yes	Yes	Some referrals developing Sharing info – some referrals on ad hoc basis.	N/A

II. Between I&R with Broader Human Resources Community

a. Rapport	Yes, in resource inventory, I&R staff training and referrals	Emphasis on on-going, regular contacts	Yes, but varies across regional I&R services	Yes	Yes, defined within the broader purpose of parent plan-ing agency	Yes, broad interest one part of I&R network	N/A
b. Provide Services	Mostly to smaller organizations on ad hoc basis	Yes, extensive range of info and marketing	Emphasis and outcomes v vary across regional services	N/A	Yes, info services mostly	Potential for info services	N/A
c. Collaboration on Projects	Coordinating emergency assistance provision	Yes, some training	N/A	N/A	N/A	N/A	N/A

1. Follows practice of referral to callers wanting resources available in adjacent counties
2. Developing toward formal relationships among specialized services and with Info Line
3. System focused on support services only; no relationships based on I&R services
4. No formal programs
5. I&R services are subcontracted to five regional providers
N/A: No available information

the larger I& R program in Humboldt share its knowledge and experience with the smaller one in Del Norte.

Model System Condition 3:
In-Place and Effective Policies
for Dealing with System Concerns

Analysis of the seven-model I& R systems shows evidence of capacity to deal effectively with a set of ongoing policy and practice concerns. These concerns include relationships among I& R interests of all types, applying policies aimed at improving performance standards of and/or data collection on all I& R services, and implementing resource saving and resource sharing measures.

Structuring Working Relationships
Among I& R System Entities

To deal with priority concerns, a model I& R system builds and maintains structured relationships among independent organizations that plan for, fund, or deliver I& R services or essential support services. These relationships provide for regular communications and for established means whereby the entities can build a consensus on needed changes in policies and practices.

Important indicators of the status of relationships are the modes of system decision-making, levels of group participation in joint ventures, and extent of formal and informal cooperation. Within systems, working relationships may be developed on vertical and/or horizontal levels.

Vertical relationships involve I& R entities at different levels. The linkages may be limited to an immediate community or may extend to regional or state-level governmental and voluntary organizations.

Linkages between the six regional subcontractors that provide generic services and the state-level Info Line of Connecticut constitute the most formally structured case of vertical relationships in the selected systems. Two of the subcontractors are community councils; one is a private, non-profit corporation established to provide Info Line service; two are multi-service organizations; and the other is a United Way. While retaining regional autonomy in delivering I& R services, the subcontractors are part of a coherent, state-level defined system with regard to use of a common resource file and data collection and analysis.

A less formally structured example of vertical relationships is that between the Information Center of Hampton Roads and southeastern Virginia city and county social service departments. The departments use a computerized resource file, produced by the center, in providing I&R services to their respective areas.

Horizontal relationships involve linkages among I&R providers and other human service providers at the same level—usually parallel organizations. All of the model systems have such linkages where there is more than one I&R provider. They also have ties with closely related services such as hot lines, ombudsman programs or crisis intervention centers. In Los Angeles County there are horizontal relationships among three independent I&R policy systems: the I&R Federation and the city and county AAAs. Geography, politics, funding, and diverse target groups require them to maintain their own autonomy although they are part of single I&R system.

Important benefits also accrue to model systems from networks of personal relationships among individuals. Ongoing contact between I&R professionals and their counterparts in other fields leads to a greater awareness of the role of I&R and its contributions to the human services. The contacts also facilitate the development of a sense of commitment to the system and to working toward common goals.

Such is the case in southeastern Virginia. The board and staff of the Information Center of Hampton Roads are represented in most major community endeavors, and the center practices widespread informal networking with service providers through joint planning and training. In Los Angeles County, staff members of Info Line have regular telephone communications with agencies and provide training to their staffs on request.

System-level consequences of ongoing professional and personal relationships are substantial. In Memphis, when LINC faced almost certain loss of funding after its original grant ended, social service agencies approached the mayor to support LINC and stressed its importance as a component of the human services community. As a result, the city agreed to fund LINC and continues to provide the sole source of support. These cases suggest that the building of personal relationships can yield benefits for the I&R system that are as real and important as the development of computerized resource files.

An I&R system with strong working relationships gives a community real advantages during period of rapid economic and social change. As most human service providers realize, the recent recession placed hardships on individuals and families who had never before looked to the human services for assistance. The demand for help—resulting from such factors as diminished mental health among unemployed adults, an increase in premature births, and malnutrition among infants—increased at the very time that budget allocations for human services were decreasing.

Community responses have varied in dealing with this situation. In Summit County, with leadership from the United Way, a coalition of human service agencies formed to collaborate in developing a coherent strategy to meet the priority needs of families with recently unemployed members. Local foundations have been enlisted to support this pilot project.

Info Line of Summit County, along with several service agencies, is preparing to target assistance in four areas: emotional support, emergency assistance, acess to social services, and job seeking and job development. Info Line's contribution will be to establish an outreach campaign for the recently unemployed, to provide quality and relevant information and referral, and to collect user data throughout the project. Obviously, Summit County's response to very difficult problems has been enhanced and facilitated by the resources of Info Line.

THE RATIONALE FOR AN EXPANDED DEFINITION
OF I&R SYSTEMS:
MEETING CHALLENGES OF A NEW ERA

Summarized above are the essential findings of a national study of model information and referral systems. The seven systems analyzed are not perfect. Nonetheless, they have achieved conditions and capacities which are exemplary relative to other systems. The evidence suggests that within most of these other systems collaborative or coordinated activities are not the norm.

One reason for the absence of extensive collaborative coordinated activities is the widespread acceptance of information and referral as a legitimate activity of the public, voluntary, and private sectors. Information providing and service referral has always been, and continues to be, a task performed by human service workers in their day-to-day operations. But anyone who has observed I&R cannot help but be intrigued by the proliferation, over the past 15 years, of information-providing, problem-solving units. Though United Way and its predecessors had a long history of I&R service to communities, their activities were supplemented by new agencies from the late 1960s onward. Political figures in many states have taken on I&R-related activities as a form of constituent service. Even local newspapers and television stations engage in citizen problem-solving as a means of enhancing their community service images.

A primary source of funding for new I&R undertakings has been the federal government. In 1978, a General Accouting Office study concluded that a number of departments and agencies were either directly engaged in, or supportive of, I&R, and, while total federal expenditures could not be determined, it estimated that hundreds of millions were spent annually. Federal involvement was so extensive that an Interdepartmental Task Force on Information and Referral was created to give special attention to the needs of the aged.

There is an irony of sorts. That a function designed to help individuals cope with the complexity of social services should itself become so complex as to elicit study by the GAO and the creation of an interdepartmental task force is a comment on public-sector capacity to plan and manage. Fragmentation—by activities, by users, by funding sources, by organizational structure, by level of government—constitutes a potentially major problem for I&R providers and especially for I&R systems. If those in need are to be served and if those in power are to be alerted to policy gaps, I&R systems need to engage in strategic thinking about planning, data gathering, and coordinating. Those in I&R leadership positions must find new ways of increasing productivity by motivating employees, redesigning technical and operating procedures, and restructuring organizational arrangements.

Calls for better planning, more efficiency, coordination, and increased productivity are not new to I&R or to human services in general. What makes the need for more effective I&R systems a priority are changes in the environment within which those systems function. Among these changes two have major implications for information and referral:

(1) As a society, we are uncertain of the results of the very substantial social spending of the past fifteen years.

(2) A central issue of government and politics during the 1980s is that of entitlement: Who in the society is deserving of public sector assistance?

The two changes are related and reflect fundamental attitude shifts in government and in public opinion. Considerable support exists in the public, the Reagan administration, and Congress for a reevaluation of the scope and level of responsibility of the federal government for social programs. As David Stockman, Director of the Office of Management and Budget, noted in 1981:

> The idea that's been established over the last 10 years, that almost every service that someone might need in life ought to be provided, financed by the Government as a matter of basic rights, is wrong. We challenge that. We reject that notion.

Such a view is not simply political rhetoric. By the late 1970s, opinion polls indicated some decline in public support for levels of federal spending on welfare. Other surveys have shown, from the mid 1960s on, a growing public disenchantment with governmental performance, levels of taxation, and bureaucratic inefficiency.

Decreased Domestic Spending

The reevaluation of governmental responsibility for social programs is due, in part, to widespread attitudinal change. It is also due to recognition that the United States has entered a period of slow economic growth and fiscal scarcity in the public sector. These two factors in combination have curtailed funding for domestic social spending. The curtailment comes, however, at the end of an extended period of growth.[4]

Increased Demand

The effects of attitudinal and funding changes on information and referral policy could be great. *The changes are occurring at the very point in time when I&R systems should be increasing their capabilities to meet new demands.*

I&R is typically a service to an entire community. While all segments of the community have occasion to use the service, some segments are more dependent on I&R, given special needs. Among the more dependent are those in the aging population.

For the elderly in a community, an effective I&R system can facilitate access to social services that supplement help from family and friends. The availability of this support often allows for a life of dignity and self-respect in familiar home surroundings. As a matter of public policy, provision of community-based services for the aging is a cost-effective alternative to institutional care.

The central role of I&R systems in maintaining alternatives to expensive long-term care is an important consideration for decision makers. Demographic trends indicate that the aging population is not simply growing in absolute numbers, but also changing in fundamental ways. It is projected that by 1990 there will be nearly 30 million people over age 65 (12.2% of total population) and by 2020 over 45 million (15.5% of total population). Presently, and likely into the future, the aging population is growing older. Because of longer life expectancy, those over 75 were 37 percent of the aging in 1979 and, according to one authority, "the population group age 85 and over grew more rapidly than any other group in the 1970s."

The essential point is a simple one. *As traditional I&R services attempt to cope with the dilemmas of reduced funding, fragmentation, and competition with other providers, challenges to the services are great.* Over the next several years it is imperative that members of the I&R community look beyond the performance of individual agencies and begin thinking in terms of system performance. The incentives to think in system terms and to address systemwide concerns are substantial. In some instances, organizational survival is at stake; despite its acknowledged importance for meeting human needs, I&R is an intermediate service and, as such, is often viewed by funders as of lower priority than direct survival services. Further incentives result from changes occurring in the national approach to social problems. Commissioner on Aging Lennie Marie Tolliver has noted: "Greater efforts must be made to foster new collaborative efforts between public and private organizations."

Such collaborative efforts do not simply appear. Their development, adoption and implementation require policies on the division of responsibilities, mechanisms for assuring cooperation and resolving conflicts, and consensus on evaluation criteria. Presently, in too many places, collaborative activities have not been undertaken or even considered, and a service designed to help people has developed inefficiencies, inadequate access, service gaps, and poorly maintained resource files. *Only by adopting a strategic approach to building I&R systems can these problems be overcome.*

APPENDIX

Developmental Histories of Seven Model I&R Systems

The seven model I&R systems selected for study represent several different combinations of service area characteristics, service delivery arrangements, and policymaking modes. Service areas of the systems range in geographic size from Connecticut's statewide system to that of a single county, and in population from more than 7 million people in Los Angeles to 150,000 residents of Humboldt/Del Norte Counties in rural, remote northern California. An overview of each I&R system is presented below.

Connecticut

Connecticut, with a population of 3,107,000 people (1980), is among the smaller states in areal size. It is one of the few states that does not have county governments. Decisions regarding human services policy, allocations, and contracts with providers are centralized at the state level.

In the early 1970s, state agencies and United Way agencies from around the state, acting independently, began to recognize a growing need for improved provision of I&R services to Connecticut's population. A statewide association of 28 United Ways proposed the development of a statewide I&R system to a newly formed governor's Council on Human Services in 1974. After study, the state and the newly formed United Way of Connecticut announced a jointly funded plan to centralize the responsibility for providing generic I&R to all segments of the population under one organization: Info Line of Connecticut. Info Line is operated by the United Way of Connecticut, Inc. A separate I&R department was established to administer this statewide system. By providing a mechanism for overseeing decisions by separate state agencies and local United Ways regarding I&R services, this agreement was an important joint venture to reduce gaps in services.

Though its jurisdiction is statewide, Info Line does not attempt to provide I&R for the entire state from a central office. Rather, I&R services are provided at the regional level under contract with six separate agencies. These agencies, while autonomous legal entities, conduct I&R programs in a consistent, if not uniform, way. All I&R policies are set by the statewide advisory board of Info Line of Connecticut, and are implemented by the I&R department working with the regional providers. The regional providers rely upon the I&R department for the maintenance of a statewide computerized resource inventory and for special reports and regional editions of the *Info Line Directory of Community Services*.

Memphis, Tennessee

The I&R system of Memphis serves the more than 900,000 residents of the city of Memphis, the rest of the central county of

Shelby, and the adjacent counties of Fayette, Lauderdale, and Tipton. I&R inquiries are also received from smaller neighborhing towns in Arkansas and Mississippi.

The development of this exemplary I&R system is characterized by two unique features. The first is that the lead agency of this system of I&R interests—Library Information Center (LINC)—is an integral part of the Memphis/Shelby County Public Library and Information Center. Established in 1975, LINC assumed from the local United Way the responsibility for providing generic I&R throughout the metropolitan area. Although specialized I&R services have since been established, contacts between them and LINC are maintained, and LINC provides necessary back-up services. By 1981, annual call volume had reached about 64,200 and is expected to reach 74,000 in 1983.

The second unique feature of this system is that the public funds used to develop greater capacity to provide I&R came from a most unexpected source: county general revenue-sharing funds, which had been withheld by the federal government. Once released, county officials earmarked the $1 million for human services. The library's I&R proposal was among those funded.

LINC was developed as a separate department within the library and has its own staff and budget. Yet LINC is also an integral part of the priority goal of the library to be a comprehensive information center for all residents of the area. All library staff members are cross-trained and LINC staff members work some hours in the library's science department. It is felt that I&R services and traditional reference services reinforce each other when answering an inquiry. LINC staff handles only those inquiries regarding the human services system and channels calls for information of a general nature to the appropriate library department.

From the beginning, LINC has made a conscious effort to be visible, accessible, and effective in meeting the expressed needs of agencies. Attention to these matters has been important because of initial skepticism on the part of human services professionals regarding the feasibility of delivering social services from such a middle-class institution as a library. Human service agencies have become significant users of LINC's services. LINC was developed as a cooperative venture with other agencies. Over the years LINC has acquired project-specific funding from the Area Agency on Aging and has jointly undertaken community projects with police, health, and other departments.

When LINC faced almost certain loss of funding two years after the original grant ended, social service agencies approached the mayor in support of LINC as an important component of the human services community. As a result, the city agreed to fund LINC and it continues to provide nearly all funding support.

Summit County

Akron/Summit County (520,000 population) is located in northeastern Ohio, just south of larger Cleveland/Cuyahoga County and just north of smaller Canton/Stark County. The downtowns of Cleveland and Canton are only 35 and 22 miles from downtown Akron. Despite geographic proximity, practically all community services, public or private, are organized separately within each county.

Within Summit County during the early 1970s, very limited I&R services were being provided by the Model Cities Program, the Summit County Department of Welfare, and the United Way. Developments between 1974 and 1976 made possible the building of a quality I&R system.

In 1974, the city of Akron created a Division of Human Resources, which retained some of the social services provided under the Model Cities Program. This division adopted access to social services as a major policy goal. Meanwhile, a four-county Area Agency on Aging was created; Summit County is the largest county in the agency's planning and service area.

City and county officials, the AAA, and United Way worked informally to consider a proposal for an independent organization to provide all I&R services. In 1974, Info Line of Summit County was incorporated. By 1976, Info Line had gained support from all four of the major organizations—the AAA, city of Akron, county Department of Welfare, and United Way.

The key responsibility for addressing ongoing systemwide concerns belongs to Info Line. Basic service delivery is one such concern; the volume of calls to Info Line has grown steadily, from 16,934 in 1974 to 41,000 in 1982 and an estimated 70,000 in 1983. On other systemwide concerns, Info Line's role has been crucial. In the absence of a structured arrangement by which major funders can discuss shared interests and varying concerns regarding I&R services, there is no negotiated public/private policy to guide the provision of I&R services within the Akron/Summit County area. As a result of Info Line's actions, the interests and requirements of individual funders have been integrated into a coherent plan for providing quality coverage of I&R services throughout Summit County. Also, Info Line has developed linkages with the broader human services system by providing a forum for those providing emergency assistance and by Info Line representatives serving on an array of committees and boards.

Los Angeles

The Los Angeles I&R system comprises all of Los Angeles County, a service area of 4,600 square miles and some 7.5 million residents. Economic and ethnic diversity as well as rural and urban populations characterize the area. Among the 83 incorporated cities in the county are Los Angeles, Long Beach, Pasadena, Compton, Pomona, Inglewood, Santa Monica, Glendale, and Burbank.

As resources became available during the 1960s, public and private organizations developed separate I&R services in particular areas. Geographic distance and population diversity contribute to further specialization. Recognizing a lack of coherency across I&R entities, the United Way of Los Angeles County and the Department of Public Social Services cosponsored a detailed study in 1976.

The study produced two important conclusions. The first was a clear consensus that specialized or limited I&R services were preferred in many instances. In-depth information on resources in their respective areas and knowledge of techniques for dealing more effectively with their particular consumer groups were viewed as strengths of the system. The second conclusion was the need to build a quality, comprehensive I&R service for all segments of the population. Subsequently such a service was incorporated as Info Line of Los Angeles county, the lead provider of generic I&R services throughout the county. Info Line is administered by the I&R Federation, a private, nonprofit organization established to achieve policy coherence.

With the I&R Federation in place, I&R service in Los Angeles County has evolved from an extensively decentralized system into a moderately decentralized system built around Info Line of Los Angeles. Also, the I&R Federation is developing linkages with specialized programs to maximize the advantages of these specialities within a comprehensive I&R network.

Three I&R policy systems operate within the county: the Los Angeles County Information and Referral Federation, which operates Info Line; the Los Angeles city AAA; and the Los Angeles county AAA. The city and county AAAs had a common I&R system—Senior Line—until 1978, when fiscal and political constraints made it necessary for the city AAA to withdraw. A close working relationship remains between the two systems, however, and each administers its own, non-overlapping service area. The city AAA was involved in the initial stages of developing the I&R Federation, with which it still maintains a cooperative working relationship.

Metropolitan Denver

Metropolitan Denver is a fast-growing four-county region of 1,620,000 people. Mile High United Way I&R Service, a department of the United Way, presently provides generic I&R to the entire region. While recognized as a leading I&R agency, Mile High United Way I&R Service is only one of several major providers of I&R to general or special populations in the region or subareas. I&R is an important service of many other agencies, including a Federal Information Center, the Denver Commission on Community Relations, the Governor's Citizens Advocate Office, "9 Wants to Know" (presented by a local TV station), and the Salvation Army, to name a few.

The building of an exemplary system in metropolitan Denver has begun based on a network of I&R interests. Mile High United Way I&R took the initiative to identify and convene all major I&R funders and providers. Some sixteen participating agencies agreed to the aims of networking when they were assured that no one agency would dictate policy to any other. An early consensus was reached that linkages would remain informal and that any innovations would result from cooperative arrangements and not consolidation of I&R services.

Establishing a comprehensive, computerized resource inventory for metropolitan Denver is currently a priority objective for Denver's I&R system. Development and introduction of the resource inventory has progressed slowly, starting with a user survey that asks all potential users of a computerized resource file what information they would like, what format they would prefer, and what they would be willing to pay for file information.

Denver's I&R system has not accomplished all of its goals yet. There is still no compilation of data concerning the extent and quality of I&R coverage across individual communities and across population groups. Adherence to, or even agreement on, appropriate standards for an I&R service—aside from Mile High United Way I&R Service—are not yet evident.

Southeastern Virginia

Southeastern Virginia's sizable service area contains 1.5 million people within its seven counties and eight cities. Since 1975, the Virginia Department of Social Services has contracted with the Information Center of Hampton Roads to provide computerized resource data to all social service departments in the Tidewater Region. The Information Center has developed relations with twenty I&R providers, including the Navy Family Service Center at Norfolk and fifteen local social service departments offering I&R to consumers within their respective communities. The Information Center of Hampton Roads is the only agency providing I&R services throughout the region; its call volume comprises about twenty percent of the system's total I&R usage, which exceeds 100,000 requests annually.

Within the Tidewater Region in southeastern Virginia, the Information Center of Hampton Roads provides centralized support services for the regional network. The center has access to its parent agency's IBM 34 computer system, which can be used to process, store, and retrieve resource and I&R operations data. Information is maintained on more than 3,000 human service agencies. Statistical compilations based on I&R user data supplied by social service agencies are performed and reports are filed with the state and made available to community organizations.

As a result of an initiative by the state of Virginia, other regional information centers have been formed to achieve more uniform provision of I&R services across planning regions. This process began in 1977, when a statewide I&R advisory council was created to consider ways to improve the quality of I&R delivery. The council's plan called for six regional information centers that, in addition to providing I&R services, would develop a comprehensive, computerized resource file for use by each regional network of social service departments in their provision of I&R. The Information Center of Hampton Roads, already an established I&R system in the Southeastern Region, served as a prototype for information centers in other regions.

Humboldt/Del Norte Counties

Northern California's Humboldt and Del Norte Counties present difficult challenges to providers of human services; the challenges are especially great for information and referral providers. The population is both small in size and dispersed. Population density ranges from extremely low in the most rural areas to modest levels in small urban communities.

Weather and transportation are viewed as the greatest barriers to effective utilization of social services. In the two-county area are five small telephone companies. Isolated persons, however, rely more on CB radio networks, and "word of mouth" is often used to reach the rural elderly.

As part of the Humboldt/Del Norte I&R system, there are two I&R providers, the Humboldt Senior Resource Center in Eureka and the Del Norte Senior Center in Crescent City. These centers provide I&R services to the elderly population. The Area I Agency on Aging is the core of this I&R system.

From 1975 to 1979, the two I&R services operated independently. Both senior centers received Older Americans Act funds in 1975, enabling them to provide services. In 1980, the Area I Agency on Aging was designated for Humboldt and Del Norte Counties. Among the first steps taken to improve the quality of I&R services were the adoption of the California Department of Aging I&R policy, monitoring of all I&R standards, and increased coordination between the two senior service centers.

This developing I&R system has three priority concerns:

(1) Improving the quality coverage of I&R services across the two counties, despite reduced funding.
(2) Increasing the number of working relationships to better coordinate the delivery of services from providers in the more populated Humboldt County to the elderly in more rural Del Norte County.
(3) Expanding outreach efforts to assure the maintenance of information contacts with the elderly in isolated rural areas.

Dealing with the priority concerns is not a simple task. For example, the sheer distance (approximately ninety miles) between senior centers in the two counties complicates coordination of programs. Discussions continue between the Area Agency on Aging and United Way organizations in both counties as to the most appropriate means for meeting the needs of the elderly. Rather than fund individual specialized I&R units, the AAA would prefer the development of a single, generic I&R service. Using comprehensive resource data with an emphasis on the elderly, such a service could assure the availability of a wide range of assistance to the aging population.

NOTES

1. In October, 1981, the U.S. Administration on Aging awarded a grant to the Alliance of Information and Referral Systems, Inc. (AIRS) for a study of Model I&R Systems. The Center for Urban Studies at the University of Akron received a contract from AIRS to provide administrative and research service. For more information write: Model Information and Referral Systems Project, Center for Urban Studies, The University of Akron, Akron, Ohio 44325 (216) 375-7616.

2. For persons interested in methodology and more detail on the individual I&R systems, consult Model I&R Systems: *Building a Bridge to the Future. A Comprehensive Report* by J. Shanahan, J. Gargan, and N. Apple (Akron, Ohio: Alliance of Information and Referral Systems, Inc. and Center for Urban Studies, The University of Akron, 1983).

3. The I&R Federation of Los Angeles Info Line is the largest single I&R service in the U.S., with a budget of approximately $1.5 million and an annual call volume of over 250,000. This relatively new service is functioning well, according to formal evaluations. While the Connecticut model with multiple, autonomous providers was an option for the I and R Federation, Info Line of Los Angeles has been successful in building one, large-volume I&R service, serving 2.5 times as many callers as the Connecticut system in total.

4. While those in the welfare and social service fields continue to see evidence of poverty and to campaign for continued publicly supported assistance, it is important that they recognize the magnitude of societal resources allocated to those in need. The emphasis given to spending cuts in selected domestic, social programs, and proposed spending increases for national defense tends to distract attention from the longer term pattern. In 1959, federal government spending accounted for 18.7 percent of the Gross National Product, of which 10.9 percent was for defense and 7.7 percent for domestic expenditures; in 1981 comparable figures were 23.4 percent of GNP, of which 7.5 percent was allocated to defense and 15.9 percent to domestic programs.

The same general pattern is evident in federal aid to state and local governments. Total federal grants-in-aid have increased from slightly more than $7 billion (or 7.6 percent of budget outlays) in 1960 to over $88 billion (or 12.1 percent of budget outlays) in 1982. Sixty-five percent of the $88 billion was distributed in 1982 to three program areas: income security (25 percent); health (21 percent); education, training, employment, and social services (19 percent). Nearly 39 percent of all federal grants-in-aid were for programs administered by the Department of Health and Human Services. The record of the past twenty years has been one of substantial increases in dollars spent as well as the numbers of social programs adopted and consumers served. It is against this background of expansion that current efforts to reduce public spending must be viewed.

REFERENCES

The Advisory Commission on Intergovern Mental Relations. (1980). *Public assistance: The growth of a federal function*. Washington, DC: ACIR.

Comptroller General of the United States. (1978). *Report to the Congress: Information and referral for people needing human services in a complex system that should be improved.* Washington, DC: General Accounting Office.

Gargan, J. J. (1981). Consideration of local government capacity. *Public Administration Review, 41,* 6 (November/December), 649-658.

The Lammers, W. W. (1983). *Policy and the aging.* Washington, DC: Congressional Quarterly, Inc.

Miller, A. H. Political issues and trust in government: 1967-1970. *American Political Science Review, 68,* 951-972.

Rosenbaum, D. E. (1981). Regan's thesis: Issue is entitlement. *The New York Times* (March 24), 10.

U.S. Department of Housing and Urban Development. (1981). *Productivity improvement for state and local government.* Washington, DC: U.S. Government Printing Office.

White, M. J., et al. (1980). *Managing public systems: Analytic techniques for public administration.* North Scituate, MA: Duxbury Press.

8

TECHNOLOGICAL ADVANCES IN I&R
An American Report

WILLIAM GARRETT

Information and referral services began in the late 1960s in the United States. It is estimated that by early 1984, 50 to 75 information and referral (I&R) services will be in operation.

Many of the computerized services have developed in a patchwork manner. Some systems began because a university or a corporation offered free low-cost access to a computer. As the system expanded, the I&R services often continued using the "subsidized" computer service for a particular function (i.e., statistical analysis) and developed in-house capabilities for other facets of I&R operations (i.e., resource file maintenance).

Few I&R services purchase their own hardware or computer equipment. Those that do purchase hardware and dedicate that hardware exclusively to I&R usually have microcomputers.[1] I&R service organizations also share the hardware with other users on a mainframe or minicomputer system.[2]

Because many I&R services are affiliated with larger organizations such as the United Way or local companies or universities, access to hardware has not been a major obstacle in computerization. Most I&R services have experienced difficulties in the areas of software development and classification systems design.

Until recently, there did not exist well-documented, thoroughly tested I&R software packages. Agencies that wanted to develop a computerized system had to design and code their own software. The cost of this effort could easily amount to over $100,000, well beyond the fiscal capabilities of the average I&R service. Within the past few years however, several software packages for I&R systems have become available. For example, the Community Service Council of

Broward County, Ft. Lauderdale, Florida, has an Agency Program Profile System (APPS), which sells for $5,000, and a client service statistical package, which sells for $3,750. These packages are fully documented, have detailed user manuals and come with technical and operational support. The Broward software was developed on an IBM System 34 and is currently the most widely used.[3] Portland, Ore., also sells software, which operates on a minicomputer, for under $5,000.

Software for I&R systems on microcomputers is still in its infancy stage, although significant progress is being made. The Maryland State Department of Education, Division of Library Services, designed and developed a software package to be used on the Apple II or Apple II Plus computer. This software sells for less than $1,000 with documentation and training. Several other I&R programs, including Link Lines in Joplin, Mo., have also developed software for microcomputers.

A second obstacle to computerization is the lack of standard classification systems that should be uniformly used by I&R agencies to categorize services. A standard classification system or taxonomy provides a common definition for each program offered by agencies. Unfortunately, achieving agreement on a common definition for a program is often very difficult since many agencies operate programs that have unique features. There are two widely used taxonomies of human services: UWASIS II (United Way of America Service Identification System) or modifications thereof, and the Louisville Classification System. Many I&R services, however, have found that either these classification systems have serious limitations or they have been forced to use state or local developed taxonomies. Several I&R services have spent much time and effort developing a suitable local taxonomy to code their service. The Westchester Library System, White Plains, N.Y.; Info Line, Los Angeles; and Link Lines, are examples of three communities in which the I&R services have developed their own unique taxonomies.

Another area of difficulty for I&R Services contemplating computerization has been the actual operating costs. Many I&R services expect to experience a decline in their operating budget when they computerize. Generally the opposite occurs. Computer hardware costs money to purchase or lease and to maintain. Software and system modifications can run into many thousands of dollars. Staff reduction seldom occurs since the computer can not perform the essential functions of the I&R service agent, who is indispensable in assessing client needs.

However, some I&R systems can justify their I&R operations on a cost basis, such as the Community Service Council of Broward County and the United Way of the Columbia-Willamette, Portland, Oregon. The Broward County system is one of the oldest and possibly the most extensive computerized I & R system in the United States. It generates revenue from the production of two types of directories ($14 for main directory; $3 for abridged and specialized directories), from sales of its software ($3,750 to $5,000 per package) and from production of special planning reports (costs vary). Portland, on the other hand, has a relative recently developed system. It has an inexpensive mode of operating the computer and does not operate online terminals. Its revenue is generated from the sales of rolodex cards ($500 for 1200 cards with monthly updates), specialized directories (from $10-$16 per copy), and mailing labels ($10 per 100).

The Computer Assistant Information & Referral Network (CAIRN) system of Boston is another system that is being designed to be economically self-sufficient. This system plans to have subscribers paying up to $500 annually for a computer-printed directory with monthly update and up to $20,000 annually for 24-hour online access to the resource file.

Most I&R services cannot use cost as the sole factor in a cost/benefit analysis to justify computerization. Improved service to clients and the community are the most important determinants in arriving at a decision to computerize. The following section of this chapter highlights some of the benefits and capabilities of computerized I&R operations.

THE STATE OF THE ART

I&R services are using computers to perform five major functions. These functions are the following:

(1) Resource file maintenance
(2) Information dissemination
(3) Online inquiry
(4) Vacancy control programs
(5) Statistical data analysis

Most computerized I&R services have automated only one or two of these functions, while some services have successfully implemented an integrated I&R service with three or more of these functions computerized. Each of these computerized components of an I&R service is described below, with examples of selected agencies that have successfully implemented these functions.

(1) Resource File Maintenance

Generally, the first priority for an I&R service is the computerization of the resource file. I&R services use computers to store, sort and retrieve data on available resources. Most I&R services organize information in three major categories:

(1) Alphabetical listing of agency names
(2) Services provided by agencies
(3) Geographic location of the services (such as zip code or county)

There are several advantages to automating a resource file. First, computerized files are easier to update. Each time an agency changes its location, hours, or services, its file has to be updated. With a manual system, the agency's alphabetical, service category, and geographical location cards each have to be completely retyped and reorganized to accommodate the new information. This is a tedious and time-consuming task. A computerized system, on the other hand, can be programmed to permit selective retyping of data and the inclusion of altered data can appear on various printouts, mailing lists, directories, and the like.

Second, a computerized file is quicker for sorting and retrieving data. Even with a well-organized, cross-referenced manual system it may take several hours or even days to retrieve a listing of all the agencies that accept Medicaid and offer a specific service. An automated system can retrieve this data in a matter of minutes if the data have been correctly encoded and entered and if the software has been properly developed.

Computerized I&R services maintain their resource files either by batch processing or online interactive input. Batch processing occurs whenever groups of data items are collected and forwarded to a computer. Batch processing normally uses punched cards or magnetic tape. Online interactive input, on the other hand, occurs when the user is in direct communication with the computer, usually through a terminal. Batch processing is the least expensive means to update a resource file, since less computer time is used and the agency need not have a computer terminal in its offices.[4] However, online interactive input is used when a terminal is readily available and updating is needed immediately. Most computerized I&R services use online interactive updating.[5]

(2) Information Dissemination

Any agency responding to information and referral requests needs access to a data base of services. In many communities, one I&R service assumes primary responsibility for the development of a centralized, comprehensive resource file. Where one centralized data base can be effectively developed and disseminated, duplication of effort is avoided. Currently, information can be distributed through the following four major media, which are discussed more fully below, printed directories, microfiche, rolodex or index cards and computer terminals.

Printed Directories

Many I&R services manually produce a detailed, comprehensive directory of services. Some communities produce pocket-size abridged directories, while other communities develop specialized directories, such as listing of services within a particular county or services for a specific target population. A few I&R services even produce customized listings detailing all agencies that meet a broad range of characteristics (for example, a listing of day care centers in zip code 77777 that serve developmentally disabled clients). Each type directory is drawn from the same data base.

The detailed, comprehensive directory may contain all data in the file while the abridged directory or the directory for a specific population contains only selected portions of the file. When manually producing these various compendia of services, each directory must be separately typed, indexed, and proofread. Hundreds of hours of staff time can be spent converting the I&R service's manual data base into a specific directory format.

Computers, on the other hand, can be programmed to print numerous types of directories from the information contained in the automated data base. The computer program can have predefined formatting rules or capitalization rules or preset typeface changes. Computer programs can be written to cross-reference the material contained in the file. For example, an alphabetical listing of agency names or a listing or services by county can be generated. These cross-references or indexes are computer generated from the data contained in the files. Therefore, while an agency name may appear several times in the directory—under the alphabetical listing, the county listing, and the agency descriptions—the staff only needs to input and proof the name one time. The other listings are generated by the computer. This represents a tremendous savings in time compared to manually produced directories.

I&R services produce printed directories using up to three types of output. The cheapest paper directory used by most agencies to produce directories in small quantities is one that is printed on preprinted forms using the agency's computer printer.[6]

If the I&R services are producing directories in large quantities, the computer printouts are given to a printer for reproduction and binding. If, however, a very limited number of copies of a particular directory are required, the I&R service simply generates an adequate

```
TCLS77     TRI-COUNTY COMMUNITY CNCL                DATE   1/27/83  PAGE    5
                                                    DIRECTORY
                                                    FOR  - P


CANDLELIGHTERS FOR CHILDREN        295-6422
                                   281-0974

0330 SW CURRY                     PORTLAND        OR 97201

GREG WIEDEMAN, PRESIDENT

RESTRICTIONS
   FAMILIES WHOSE CHILDREN HAVE     HRS 24 HOURS DAILY
   OR DID HAVE CANCER. MAY ALSO
   CONTACT GROUP THROUGH AMERICAN
   CANCER SOCIETY.
                                    FEE NONE

SERVICES
   MONTHLY NEWSLETTERS AND MEETINGS.  BOOK/TAPE
   LIBRARY.  SELF-HELP RESOURCE FOR FAMILIES WITH
   CHILD CANCER VICTIMS.  EMERGENCY FUNDS FOR LOW-
   INCOME FAMILIES TO HELP DEFRAY COSTS OF STAYING
   NEAR CHILDREN HAVING CANCER TREATMENT AT MAJOR
   CENTER. STATEWIDE GROUPS.

ACCESS

FOCUS




CAR SEATS FOR INFANTS              248-3704 MULT
MULT & WASH CNTY HEALTH DEPTS      648-8881 WASH

ADDRESS VARIES

PEGGY STOLTE, MULT CTY COORD     MARGE LARSON, WASH

RESTRICTIONS
   MULT CNTY PROG HAS INFANT        HRS MULT - M-F 9A-
   SEATS FOR CHILDREN UP TO 20LBS       4*30P/CLACKA -
   & TODDLER SEATS FOR CHILD UP         8A-5P - CALL
   TO 45 LBS. WAITING LIST FOR
   TODDLER SEATS. SERVES MULT &     FEE $8 - POSSIBLE
   CLACKA CTY.                          $5 REFUNDABLE

SERVICES
   LOW COST INFANT AND TODDLER CAR SEAT RENTAL.
   WASH CTY PROG HAS CAR SEATS FOR INFANTS ONLY.
   NO GEOGRAPHIC RESTRICTIONS.


ACCESS

FOCUS    LOW INCOME
```

Figure 8.1: Directory Printed from In-House Printer (Dot Matrix)

number of copies of the computer printout to meet the needs of the community. Figures 8.1 and 8.2 contain samples of their type of output.

A small number of I& R services produce directories from high-speed printers (usually a laser printer). These output copies are of a high quality and more readable than one produced from a standard computer printer. I& R services that use a laser printer generally print sufficient copies of their directory directly from the printer. A commercial printer is not required to reproduce the book. Laser printers are cost-effective if a limited number of copies (under 500 copies) of a directory is being produced and a high-quality output is desired. The CRIB system in Los Angeles and the Westchester Library System, White Plains both use the laser printer. Figure 8.3 displays this type of print quality.

The final type of output for a paper directory is called "camera-ready copy." Here, the I& R service develops a computer program to create a magnetic tape or diskette of information of the data base to be included in the directory. This tape is then given to a commercial firm for phototypesetting. This process, which requires no manual intervention by the I& R service or the phototypesetting firm, results in the production of highest quality output, which is ideally suited for reproduction by a commercial printer. Production of camera-ready copy is generally the most expensive means of producing a directory. Software must be developed by the phototypesetting firm to accept and typeset the data given to it by the I& R service. It should be noted that camera-ready pages cost over $5 per page to produce, whereas a laser printer can produce a page for less than 2¢. However, camera-ready copy is the most suitable output for reproducing a large number of copies of a directory. It is cost-effective if over 2,000 copies of a directory are produced, since the original coy maximizes the amount of words per page, thereby reducing the number of pages required in a directory. United Way of Minneapolis and the Greater New York Fund/United Way are among the agencies that use this process. Figure 8.4 is an example of camera-ready output.

Microfiche

A second medium for dissemination of a computerized data base is through microfiche. Microfiche is a miniature photographic image of output that must be viewed by a microfiche reader that amplifies the output. The process of producing microfiche is called COM or Computer Output to Microfiche. The process is similar in nature to the

BOY SCOUTS OF AMERICA

ADDRESS 2)47   AIRLINE   HW
METAIRIE   LA 70004   **TELEPHONE** 837-0780

NAME FRANK   LAWRENCE   SCOUT EXECUTIVE

HOURS 08 30 A.M. TO 05 30 P.M.
DAYS   MON TUE WED THU FRI

**AREA
SERVED** REGIONAL AREA

SERVICES
1   ACTIVITY GROUPS-YOUTH

ELIGIBILITY   AGE LIMIT

FUNDING   PRIVATE NCN-PRCFIT

**GENERAL
INFORMATION** YOUTH ACTIVITY GROUPS FOR MALES AGES 7-18   AP-
PLICATION REQUIRED.

* * *

BOYS' CLUBS OF GREATER NEW CRLEANS, INC.

ADDRESS 211   CAMP   ST
NEW ORLEANS   LA 70130   **TELEPHONE** 524-0357

NAME M DON   HELMS   EXECUTIVE DIRECTOR

HOURS 09 00 A.M. TO 05 00 P.M.
DAYS   MON TUE WED THU FRI

**AREA
SERVED** METRO AREA

SERVICES
1   ADMINISTRATION

ELIGIBILITY   NO RESTRICTICNS

FUNDING   PRIVATE NCN-PRCFIT

**GENERAL
INFORMATION** SPANISH SPEAKING STAFF AVAILABLE. ELEVATORS,
REST ROOMS, CURB RAMPS AND A FRONT LOADING EN-
TRANCE AVAILABLE FOR ELDERLY AND HANDICAPPED
CLIENTS. FOR MORE SPECIFIC INFORMATION, CALL
VIA AT 525-7131.

Figure 8.2: Directory Printed from In-House Printer (Pre-Printed Pages)

WHITE PLAINS CTR FOR NURSING CARE   AGENCY ID#: NH 0002 000

220 W POST RD
WHITE PLAINS   NY 10606

ADMIN PHONE: 914-946-8005   MON-SUN 9AM-5PM
EMERG PHONE: 914-946-8005   24 HRS, 7 DAYS A WEEK

ADMINISTRATOR: DULCEY B MILLER

        AGENCY TYPE: PRIVATE   FOR PROFIT   LICENSED: YES

        DESCRIPTION: AN 88 BED SKILLED NURSING FACILITY;WILL ACCEPT DIFFICULT
                      PERSONALITY,MENTALLY/INTELLECTUALLY IMPAIRED,ACUTELY
                      ILL,SHORT TERM CARE;KOSHER FOOD PACK AVAILABLE

        AREA SERVED: ALL WESTCHESTER

        TRAVEL INFO: BUS:#40;NEAREST STOP:FRONT OF BLDG;TRAIN:HARLEM LINE TO WHITE
                      PLAINS;MAJOR INT:W POST RD & QUINBY AVE

FOREIGN LANGUAGES: ITALIAN   SPANISH

ACCOMMODATIONS FOR   RESERVED PARKING   ENTRY RAMP/NO STAIRS
DISABLED PERSONS: ENTRY ASSISTANCE AVAIL   INDOOR RAMPS/NO STAIRS
                        BARRIER FREE SERVICE AREA   ELEVATORS
                        LOWERED ELEVATOR CONTROLS   LOWERED PUBLIC PHONE
                        ACCESSIBLE RESTROOMS

CLIENT CONVENIENCES: PARKING AVAIL   PUBLIC PHONE   RECREATION
                      TRIPS   LIBRARY

                                      --SERVICE SITES--

                    THIS IS A SINGLE SITE (LOCATION) AGENCY

                                  --SERVICES PROVIDED--

RESIDENTIAL CARE/TREATMENT

SKILLED NURSING CARE-RESIDENTIAL

    PROVIDES 24 HR NURSING CARE TO THOSE REQUIRING CONTINUOUS
    NURSING SUPERVISION & FREQUENT MEDICAL ATTENTION & SERVICES

        --ELIGIBILITY--   --APPLICATION--   ------FEES------   ----PAYMENT----

        MEDICAL DIAG   REFERRAL REQ $74-86/DAY   MEDICARE
                             INTERVIEW REQ   MEDICAID
                             AT-HOME INTAKE   VETERANS ADMIN
                                                                       CLIENT MAY PAY

                                    1,556

Figure 8.3: Laser Printed Directory

179

0021 AHI

0021   last survey: 7/83

AHI EZER CONGREGATION
2433 OCEAN PKWY
BROOKLYN, NY 11204
(212) 833-1400

Programs
TAX PREPARATION AND INFORMATION
  ELIGIBILITY: AGE 60 AND OLDER
  DOCUMENTS: PROOF OF AGE
  FEES: NONE
  REFERRAL METHOD: TELEPHONE, WRITE, WALK-IN
  GEOGRAPHIC RESTRICTIONS: SERVES NYC RESIDENTS
  SERVICE SITE(S): 1

SENIOR CENTER ACTIVITIES
KOSHER MEALS/DANCE/CRAFTS/FINE ARTS TAUGHT BY PRATT
TEACHER; MENTAL HEALTH COUNSEL FROM S BEACH PSYCHIATRIC.
SEWING/DRAMA/CHORUS.
  ELIGIBILITY: AGE 60 AND OLDER
  DOCUMENTS: PROOF OF AGE
  FEES: NONE
  REFERRAL METHOD: TELEPHONE, WRITE, WALK-IN
  GEOGRAPHIC RESTRICTIONS: SERVES NYC RESIDENTS
  SERVICE SITE(S): 1

Service Sites
• 1 SEPHARDIC MULTI-SERVICE SENIOR CITIZENS CENTER
       2165 71 ST
       BROOKLYN, NY 11204
       (212) 259-0100
       (212) 833-1400
       HOURS:
         MON-FRI: 8:00 am - 4:00 pm
         CLOSE AT 3:00 PM ON FRIDAYS DURING WINTER
       TRANSPORTATION: BUS, WITHIN 3 BLOCKS; TRAIN, WITHIN 3
       BLOCKS. AVE R MEDICAL CTR OFFERS FREE TWO-WAY
       TRANSPORTATION; AGENCY VAN AVAILABLE
       LANGUAGES: FRENCH, YIDDISH, HEBREW

0022   last survey: 7/83

AIMS OF MODZAWE
115-62 SUTPHIN BLVD
JAMAICA, QUEENS, NY 11434
(212) 528-6279

Programs
ARTISTIC PARTICIPATION ACTIVITIES
AFRICAN DANCE, MUSIC (DRUMS, OTHER PERCUSSIONS), LANGUAGE
(GHANIANTWI) HISTORY. AFTERSCHOOL 4-6 PM. AGES 6-15.
INCLUDES ARTS AND CRAFTS; EVENINGS AGES 16 +
  ELIGIBILITY: AGE 6 AND OLDER
  DOCUMENTS: NONE REQUIRED
  FEES: NONE
  REFERRAL METHOD: TELEPHONE, WRITE, WALK-IN
  GEOGRAPHIC RESTRICTIONS: SERVES QUEENS RESIDENTS
  SERVICE SITE(S): 1

Service Sites
• 1 AIMS OF MODZAWE
       115-62 SUTPHIN BLVD
       JAMAICA, QUEENS, NY 11434
       (212) 843-6213
       (212) 528-6279
       HOURS:
         MON-FRI: 4:00 pm - 6:00 pm; 7:00 pm - 10:00 pm
         SUMMER HOURS 10 AM - 4 PM AND 6 - 8 PM MONDAY-
         FRIDAY
       TRANSPORTATION: BUS, WITHIN 3 BLOCKS
       LANGUAGES: AFRICAN

0023   last survey: 7/83

ALFRED ADLER MENTAL HYGIENE CLINIC
37 W 65 ST
NEW YORK, NY 10023
(212) 874-2427

Programs
MENTAL HEALTH DAY TREATMENT
FULL-DAY ACTIVITIES PROGRAM FOR FORMER PSYCHIATRIC PATIENTS.
  DOCUMENTS: MEDICAID CARD
  FEES: SLIDING SCALE, $20 TO $40/SESSION
  PAYMENT METHOD: MEDICAID, PRIVATE INSURANCE
  REFERRAL METHOD: TELEPHONE, WRITE, WALK-IN
  GEOGRAPHIC RESTRICTIONS: NO RESTRICTIONS
  SERVICE SITE(S): 1
PSYCHIATRIC SERVICES, OUTPATIENT
  DOCUMENTS: MEDICAID CARD
  FEES: SLIDING SCALE, $18 TO $40/SESSION
  PAYMENT METHOD: PRIVATE INSURANCE, MEDICAID
  REFERRAL METHOD: TELEPHONE, WRITE
  GEOGRAPHIC RESTRICTIONS: NO RESTRICTIONS
  SERVICE SITE(S): 1

Service Sites
  1 ALFRED ADLER MENTAL HYGIENE CLINIC
       37 W 65 ST
       NEW YORK, NY 10023
       (212) 874-2427
       HOURS:
         MON: 9:00 am - 9:00 pm
         TUE: 9:00 am - 9:00 pm
         WED: 9:00 am - 9:00 pm
         THU: 9:00 am - 9:00 pm
         FRI: 9:00 am - 5:00 pm
         SAT: 9:00 am - 5:00 pm
       TRANSPORTATION: BUS, WITHIN 3 BLOCKS; TRAIN, WITHIN 3
       BLOCKS
       LANGUAGES: FRENCH, SPANISH, YIDDISH

0024   last survey: 7/83

ALL SAINTS EPISCOPAL CHURCH
2329 VICTORY BLVD
STATEN ISLAND, NY 10314
(212) 698-1338

Programs
RECREATION FOR CHILDREN OR YOUTH
1 GATHERING A MONTH FOR SOCIALIZATION AND RECREATION.
MEETING SCHEDULE FLEXIBLE.
  ELIGIBILITY: AGE 14 - 18
  DOCUMENTS: NONE REQUIRED
  FEES: NONE
  REFERRAL METHOD: TELEPHONE, WALK-IN
  GEOGRAPHIC RESTRICTIONS: NO RESTRICTIONS
  SERVICE SITE(S): 1
SELF-HELP GROUPS (GENERAL AND SPECIALTY)
SUPPORT GROUP FOR WIDOWS/WIDOWERS MEETS SECOND SUN OF
EVERY MONTH AT 2 PM. GROUP ALSO AVAILABLE FOR FOSTER
PARENTS OF CHILDREN OF SEAMEN'S INSTITUTE.
  DOCUMENTS: NONE REQUIRED
  FEES: NONE
  REFERRAL METHOD: TELEPHONE, WRITE, WALK-IN
  GEOGRAPHIC RESTRICTIONS: NO RESTRICTIONS
  SERVICE SITE(S): 1
SELF-HELP GROUPS, HEALTH RELATED
WORKSHOPS FOR DEAF AND BLIND PERSONS.
  ELIGIBILITY: MUST BE RESIDENTS OF WILLOWBROOK
  DEVELOPMENTAL CENTER
  DOCUMENTS: NONE REQUIRED
  FEES: NONE
  REFERRAL METHOD: REFERRAL REQUIRED FROM MUST BE
  REFERRED BY WILLOWBROOK STAFF
  GEOGRAPHIC RESTRICTIONS: NO RESTRICTIONS
  SERVICE SITE(S): 1

•   denotes a service site which reported accessible entry for the disabled in wheelchairs.
See User's Guide for explanation.

PAGE COMPOSITION BY PHOTOTYPESETTING SYSTEMS, INC

Reprinted by permission © City of New York and Greater New York Fund/United
Way.

Figure 8.4: Camera-Ready Copy

procedures used to produce camera-ready copy. A tape of the data
base is created and given to a COM vendor. This vendor develops
software to accept data from the tape and produce the microfiche.

   Microfiche is a cost-effective way to distribute large quantities of
data. Most vendors use microfiche that can hold up to 258 pages of

information on one fiche. Copies of fiche cost between 15 and 20¢ each, considerably cheaper than the cost of reproducing 258 pages. Also, the microfiche is very light and therefore less expensive to mail than paper directories. Set-up charges for microfiche generally cost less than $2,000 for each new set. I&R services that produce microfiche usually update their entire set of microfiche either monthly or quarterly.

Unfortunately, microfiche has not been well received in most communities. For a variety of reasons, not the least of which is the slow retrieval of data by microfiche, the cost of the microfiche readers (approximately $200), and the poor visibility of the reader, many I&R workers will not use microfiche. Several communities, however, use microfiche with varying levels of success.[7]

File Cards

A third medium for information dissemination is through file cards. Since many I&R workers had effectively used manually developed rolodex cards before computerization, it seemed natural to produce file cards by the computer and thereby minimize the amount of disruption to standard practices for the I&R worker. Unfortunately, the production of rolodex cards is expensive and not practical in larger communities where thousands of cards would be needed for each worker. Nevertheless, several communities do generate cards from their computerized data bases.[8]

(3) Online Inquiries

Computer terminals are the most sophisticated and controversial medium currently in use to disseminate human resources data. As was noted earlier, most I&R services sort and retrieve data by alphabetical order, service category, and location. The more sophisticated systems have developed software to sort and retrieve by such criteria and combinations of criteria as these noted below:

(1) Eligibility criteria (age, sex, marital status, income level)
(2) Key words (such as target groups)
(3) Type of service provider: governmental, private, voluntary
(4) Accessibility to the handicapped
(5) Hours of operation
(6) Languages spoken by service providers
(7) Forms of payment (such as Medicaid or Medicare)
(8) Affiliation (such as membership in a sectarian federation)

For example, a program can be developed to retrieve a listing of agencies in a particular geographic area that offer day care for a multiple-handicapped child who only speaks Korean.

While computer terminals are widely recognized as the most effective way to retrieve complex data on human service organizations, they may not necessarily be cost-efficient. For an online computer terminal, the cost of access to a data base of human services can be anywhere from several thousands dollars per year to well over $25,000 per year. Costs include the terminal itself (purchased or leased) communications equipment costs (if remote terminals are needed), printers, and access time to the computer. The computer terminal may cost as much as one staff members salary. Many I&R workers would argue that the money could be better spent on training and on increasing the number of staff members to respond to client needs rather than developing more sophisticated tools for the worker. Several communities already have found that the cost of extensive online access was more than the social service agencies could afford and therefore abandoned online systems due at least in part to costs.[9]

Only a few I&R services use computer terminals as mechanisms for retrieving data.[10]

The CAIRN system in Boston, plans to have online access when it becomes operational. This system will have a unique capability whereby workers can add confidential personal notes to an agency's description for their future viewing. For example, a worker may want to note the name of a particularly helpful employee at an agency. The CAIRN system will permit this information to be added to a screen and retrieved at a later data.

The Broward County system offers community agencies remote access to the data base. Currently, 18 agencies are paying approximately $10,000 per year each in hardware cost for such remote access. The CAIRN System in Boston will be charging $20,000 (plus hardware cost) per year for 24-hour access to its to-be-developed resource file and has attracted over a dozen interested hospitals and social agencies.

(4) Vacancy Control Program
or Service Opening Registry

One of the most frustrating experiences for an I&R worker is to spend time tracking down a service for a client only to find out that the agency is operating at capacity and therefore cannot assist the client. This most frequently occurs with such services as day care, nursing homes, emergency food and shelter, senior meal programs, subsidized housing, or employment training opportunities. To facilitate the efforts of I&R workers, communities have established computerized vacancy programs which provides up-to-date information on openings within these services.

Conceptually, the computerized vacancy program is similar to the airline reservation system. A call is received, a search is conducted and, if the caller satisfied, a reservation is made. Unfortunately, the vacancy program is not as sophisticated as the airline's system. With the vacancy program, much of the data are gathered manually (e.g., each week local day care centers must be called for openings). The filling of vacancies also must be done manually, with the I&R service or client calling the agency to register for the service.

Due primarily to the expense of properly maintaining and updating the vacancy system, few communities have implemented this type of program. In the case example section, the-now defunct Philadelphia vacancy system and the still operational day care and shelter bed space system of Seattle are described.

(5) Statistical Analysis of Data

For planning purposes, many I&R services collect data about the client who calls for assistance. Listed below is the general type of information that is gathered:

(1) Demographics (age, sex, income, etc.)
(2) Client problems/needs
(3) Services recommended
(4) Agencies recommended to the client for service
(5) Time call received
(6) Amount of time worker spent on call

Most I&R services also perform follow-up to ensure that a client referred for service did in fact receive the service, and, if not, reasons for unmet needs are documented.

Analysis of a large volume of data is difficult to manage manually. An automated system, on the other hand, can easily manipulate data to produce a variety of useful reports.

Various I&R providers use their computerized systems to develop statistical reports that are useful for internal management and community planning. Some I&R services use the computer to convert data to easily readable graphs or charts. Such reports include these:

(1) Peak days/hours of calls received
(2) Volume of work for each staff
(3) Unresolved cases by worker
(4) Reasons for unmet needs in the community
(5) List the names of agencies to which clients were referred
(6) Calls received by geographic area ethnic group, age, sex, or income status
(7) Types of service requested by various demographic groupings

Most agencies fill out client intake forms which are then keyed into the computer file. Houston has developed a form which can be input by an optical scanner, thereby saving many hours of clerical time.[11]

FUTURE APPLICATIONS

During the past few years there has been rapid advancement in the communications component of the computer industry. Two important developments include cable television and videotex. I & R services are now beginning to become involved with these communication vehicles.

The Volunteer and Information Agency, Inc. (VIA), of New Orleans is working to provide human service information on cable television. In negotiating to win the franchise to provide cable television, Cox Cable agreed to dedicate a part of subscription fees to promote community access programming. These funds are administered by a city agency, which awards grants to community organizations. A nonprofit organization was formed, Human Services on Cable, Inc. (HSOC), and has been awarded a grant to design a unique program service on Cox's two-way interactive cable TV service, INDAX. Through a computerized retrieval system, information on local services will be available in text form to subscribers at the workplace and at home. Provisions have also been made to establish volunteer-staffed "Neighborhood Viewing Centers" in low-income areas to serve residents who cannot afford cable access. VIA will be responsible for maintaining the data base.

The HSOC service will be known as KEYFACTS. Subscribers will be given a small hand-held keypad to be used in conjunction with their cable television sets. A user of the HSOC system will be given a list of subject headings (i.e., (1) food, (2) clothing, (3) housing) to choose from by pressing the number on the keypad that corresponds with the described subject headings. A second screen will then appear which will detail the major subject heading (i.e., food) into subheadings of discrete services (i.e., (1) Emergency Food, (2) Free meals, and so on). By pressing the number on the keypad that is associated with the desired service, a listing of agencies that offer the service will appear. Further details about any particular agency can then be viewed by pressing the appropriate number for the agency.

Due primarily to cost consideration, the KEYFACTS system has not yet been implemented. It is anticipated that the system will be operational by 1985.

A second high-technology application for I&R is in videotex. Videotex, which has been termed "interactive television," is a merger of the computer and telecommunications technology. It is telephone-based, two-way interactive service that allows for remote banking, shopping at home and electronic mail. Someone with a videotape system will be able to read the pages of the morning newspaper, review the current stock market, or make airline reservations. Videotex allows the user access to several different computerized data bases—stock market, airline reservations, and so on—all through one terminal. Data are then displayed on the screen using a combination of colored charts and graphics.

Videotex was conceived in England over a decade ago. Today Britain's largest videotex system has over 250,000 users. West Germany, Holland, Japan, Canada, Switzerland, and France all have various operating videotex systems. The United States has only recently become far more involved with videotex technology.

The Community Information Center of Metropolitan Toronto is the foremost user of videotex, and has developed an interactive system known as Telidon. Through grants from the Federal (Canada) Department of Communications and Bell Canada, the center has produced over 2,500 pages of information on community services in Metropolitan Toronto. Using the Telidon system, the information includes the following items:

(1) a description of the center and its services
(2) a map and listings of the 18 local Community Information Centers in and around Metropolitan Toronto
(3) a listing of emergency (24-hour) community services

Information appears in pictures and words, both of which can be enlarged for the visually impaired. Over 200 terminals are available in public places such as shopping malls, hotels, government information centers, libraries, and transportation terminals.

Knight Ridder and AT&T have begun to provide a videotex service in the Ft. Lauderdale-Miami area. The Community Service Council of Broward County will be providing the videotex network with periodic tapes of its human resources data base for video use. Knight Ridder and AT&T hope that the Broward County data base will be a marketable item in approaching corporations for subscriptions to their videotex system.

The videotex system design is similar in operation to the KEYFACT system in New Orleans. The major difference is in the mode of communication. In New Orleans, cable lines, television sets, and keypads are used. In Broward County, telephone lines, a videotex terminal (purchase price—$525), and a keyboard is used.

SUMMARY AND PROJECTIONS

Use of computers by information and referral services will continue to expand over the next several decades. Among the factors contributing to this expansion are:

(a) Decreasing cost of hardware
(b) Greater availability of tested and affordable software
(c) Better understanding and training of staff in the use of computers
(d) Increase in availability of easy-to-use computers and software

Further growth in the use of computer terminals appears virtually assured because of two converging forces. First is the continual decline of computer hardware prices that will bring this technology more in line with social agencies' budgetary constraints. Second is the gradual acceptance of the system approach of I&R delivery, whereby one I&R service takes a primary responsibility for development of the resource file and all other I&R service share in the cost and use of the file. (See Chapter 7 by J. Gargan and J. Shanahan for more details on the system approach.)

Computers can only augment the development of I&R systems, since the computer can permit one comprehensive data base to be organized to meet the specific needs of many diverse groups. A single computerized, comprehensive resource file will satisfy the information needs of a generic I&R worker; it will also meet the requirements of a specialized I& R professional who must extract only portions of the file.

Many communities will find that their manual systems are adequate for their needs. So be it. Do not attempt to fix that which is not broken! If, however, an I& R service does decide to automate, it should be noted that the technology must serve the goals and objectives of the organization. Professional consultants and computer experts are frequently needed, not necessarily hardware or software sales persons. Managers and line staff who are trained, experienced, and committed to effective service must also assume the responsibilities of planning, designing, and implementing the computer system. For a computer to be truly useful, the planning for that system must be retained by the staff of the I& R service, not outside computer experts.

I& R services are cautioned against "technology for technology's sake," bearing in mind that the goals of I& R services are

(1) to link the client with services and
(2) to provide meaningful data to planners on demands, gaps and duplication of services

The computer can be a valuable tool in the accomplishment of these goals. However, without well-trained, conscientious staff, comprehensive listing of services, and effective management, the computer will be useless. I& R is primarily a "high touch" business. Human relations and interaction are paramount to the successful delivery of services. Diagnostic and listening skills are the cornerstones of success, not technology. Service to clients must continue to be the bottom line for human service organizations and professionals.

ADDENDUM: A REPORT OF SIX CASE STUDIES

Six case studies are presented to demonstrate the successful as well as unsuccessful implementations of computerized I& R systems. The communities chosen represent a diversity of locations, size of population served, years of experience with automation, functions computerized, and funds spent on computerization. Case studies are offered for Philadelphia, Phoenix, Seattle, Minneapolis, New York, and Houston. Figure 8.5 shows the locations of these centers.

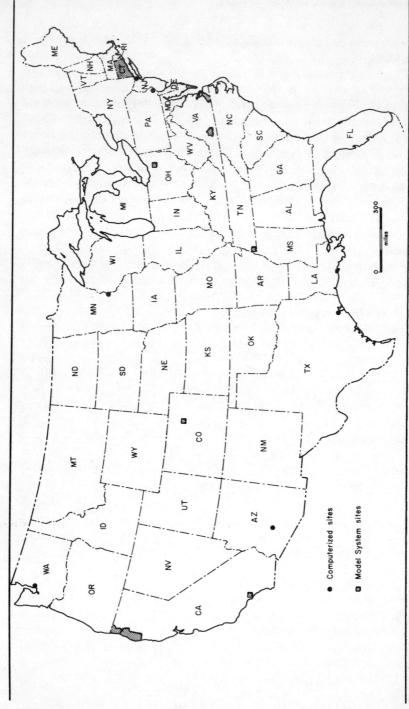

● Computerized sites

⊗ Model System sites

Figure 8.5: Location of Computerized and Model System Sites

Community Service Planning Council, Philadelphia

The Community Service Planning Council became involved with computerization in early 1970s. Its initial attempt was to have an online computer system available to the I&R services of Philadelphia. Although more than $1 million was spent on this effort, it never became operational. One major problem was that the computer programs were to be developed, tested, and debugged by a computer consultant hired on a fee-for-service basis. The programs were never completely debugged by the time the funding commitments were exhausted.

The administrative structure also created difficulties. This project was jointly administered by the Community Service Planning Council and the United Way of Southern Pennsylvania. As so frequently happens with dually administered projects, this structure did not facilitate timely decision-making, thereby further impeding the success of this overly ambitious undertaking.

In 1974-1975, Philadelphia developed the online service opening registry (SOR). This computerized operation was designed to provide up-to-date, accurate information on openings in day care, nursing homes, and low-income housing. Clients could call in for any one of these services and indicate their desired locations, level of fees they were capable of paying, and mode of payment (i.e., Medicaid or Medicare). Based on the clients criteria a list of agencies with openings would be generated. In the mid 1970s a microfiche catalogue of services was also developed by the council. At its zenith, 140 subscribers used the microfiche system containing data on human service organizations.

By 1980, both the SOR and microfiche system were abandoned. The cost of maintaining the SOR system, which had to be updated at least weekly, was beyond the limits of the agency. The microfiche catalogue was deemed of limited value to the I&R community after extensive testing in the user community.

Currently, the Community Service Planning Council has its resource file computerized on a IBM 3033 through a time-sharing arrangement. The data are batch entered (although online editing is possible at the site of the time-sharing company). Printed copy directories can be generated using a laser printer to produce a master copy suitable for large-volume reproduction. The directories can be sorted by county and/or service.

In addition, the council can extract planning reports listing agencies by any combination of the following variables: service, target group, location of service, or fees. Client statistics for the 15,000 I&R-received calls each year are also maintained on the system and used to generate reports for the annual report. No online onsite retrieval of data is possible.

The cost for the current operation is $22,000 a year for time-sharing expenses and $8,000 a year for keypunch. Revenue from directory sales offset some of these charges.

Community Information
and Referral Services,
Phoenix

In 1978 the Honeywell Corporation offered to provide the Community I&R Services with full computer assistance. The community resource file was stored on the Honeywell mainframe via a remote online terminal in the I&R offices. On a monthly basis microfiche was produced for sale to 12 subscribers. The Honeywell system also created a magnetic tape of the data base, which was given to a printer for typesetting of a biannual directory of human service organizations.

The Community I&R Services had decided by 1981 to purchase two Nippon Electric Corporation microcomputers. A computer consultant was hired to program these computers. Currently Phoenix is maintaining its major resource file on the Honeywell mainframe and an alternative resource file (i.e., church groups, local clubs, and so on) on the microcomputers. This division of the resource file data was necessitated by several factors: (1) The microcomputers did not have adequate storage capability to retain the full resource file, and (2) the Honeywell offer of free storatge and microfiche production could not be beat.

The in-house microcomputers have provided the Community I&R Service with a great deal of flexibility. The microcomputers can be used to modify or retrieve data on the alternative resource file. They also can act as terminals to communicate with the Honeywell mainframe for data input to the main resource file. The microcomputers also store client demographic data and are used to generate monthly statistical reports. Finally, the software for the mainframe computer allows for the generation of customized mailing labels and computer lists.

Community I&R Services has spent less than $30,000 for all software development and hardware purchased. In part this figure has been kept to a minimum through the in-kind support of the Honeywell Corporation.

Crisis Clinic Inc., Seattle

The Crisis Clinic has the distinction of being the only I&R service in the United States with a minicomputer dedicated solely to information and referral. The clinic owns a Prime 1000 computer with 12 local terminals and one remote terminal. This system cost approximately $190,000 to purchase plus $1,000 per month to maintain. The software to operate the system was developed by a consultant firm at the cost of $50,000.

The system provides phone workers with primary access to data through service categories. The Workers are given a menu or list of options to choose from on the screen. The workers select the option that best meets the clients' needs (similar to the cable system described for New Orleans). Before requesting a list of agencies offering a specific service, workers are permitted to refine the list by specifying one of the following: target group, hours, fees, and geographic area. After the workers review a listing of agencies that offer a specified service, they can go to detailed agency information, such as name, also-known-as-name, address, phone, branches, services, eligibility, hours, fees, application procedures, funding, and staffing.

Access to the file is also provided by typing one or more words or abbreviations in the name or also-known-as name of the agency. This step will cause a listing of agencies with the typed word(s) in its name or also known-as-name to appear. From this list the workers can obtain a detailed description of the agency.

The Crisis Clinic has modified its basic resource file to serve as a vacancy tracking system for day care and shelter bed space. Area day care centers and shelters which have vacancies contact the clinic regarding their openings. Notifications of openings are placed on the system and automatically removed after one week, thereby minimizing the level of manual maintenance of the file. Data are maintained on the system and can be retrieved through the search restrictors noted above; namely, target group, hours, fees, and geographic area.

The Crisis Clinic has also developed a unique feature to its computer system called "protocols." Protocols are detailed descriptions of services or problems to aid I&R staff in taking appropriate action. For example, one protocol is on poison. When workers access this protocol, they are given information on the screen regarding what to do for various types of poison situations. Emergency numbers are also contained on the protocol screen. These protocol screens are very useful for inexperienced staff and volunteers who must deal with a crisis situation or handle a case involving complex systems like AFCD or Medicaid.

Another attribute of the Seattle system is the collection and analysis of demographic data. Statistics on callers (i.e., duration of call, sex, age, income, geographic area, problem, and so on); disposition of call (i.e., referrals made) and level of call (i.e., information only, problem-solving with referral, crisis, and so forth) are maintained by completing an intake form for key entry. A standardized monthly report is generated after the data have been entered into the computer. Specialized reports of callers combining any of the variables noted above can also be extracted using an English-like programming language available on the Prime 1000.

The Crisis Clinic can generate mailing labels, rolodex cards, and printouts of agency profiles, indexes, protocols, and directories—either listing the entire file or special subsections. The clinic, like many other computerized systems, uses the agency profile printout to mail to the agency for updating. The Crisis Clinic has the ability to add a brief note to the agency profile printout, thereby eliminating the need for a cover letter. The agency profile printout exhibits the agency's address in a manner suitable for enclosure in a window-envelope, thereby saving the time and expense of labels.

The Crisis Clinic computer system is clearly one of the most sophisticated and flexible online systems. It was developed after many hours of involvement and planning by the clinic staff members, who were familiar with their needs.

United Way of Minneapolis

The United Way of Minneapolis's First Call for Help developed its computerized resource information systems in 1973. With input from the United Way staff, the system was designed, programmed, and maintained by the Honeywell Corporation. In 1981, the data base was converted from the Honeywell system to the Twin Cities United Way Data Processing Center.

The system designed by Honeywell in 1973, and currently in use, is a batch retrieval system. It produces a resource file on microfiche that is updated on a monthly basis. A copy of the microfiche file and reader are located at the desk of each Information and Referral specialist for use in responding to the needs of callers. Directories available for sale to community agencies also are produced from the computer file. Both the directories and the microfiche are generated by this process: First a magnetic tape of the data base is produced, containing all data to be included in the directory or the microfiche. The tape for the directory is then given to a commercial firm to produce "camera-ready copy." Some 5,000 copies of the directory, which list more than 750 of the 2,500 resources contained in the data base, are produced biannually. The tape for the microfiche, on the other hand, is given to a COM vendor, who creates the monthly microfiche list of all 2,500 community resources.

By 1984 the modus operandi of First Call for Help will change. The United Way has received a $196,000 grant from the McKnight Foundation to convert its batch system into an up-to-date, online interactive system and to connect the East Metro Information and Referral Center of St. Paul to the data base. The new system will be structured as follows:

(1) The information resource file will continue to be maintained on United Way's Data Center computer system, IBM System 38. Maintenance of the file will be performed interactively at two computer terminals, one located at the offices of Minneapolis First Call for Help, the other at the East Metro I&R Center.

(2) At Minneapolis First Call for Help a number of computer terminals will be installed with online interactive access to the data base.

(3) The East Metro Information and Referral Center will be linked interactively to the United Way Data Center's System 38. The Information and Referral Center will have five interactive terminals for retrieval, with one having data entry capacity.

This configuration will provide First Call for Help and East Metro I&R Center with maximum computer power at a reasonable price. Because the McKnight grant will permit the United Way to purchase all equipment, the operating costs should be manageable.

Greater New York Fund/United Way

The history of developing a computerized resource file for New York City has been a long one. In the mid 1960s the city government began a project called IRMA (Information and Referral Manual). The project, during its 16-plus-year history, succeeded in developing citywide microfiche listings and computer printouts for each of 59 community districts (a community district is a political subdivision of the borough or counties). IRMA developed its own taxonomy of services through a grant received from the U.S. Department of Health, Education and Welfare.

By the late 1970s it was apparent that IRMA was not meeting the needs of the community, particularly the public agencies it was primarily intended to serve. In 1980, the Greater New York Fund/ United Way and the City of New York Human Resources Administration decided to coordinate their efforts to develop an effective online interactive system for New York City. For 18 months, an extensive planning and community input process was undertaken. Over 40 public and private human service organizations participated in designing a computer system. This design lead to the formation of the Service Agency Inventory System (SAIS). The goal of this project was to develop a computerized comprehensive resource file for New York City.

At the end of 1983 the SAIS project has achieved the following:

(1) The development and semiannual updating of a computerized resource file of almost 5,000 locations of service.

(2) The production of a directory of service listing over 1,700 human service organizations. The directory is created from "camera-ready" output and sold by a commercial firm which pays SAIS royalties.

(3) The capability to generate computer listings or mailing labels based on any combination of up to 40 variables, including location of agency, language spoken, handicap accessibility, target group served, and programs offered.

(4) Development of an online system, currently only available in-house, that has the capability to retrieve data base on any combination up to 40 variables. This capability allows workers to request agencies that met the client specific need. For example, rather than search through a list of some 1,500 day care centers, the worker can specify exactly the type of center required—day care for a developmentally disabled blind child who speaks Russian or a senior center in zip code 10016 for Jewish women only. Primary access to the system is provided by typing in the agency name or popular name, or part thereof; or by typing a general or specific service category.

(5) Development of complete documentation and a detailed training program for future system users.

The City of New York Human Resources Administration, has also been pilot-testing the online retrieval of the computer resource file by its office workers throughout the five boroughs. When fully implemented, some 1,000 computer terminals connected to the Human Resource Administration mainframe will have remote access to the data base. The Human Resources Administration files will be kept up-to-date through receipt of a monthly tape of the file maintained by SAIS. SAIS, which is jointly funded by the Human Resources Administration and the Greater New York Fund/United Way, has expended over $300,000 in computer time-sharing fees and programming charges. The software has been developed and maintained by the United Way of Tri-State on an IBM System 38.

United Way of Texas Gulf Coast, Houston

In 1976, the United Way of the Texas Gulf Coast began development of its automated system. The I&R system has a sophisticated online retrieval package programmed on an IBM mainframe. Users can retrieve data by target group, service category, geographic area agency name, or office name. Detailed information on the agency (name, address, phone numbers, director's name, budget sources, and so forth); services offered (service associated eligibility requirements, intake worker for service, referral method, fees, and so on); and offices (services provided from each office name, addresses, hours, transportations, language spoken, handicap access) are given.

The online data base, which is updated every 12 months, is currently being used on six in-house terminals. No remote terminals exist to date.

A computer-generated directory is also produced on the in-house printer. This self-sufficient directory is published every two years and 3,200 copies are sold.

The Houston system also has a machine-readable client case log form. Workers complete one form for each case indicating such data as worker number, date, race of caller, age of caller, sex of caller, problems encountered, referrals made, time spent on referral, and follow-up made. These forms are completed by darking the appropriate circle(s) on the form. The forms are then ready by an optical scanner and numerous types of monthly reports are produced, including number of calls by problem areas, number of cases referred to specific agencies, demographic data (age, race, sex of callers), follow-up results by agency referred to; follow-up by client, and reasons for unmet needs.

The software for the system was developed by Arthur Andersen and Company. The cost to the United Way was $25,000 for development and limited ongoing maintenance. This fee represents a significant subsidy from Arthur Andersen and company.

GLOSSARY

Batch Processing (also termed sequential processing): A method of processing groups of data that are accumulated and forwarded to a computer.

Central Processing Unit: "Brains" of the computer. Manages all arithmetic/logic functions, storage units and control units.

Classification System: A method of organizing services according to certain characteristic so as to be meaningful to the user.

Computer: A device which can perform calculations (such as addition and subtraction) and logic operations (less than, equal to) without human intervention.

Computer Output Microfiche (COM): A technique used to record output from a computer as very small images on sheet film.

Data: A representation of facts for communication, interpretation, and processing by humans or machines.

Data Base: A collection of interrelated data stored together with a minimum amount of redundancy to serve multiply users.

Debugging: To isolate and remove malfunctions from a computer program.

Hardware: Physical equipment or components of a computer system. Includes central processing unit, printers, terminals, tape drives.

Laser Printer: A type of printer that combines laser beams and electrophotographic technology to form images on paper.

Local Terminals: Terminals connected by wires or cables to the central processing unit.

Magnetic Tape: A half-inch-wide storage medium on which data can be stored electronically. Typical length for tapes are 600, 1200, and 2400 feet.

Magnetic Disks: A storage medium in which data is retained on rotating disks.

Mainframe: Large, expensive computers that are capable of processing vast amounts of data at very fast speeds.

Microcomputer: (also termed "personal" computer): A small computer generally costing less than $10,000.

Minicomputer: A computer with slower processing speed, smaller storage capacity and lower cost than a mainframe, but greater capabilities and higher cost than a microcomputer.

Online: Being in direct communication with the computer as a customer is with a telephone operator.

Optical Character Reader: A devise which reads the data on a document by scanning the location or shape of the data.

Remote Terminal: A terminal that is some distance for the computer and is connected to the Central Processing Unit by a communication channel, generally a telephone line.

Software: Program or instructions written for the computer system which are designed to solve problems of a specific nature—i.e., payroll preparation.

Terminals: (also termed a Cathode Ray Tube): A device that contains a television-like screen for displaying data, with a typewriter-like keyboard for input of data.
Time-sharing: An arrangement whereby two or more independent users can access the central processing unit at the same time.
Videotex: Telephone-based, two-way interactive service utilizing a videotex terminal to communicate with a centralized data base.

NOTES

1. Among the microcomputer users are Community I&R Services in Phoenix and several public libraries in the state of Maryland.

2. Examples of users of minicomputers include the United Way of Broome County, Binghamton, N.Y.; First Call for Help, Morristown, N.J.; Info Line, Akron, Ohio; and United Way of Columbia-Willamette, Portland, Ore. Users of mainframe computers include the Westchester County System, White Plains, N.Y.; the United Way of the Texas Gulf Coast, Houston, Texas; the Community Service Planning Council, Philadelphia, Pa. and the Volunteer and Information Agency, Inc. in New Orleans, La.

3. Installations of the Broward software have been made in Baltimore, Binghamton, Indianapolis, Providence, and Orlando.

4. Agencies that use batch processing include the Community Chest and Council of Greater Cincinnati; the Health and Welfare Council of Nassau County, Hempstead, N.Y.; Volunteer and Information Agency New Orleans; Info-Line, Hartford, Conn., and Portland, Oregon.

5. Agencies that operate online systems include Community Information & Referral Service the United Way of Chicago; The United Way of Broome County, Binghamton, N.Y.; Morristown, N.J.; Joplin, Mo.; Akron, Ohio, and White Plains, New York.

6. Directories produced by agency-computers include Broward County, Fla.; Binghamton, N.Y.; Hartford, Conn.; New Orleans, La., and Portland, Ore.

7. Microfiche systems are used by I&R systems in Hempstead, N.Y.; Phoenix; Chicago, and Minneapolis.

8. Communities that utilize card files from their computerized data bases include Morristown, N.J.; Portland, Ore.; and the Crisis Clinic in Seattle.

9. Communities that have abandoned online systems include the United Way of Dade County, Miami; the Department of Social Services, Lansing, Mich.; and the Community Service Planning Council, Philadelphia.

10. Computer terminals used for retrieval are reported by the following communities: Cincinnati; Morristown, N.J.; Seattle; Joplin, Mo.; Minneapolis; Akron, Ohio; Houston, and White Plains, N.Y.

11. Among the I&R services that have computerized their statistical analysis of data are: Akron, Ohio; Morristown; Portland; Cincinnati; Broward County; Seattle; Houston; Chicago; Minneapolis; Cleveland, and Joplin.

REFERENCES

Bowers, G. E., & Bowers, M. R. (1977). *Cultivating client information systems* (series no. 5). Washington, DC: DHHS, Office of Intergovernmental Systems, Project Share Human Services. Monograph Series.

Mandell, S. L. (Ed.). (1979). *Computers and data processing: Concepts and applications*. St. Paul, MN: West Publishing Co.

Miller, F. W. (1983). Micro mini info: Here, there, everywhere. *Info Systems, 30,* 4, 28-32.

Naisbitt, J. (1982). *Megatrends.* New York: Warner Books.

Schoech, D. (1982). *Computer use in human services: A guide to information management.* New York: Human Sciences Press.

Segelstein, B., & Segelstein, S. (1976). *Data processing contracts: Structure, contents and negotiations.* New York: Van Nostrand Reinhold.

Shelly, G. B., & Cashman, T. J. (1980). *Introduction to computers and data processing.* Anaheim, CA: Anaheim Publishing Company.

Slavin, S. (Ed.). (1982). *Applying computers in social services & mental health agencies: A guide to selecting equipment, procedures and strategies.* New York: Haworth Press.

Taylor, J. B., & Gibbons, J. (1980). *Microcomputer applications in human service agencies* (series no. 16). Washington, DC: DHHS, Office Intergovernmental Systems, Project Share Human Service Monograph Series.

9

IMPACT OF ADVANCED TECHNOLOGY ON I&R IN A CANADIAN PROVINCIAL CONTEXT

DONALD F. BELLAMY
DONALD J. FORGIE

The focus of this chapter is the Community Information Center of Metropolitan Toronto (CICMT) in its urban and larger provincial environment and its response to new communication technologies. The CICMT was chosen because it is the major node in an Ontario I&R network; it has the longest history and the largest size in terms of budget, staff, and population served; and it is currently engaged in experimenting with advanced information technologies.

From a constitutional point of view, the ten provinces undertake the primary responsibility for delivery of health, education, and social welfare services. As Canada became increasingly industrialized, with attendant problems, direct initiatives in the social services were taken in more recent times by the federal authorities.

Personal social services may be provided in Canada provincially or municipally, or by non-governmental bodies under charitable auspices. The tradition of using both government and voluntary auspices is found in the case of I&R services.

AUTHORS' NOTE: *The authors acknowledge with appreciation the assistance of, among others, Ms. Elizabeth Wray (CICMT); Ms. Linda Church (Ontario Ministry of Citizenship and Culture); Ms. Ann Kemp (Citizen's Inquiry); and Ms. Ernestine Van Marle and Ms. Terri Noseworthy (Rexdale CID) in the preparation of this chapter.*

VOLUNTARY I&R CENTERS IN CANADA

An accurate census of voluntary I&R centers in Canada's provinces and territories is not readily obtainable due to differences in reporting and definition. A recent compilation by the Association of Community Information Centers in Ontario identified 123 centers across the country. According to this inventory, two Atlantic provinces (Newfoundland and Prince Edward Island) and the Yukon and Northwest Territories do not have I&R centers. The provinces of New Brunswick, Nova Scotia, Manitoba, and Saskatchewan have 7 centers between them. The Province of Quebec has 5, British Columbia 28, Alberta 30, and Ontario 53. Outside of Alberta and Ontario, which both have major programs of provincial financial support, only 8 centers enjoy provincial subsidies. It should be noted that some of the centers listed outside of Ontario are either government information agencies, service centers, or specialized I&R centers, designed to serve particular groups on the basis of age, health condition, or ethnicity.

I&R DEVELOPMENTS IN ONTARIO

Building Toward a Provincewide Network

Between 1952, when CICMT began operating, and 1970, a loose network of centers developed in the province, and this group began the work of building a provincewide association. The association of Community Information Centers in Ontario was formally established as recently as 1977. It came into existence in order to give its members a unified voice in seeking provincial and other sources of financial support and to give the members an opportunity to debate such mutual concerns as long-range planning (Martins, 1979). Today, there are 53 member centers in the association, which restricts admission to general information and referral centers (Profiles, 1982).

Between 1971 and 1974, 28 of the 53 centers came into existence, coinciding with Ontario's support for voluntary I&R centers. On the other hand, only 2 member centers have been created since 1978. The geographic distribution of these centers, not surprisingly, follows Ontario's uneven population distribution, with most centers in the most heavily populated central and southwestern parts of the province.

The most firmly established of all these regional groups is in Metropolitan Toronto. In this metropolis (2.2 million population), a group of 14 centers, which provide generic information, has been called officially the Federation of Community Information Centers (FCIC) ever since it was established in 1973 (Policy and Procedure Manual, 1978). The federation has worked effectively to promote high standards and support for its own members and those of association members. Efforts of both the federation and association to ensure adequate and stable financial support have been less successful.

Statistical Reporting

In addition to its other activities, the Ontario association developed, with the aid of a provincial grant, a uniform statistical reporting system for I&R centers. Among the objectives of this project were improved accountability to center boards and funding bodies; improved internal planning of centers; identification of emerging service trends in the centers; identification of needed or redundant community services; and improvement of communication between centers through the use of commonly accepted terms and forms of reporting (Wray, 1977).

The primary unit of service data in the statistical system is the inquiry—a request for information by a user. This initial request may generate any number of additional contacts with the user or collateral sources. Problem classification in the statistical system is based on up to 1,000 cross-indexed data dictionary codes. Unfortunately the maintenance and effective use of the system to its full potential requires considerably more financial resources than the association has available. In the absence of a central control system, individual centers are left to make their own local arrangements for data tabulation and analysis with educational institutions or firms, or else undertake tedious manual work themselves. Statistical outputs accordingly vary in extent from center to center, with small ones producing only summary statistics monthly or yearly concerning the number of inquiries received. More complex output statistics, such as cross-tabulations of problems identified with resources referred to or available, have been difficult to obtain. Some centers use their own output figures to support local demands for service development.

There have also been a few collective efforts by the association to produce special tabulations on timely provincial policy areas such as child day-care. The association has gone to great lengths to develop a training kit to increase the reliability of statistics collected. Much more than this will require a statistical worker who can advise and assist local centers, thus helping to ensure a more uniform and effective use of the system.

But generally, identification of service gaps and planned strategies to fill them have become low priorities in today's economic climate. Maintaining the essentials already in place has become the primary concern, as it has in other countries. These priorities are understandable, too, not only in terms of the economic environment, but also in terms of provincial expectations and funding criteria. The primary function of I&R centers is the provision of information and the improvement and extension of information services where gaps are found (The Association, 1979). The identification of needs and gaps in direct human services may occur as a by-product of this primary information function. The I&R centers are not expected to go beyond social reporting to appropriate planning bodies and become involved in the direct provision of human services within the terms of the grant from the province.

Funding the I&R Centers

As indicated in the introduction, although the federal government originally had only a minor function in social service provision, it has expanded its role to meet modern requirements. Recent examples are the need to intervene in the problems of unemployed youth, expand employment opportunities generally, assist immigrants, and deal with consumer problems. The interventions often have taken the form of grants to approved organizations to hire students or other staff on time-limited contracts; these programs tend to be implemented on an annual basis. The Ontario Ministry of the Attorney General has fully funded legal clinics attached to two of the I&R centers. The stability of these arrangements, and the demand for legal service, has led to the clinics becoming a major function of those centers.

The lack of long-term funding commitments in the case of some government grant or purchase-of-service arrangements is a recurring issue. Without such stability, centers have a weak base for the future. Conflict between case accountability to the funder and case confidentiality has been contentious, particularly in contracting to supply services to immigrants on behalf of federal immigration authorities. Users who are liable to be deported from the country in the event of economically dependency or irregular status as immigrants can be identified in the event of a government audit of files. The tendency now is not to enter into this particular arrangement.

Common core funding sources of the I& R centers are the following:

(1) *United Way*. In 1981, 21 of the 53 member centers of the association received a total of approximately $1.1 million. In communities without a United Way campaign, centers often conduct their own fund-raising drives locally.

(2) *Local government*. Local elected councils are permitted under provincial legislation to make discretionary grants to charitable organizations. The councilors must reconcile the competing demands of any number of organizations in the process. All but eight or nine centers received these discretionary municipal grants in 1981, to a grand total of $560,000.

(3) *Provincial government*. The Ministry of Citizenship and Culture supports a Community Information Services Program through which discretionary grants are made to approved centers based on a proportion of actual expenditures (up to 33 percent). For 10 years, provincial authorities have accepted FCIC membership criteria as the basis for funding centers. The intent of the grant program is to underwrite and make consultation available to a provincewide network of local I& R centers. Its inclusion in the particular Ontario ministry is viewed as an efficient way to effect the ministry's mandate of educating people as to their citizenship rights and responsibilities through enhancing volunteer involvement in the community, stimulating the formation of self-help systems, and supporting access to personalized information. Since another ministry, The Ministry of Community and Social Services, has the primary operational responsibility for provincial government social welfare programs, there is a clear separation between the provision of those services and community information services.

The Community Information Services Program does not have continuity through legislative enactment, and the government must allocate the funds through an annual vote. Further, the 33 percent limit set for grants to individual I& R centers is conditional on the remainder being available from other sources. The grant program, thus, will not support a poorly funded center (The Association, 1979).

Currently, about 60 percent of members of the Ontario Association receive the maximum 33 percent grant. About 10 other centers receive below this figure, while only 4 centers received no grant in 1981. The total sum received by the centers in that year was approximately $725,000.

Location and I&R Access

Until recent years, most new I&R centers were established in offices, storefronts, and various public buildings, frequently at a modest rent or none at all. Several centers operated autonomously in public libraries. There is now a tendency to establish I&R centers under local public library boards, in which case provincial authorities expect the I&R function to be identifiable and placed under a management committee or similar structure of the library board. Some of the advantages claimed for I&R centers that operate as a component of the library are greater visibility and walk-in access and more extended hours of I&R service. An increasing number of centers are associated with multiservice centers in Ontario, but there are relatively few such interorganizational structures in Ontario. They have not been publicly supported to the extent they have in the United States.

In many communities across the province, I&R services are not available outside of regular working hours on weekdays. A few centers are open one or more evenings a week, and fewer are open on Saturdays. To compensate, a few centers have installed messaging equipment or telephone answering services, but unfortunately the use of this service enhancement seems to be declining, perhaps a victim of the economic environment and the adverse impact of scarce resources. The central services in Toronto (CICMT) and Windsor-Essex (Help Services) are the only ones that operate after-hours information services; together with their regular service, these two centers have 24-hour coverage seven days a week (Profiles, 1982).

Staff in the Centers

The total number of personnel employed full-time by the association member centers has remained fairly constant over the most recent four-year period. Altogether, 107 full-time staff members were employed in 1982, an increase of only 7 in the same period. Since about half of these are in Toronto, it is clear that a great many centers have 1, 2, or, occasionally, 3 such staff members. Only a handful have as many as 5. It is not surprising that many centers of such size place their highest priorities upon serving their users, interacting with local human services, and participating in wider I&R networks only if time and resources allow. Increasingly, centers are turning to employing their staff on short contracts rather than permanent status. Many centers have come to rely upon part-time staff: the total number rose from 24 in 1978 to 42 in 1982. Almost all centers have volunteer assistance, a total across the province of about 750 currently (Profiles, 1982). Hiring students or other casual workers under federal and provincial employment expansion programs has been popular with most centers. As the numbers vary from year to year, this is an unreliable means of procuring staff expertise.

I&R Center Functions

In Metropolitan Toronto, CICMT is the only member of the federation that serves as a central service, and its activities are purely I&R. By this last term is meant activities that are identified as "Information; Interpreting; Form Filling, Direction; Consultation/ Liaison; Referral; Crisis Intervention; Advice, Guidance, Listening; Clarification of Rights and Intervention Adequacy" (The Association, 1978). In the remainder of the province about half are central services and the other combine the I&R functions with such direct services as income tax and legal aid clinics, landlord/tenant assistance, translation, consumer advocacy, transportation coordination, operation of various registries, and clothing depots. Few offer extended counseling. Suicide and distress calls tend to be taken by specialized agencies in the larger urban centers.

Many centers in Ontario's smaller towns and cities have assumed a variety of such concrete service functions in response to community initiative. In those places, very often there are few formal voluntary social services that are accessible to the general population. These community initiatives appear to fill a serious gap (Profiles, 1982).

Community Information Center of Metropolitan Toronto (CICMT)

The CICMT was the first major centralized metropolitan I&R center in Canada when it was established as a full-time service in 1952.[1] For many years it was a department of the Toronto Welfare Council. The center became incorporated as an independent social service in 1970, having its own board of directors and quarters in a downtown office building. Its main goal then was, and remains, to provide individualized information about social resources to individuals and organizations, and through doing so to identify trends, social needs, and service gaps. Although Canadian legislation does not by any means completely support the notion, the center functions on the basis of the right of people to obtain free, accurate, and effectively communicated information in confidence (MacFarlane, 1978).

Services of CICMT

Telephone/voice communication is the primary mode of delivering information from this central service. Office interviews account for no more than 2 percent of the inquiries handled by the center. Full-time paid telephone information counselors are employed, aided by some experienced volunteers; some of these are multilingual. This service is available from 8:30 a.m. to 6 p.m. on weekdays. Telephone access is gained via six lines, though not all can be open all the time owing to workload scheduling; tests indicate that the system is overloaded at peak times of the day. The total volume of inquiries dealt with by this regular daytime service was more than 87,000 in the year 1981. It is estimated that over 20 percent of these calls are made by other information providers or persons referred by professional practitioners.

A separate telephone after-hours emergency information service handled 12,000 inquiries in 1981. This service is undergoing changes that are discussed below.

The second mode of communication with CICMT users is print. A directory of community information services, popularly known as the Blue Book from its blue cover, is the primary resource. This is widely purchased by social service agencies, professionals in private practice, and libraries. The Blue Book has been extensively supplemented by smaller, specialized directories and pamphlets aimed at special-interest groups and service providers; examples are directories in the field of child day-care, services for seniors, and summer camps. Publication sales account for over 5 percent of CICMT revenues.

A community education division of CICMT has the objective of assisting organizations through consultation, training, and classroom work in using community resources and also teaching users how to search for information themselves.

Resource Bank of CICMT

The main files of CICMT are maintained on a card system containing information on more than 4,000 services in Metropolitan Toronto. Included are services offered by governmental and voluntary agencies, self-help groups, and similar bodies. Commercial providers are excluded unless nonprofit organizations cannot meet the need for a particular service. In addition to routine daily checks in the media, systematic checks with service providers take place yearly, when 70 percent of agencies submit amended information.

About 750 entries taken from the CICMT resource bank are published in the Blue Book. The selection of services to be included in the directory takes into account the wishes of some organizations to be able to control the pressure on their own delivery systems through not being publicized. Supplementary pamphlets, some of which contain 300 to 400 entries, provide specific service locations not given in the Blue Book.

Financing CICMT

Like other centers in the province, the CICMT is dependent upon a variety of funding resources. Of total revenues in 1981 amounting to $644,000, $441,000 consisted of grants. The Province of Ontario, through its discretionary grant program to I & R centers located in the Ministry of Citizenship and Culture, contributed the largest single amount, $157,000, equal to 24 percent of total revenues. This was followed closely by the Municipality of Metropolitan Toronto, which contributed $150,000. The United Way gave $125,000. An additional small sum was received from Wintario, a provincial agency that operates a lottery by that name, the proceeds of which may be used for grants to charitable organizations conditional upon equal matching donations by private resources. Sales of publications, as mentioned before, brought in $98,000. Most of the revenues remaining came from donations, fees, and interest.

Some special project support also came from Bell Canada and the Department of Communications for experimenting with applications of new technologies for community information services, particularly Telidon.

The year 1982 saw a marked expansion of project funding from the Wintario lottery and the Federal Department of Employment and Immigration for the purpose of developing a technological capability to provide information using a Telidon data base created by CICMT.

Staff Resources of CICMT

The full-time staff complement during the regular working hours was 28 as of December 1982 in four administrative divisions. Eleven

worked in Inquiry/Education and seven in Publications and Resources. Seven staff members worked in a special Telidon project,
discussed below. Management was by three persons.

In 1982, in addition to the above personnel, four summer students
were employed, and ten persons were engaged in the after-hours
emergency information service.

New Directions at CICMT

Development of After-Hours Service

As noted in the earlier discussion of services, for many years
CICMT offered an after-hours emergency information service, which
has dealt with telephone inquiries outside regular working hours. It is
staffed by a roster of 10 persons on a purchase-of-service basis. The
sheer volume of inquiries alongside recent information about service
inaccessibility indicated the need for further development. In addition to a 1981 volume of 12,000 CICMT inquiries after hours, it is
estimated that as high a proportion as 80 percent of calls taken at the
Public Emergency number (911) for fire, police, and ambulance, concern social service matters. In 1982, CICMT conducted a feasibility
study to determine the readiness of governmental and voluntary
services to participate in establishing a demonstration project of
centralized service delivery after hours.[2]

Currently, this study has moved to the proposal stage, which
would involve an initial first-year outlay of about $420,000, and a
projected volume of more than 70,000 inquiries. Approximately 25
agencies are now considering the nature of their after-hours requirements and the legal ramifications of contracting with CICMT. The
latter would receive calls to agencies and tie together the participating
agencies not only by telephone/voice communication, but might also
allow CICMT to give information on local video display terminals.
The multiservice center would then be not just a one-stop service in a
single geographic location, but a service network interacting electronically. This degree of cooperation would provide a testing ground for
other forms of collaboration during regular working hours.

Use of Advanced Technology

The CICMT made its first move away from complete reliance on
conventional and manual forms of information production and dissemination in 1980 with the purchase of Micom word processing

equipment. The impact of this was to improve quality, expand the publication program, and allow CICMT to maintain a frequent updating cycle. The improved capabilities have allowed CICMT to recover much of the cost through charges, with the effect seen in substantially higher revenues derived from publication sales as reported earlier.

The second step into advanced technology was a major move into the use of Telidon after a period of study of videotex and related technologies in the 1970s. For some years, the Canadian Department of Communication has been conducting research into the development of a high-quality videotex system that would permit its users to interact with a data base and allow the transmission of quality color graphics and text using any of the common carriers such as the telephone network with display capabilities added to the home color television set. When it was released, the Canadian development, Telidon, had the advantages of simplicity of use, currency for updates, and an opportunity for the Community Information Center to create its own data bases related to local user needs. Along with the British Prestel and the French Antiope, Canadian Telidon became a videotex standard for testing in the international marketplace. When a number of field trials were begun in 1981, CICMT decided to participate in the largest of these, the Vista trial directed by Bell Canada. Funding was secured from federal and provincial sources in addition to Bell Canada for the development of a CICMT data base in the field trial.

Why did CICMT become interested in Telidon? First, the center was concerned that noncommercial interests have an important part to play in what could otherwise become a new medium dominated almost exclusively by commercial enterprise. By demonstrating its responsiveness to people through the dissemination of public service information, CICMT was able to participate in and help formulate and shape the development of the new medium.

GOVERNMENTAL SYSTEMS

Both the Ontario and the Canadian governments have been concerned about access by the public, elected members, and public servants to information and referral to particular programs and services available through government.

A central provincial information agency known as Citizens' Inquiry was begun by the Ontario government in 1972 (MacFarlane, 1978). It is located in Toronto under the jurisdiction of the Ministry of

Government Services. By confining its work to referral whenever inquiries do not involve provincial responsibilities and to facilitating direct user contact with provincial officials when necessary, Citizens' Inquiry appears to have built up effective interrelationships with such complementary systems as the voluntary I & R centers and offices of public officials. Its annual volume of calls is 50,000 currently, about 90 percent by telephone. There is a staff of 11 persons employed full time: 2 in administration, 5 for data base and directory work, and 14 in the inquiry offices. Three part-time interpreters also are employed (Citizens' Inquiry, 1983).

Among developments are the use of Zenith or 800 exchange numbers that allow persons in smaller centers and rural areas to call government switchboards at district offices without incurring long-distance charges. The channel for such information in the north country is provided by 31 district offices of the Ministry of Northern Affairs.

If the Zenith number is not available to the caller, "Zenith Ontario" has been established to assure full free access to directory numbers. Most ministries have undertaken to accept toll-free calls from members of the public who proceed with the request for services information or other assistance. Blue-colored government pages are included in local telephone directories, listing departments and toll-free numbers.

In order to back up its own I & R work and that of others in the field, both in the provincial district offices and voluntary I & R centers, Citizens' Inquiry publishes a "KWIC Index" of provincial services and access locations. This is available in both written form and at the central office online. This publication and voluntary I & R directories such as CICMT's Blue Book have complementary uses.

The Canadian government has published Zenith numbers to assist members of the public in gaining toll-free access to information and services from distant points. Further centralization of Ontario and Canadian government information access seems likely to occur through the utilization of "Zenith Ontario" by both governments for the benefit of all members of the Ontario public. This degree of centralization would contrast sharply with the highly decentralized system of voluntary I & R centers. In addition to the Zenith systems, the Canadian government has a Telidon data base with free terminals located in a number of public places across the country such as post offices, Canada Service Centers, and shopping centers. Government information and a job information service are examples of the public interest information obtainable, and the Ontario government is also participating. Access to the visual displays is obtained by selecting numbers on a keypad. This public information system, along with various commercial data bases on Telidon, is currently being managed by Infomart, a Canadian company actively engaged in the development and marketing of Telidon based services locally, nationally, and internationally.

In the future, as provincial and federal government information available through their Zenith numbers is more frequently accessed, a logical step would be the integration of local information data bases in order to simplify public access not only for voice communication but also for data, records, and graphic communication.

In addition to telephone-based networks, TV Ontario and the Canadian Broadcasting Corporation (both government agencies) are experimenting with Telidon-based systems using broadcast networks.

FUTURE ISSUES

Community information and referral services in Canada are ready to respond to the inquiry of an individual or any professional. The questions asked are concerned with specific human needs, local community conditions, and short-term or immediate decisions requiring action.

The ecological approach is one in which not only individual concerns are of interest, but also the interrelationships between individuals, groups, communities, provinces, and states, as well as national and international bodies. An ecological approach also attempts to anticipate, not only the immediate effects of, for example, the availability of day care in a specific borough of a metropolitan center, but also the ramifications that availability or lack thereof may have upon both parents and young children in years to come.

These concerns that extend beyond present community requirements and involving future generations are difficult to deal with. For many, they also become irrelevant speculation, standing in sharp contrast to crisp, specific, current human needs (Smith, 1982). Issues of major concern having long-range impact upon individuals and society often fail to reach the agendas of those planning future I & R services locally or even at senior government funding levels. Some issues, however, may have a greater effect upon future access to information and services in our society than any of the immediate problems such as funding, staffing, and service levels. The application of computer/

communications technologies by our society is one such issue (Cameron, Telidon, 1/14/80, 75).

The Impact of Advanced Technology and the Growth of Ignorance

Ignorance is seldom linked to the public image associated with societal developments in the 1980s and 1990s (Telidonic Information Systems, 1981). Before literacy, the idea of ignorance was of limited significance, but the introduction of reading, writing, and printed books and newspapers left those who could neither read nor write in a disabling stage of ignorance. A social phenomenon of growing significance today in Canada is functional illiteracy, which occurs when adults do not have sufficient skills in reading and writing to permit them to function in our society. The problem is greatly magnified by the rapid introduction of advanced technology in communication because many adults, even highly educated adults, are not familiar with the application or potential of the new technology.

In some form, computer and related communication technologies such as fiber optics and satellite transmission are now having specific and likely lasting implications for I & R services, the agencies concerned with I & R, and those who might make an inquiry from any I & R center. In Canada, a variety of technologies have had a profound impact already on both access to information and I & R services. These include the use of word processors and microcomputers, and developments in radio, television, cable, and telephone networks permitting local access to text and graphics. There have been attempts to develop community information data bases and networks and to introduce Telidon as a vehicle for public information. Access to information requires that either the professionals or their clients have access to the information storage and delivery medium— whether this is a human being alone, a human using the telephone network, a printed source, or a TV display unit. Thus, whole sectors of users can be denied access if they cannot reach an information source due to lack of available technology or ignorance concerning its use. At this time in Canada, remote access to I & R services using the telephone is the basic form used. Relatively few individuals in the community lack the ability required to use a telephone; where there is a language barrier, multilingual information counselors help to make access effective. As individually operated computer data base retrieval systems are introduced—with added equipment costs, fees for service, and a lack of individual knowledge of data base access and operation—serious barriers between users and providers of information can arise. Thus, an issue of substance is the degree to which new computer/communication capabilities will be made available to the public generally. At what price will service barriers arise; that is, what level of cost is associated with access? What training and development of programs will be designed to make these "user friendly" systems generally accessible?

Accessibility is also related to system design and the understanding of the new capabilities by those creating new information resources. Telidon, for example, provides an extremely versatile, high-quality capability for providing both text and graphics on a color video display unit. It is capable of transmitting by any common carrier and can be used in any computer system adapted for its use.[3] This means that Telidon graphics data bases can be stored in such micro-computers as the Apple, that information provider terminals can be located in community information centers, and that remote updating of data bases can be carried out at the information source (Chang, 1981). Information counselors with access to a Telidon data base, or another community information data base without graphics, can retrieve information directly on their screens, as is done in airline reservation systems. Where the inquirer, a professional, or other individual also has access to both a telephone and a data base display terminal, discussions of essential information can occur in what is known as common visual and acoustic space (Thompson, Telisis 1).

Telidon fields trials in Canada in 1981 were limited to data base access systems using menu-driven tree structures without linking these capabilities with the present highly efficient telephone answering systems. New system capabilities and networks have traditionally been "grown" as interested parties identify new and cost-effective ways to make use of new capabilities (Pierce, 1969). The initial stages of such developments for community information services are being explored in many parts of Canada by both libraries and I&R centers. Such exploration has taken place in both large and small centers, including Toronto, Hamilton, Barrie, Fredericton, and Vancouver.

Cable Television is being used now by the hearing-impaired for specialized information. Developments such as the "visual ear" or "power-phone" are in use to provide visual telephone access. The extent to which these capabilities are available in I&R and library-based information centers is, at present, unfortunately, not widespread.

As indicated earlier, much of the organizational infrastructure exists to permit I&R services in Canada to take advantage of electronically based computer/communications technologies. Limiting factors include limited access both by the public and professionals to new capabilities located in government and public or volunteer centers; limited experience with the new technologies and their applications potential by experienced staff; pre-eminence of concern with commercial development of systems and rate structures without sufficient attention to social impact; lack of awareness of the meaning of fully interactive communication that combines print, sound, and graphics displays in common and shared visual space; and the effects of this capability upon existing geographic, political and knowledge boundaries (Lancaster, 1982). To these must be added an overconcern with hardware and software instead of human services (Forgie and Thomas, 1982). Finally, there are financial barriers for the private individual consumer, which appear in user fees or other charges, either direct or indirect.

A critical issue in Canada is the potential use of computer/communications technologies to link centers of information into a coherent pattern of nodal centers with personnel trained in both traditional and emerging methods for storing, accessing, verifying, and networking information resources that are important to the public. Such developments create an ecological context for information sharing in which the short-term and long-term implications become more easily grasped and internalized into the evolving network structure.

NOTES

1. Except where noted otherwise in this section on (CICMT,) information was secured from several sources, notably: Community Information Center of Metropolitan Toronto, "Annual Report, 1981", Toronto: CICMT, 1982; D.J. Forgie, D. F. Bellamy, C. C. Gotlieb, C C. Packer, "Community Information Center of Metropolitan Toronto: Application of Telidon-based Information Services for Community Information" (Research Report for Department of Communications, Ottawa, Canada under Contract OSU81-00233), Ottawa: 1982, also interviews with Elizabeth M. Wray, Executive Director, CICMT, December 1982 and January 17, 1983.

2. Interview with Ms. Ann Kemp, Coordinator, Citizen' Inquiry. Jan. 20, 1983.

3. Advanced Communicating Laboratory, "Telidonic Information System", Conference sponsored by Advanced Communicating Laboratory, Faculty of Library and Information Science, University of Toronto, 16-17 October 1981.

REFERENCES

The Association of Community Information Centers in Ontario (1978-1982). *Profiles.*

Cameron, C. A. (1980). Telidon: Social impact and policy questions. In the Social Imports of Computerization: Proceedings of the Forum held at the University of Waterloo (January).

Chan, E. J., & Godfrey, S. D. (1981). *Open networks and videotex.* Victoria: Department of Computer Science, University of Victoria.

Community Information Centre of Metropolitan Toronto. (1982, October). *Community services after hours: A proposed model for a central after hours clearinghouse for human services in metro toronto.* Toronto: CICMT.

The Federation of Community Information Centres (1978). *Policy and procedures manual.* Toronto: The Federation of Community Information Centers.

Forgie, D. (1981a). Videotex research and development: The Canadian context and contribution. *The Canadian Journal of Information Science,* pp. 25-34.

Forgie, D. (1981b). *Library service for the hearing and speech impaired.* Toronto: Advanced Communicating Laboratory, Faculty of Library and Information Science (ACL Report No. 8101).

Forgie, D., & Thomas, K. (1982). Not either or, but not only, but also, and. *The Canadian Journal of Information Science, 7,* 123-125.

Lancaster, F. M. (1982). *Libraries and librarians in an age of electronics.* Arlington, VA: Information Resources Press.

McFarlane, A. (1978). Citizens' inquiry branch: History and principles. *Canadian Journal of Information Science, 3,* 148-157.

Martins, D. K. (1979). *A history of the Association of Community Information Centres in Ontario.* Toronto: The Association of Community Information Centers in Ontario.

Pierce, J. R. (1969). *Waves and messages.* Garden City, NY: Doubleday.

Smith, A. (1982). Information technology and the myth of abundance. *Daedalus* (Fall): 15.

Thompson, G. B., & Westleman, M. (1968). Scribblephone: Extending man's powers of communication. *Telisis, 1* (September), 74-79.

Wray, E. M. (1977, May). Why do we want a uniform statistical system? Toronto: Community Information Centre of Metropolitan Toronto.

10

AID OF EDMONTON
An Expanding Canadian I&R Service

BARBARA ANN OLSEN

In Edmonton, Alberta, Canada, as in many other cities worldwide, there was a rapid proliferation of social service agencies after World War II. However, even with the multiplicity of new welfare programs, Edmontonians had great difficulty in finding those appropriate to their needs. Thus, in 1958, the Edmonton Council of Community Services (now the Edmonton Social Planning Council) undertook a study to determine a solution to this problem.

The results of this study indicated that the majority of individuals and organizations in the community were *not aware* of the existing helping agencies and the services they provided. Respondents felt overwhelmingly that a central information and referral service should be established that would identify agencies and maintain up-to-date descriptions of all program activities. There was also consensus that the service should be attached to the Edmonton Council of Community Services, that extensive publicity should accompany its launching, and that ongoing, concentrated public education should be part of its mandate.

About this same time, a tragic incident occurred—a young boy died as the result of abuse. The entire Edmonton community found itself greatly shaken and concerned about the adequacy of protection services for children.

Through the Youth Services Division of the Council of Community Services, a study was undertaken to determine whether a Society for the Prevention of Cruelty to Children was needed. The results of the study indicated that Edmonton's child protection services were adequate, but that the community *was not aware* of them or what they actually did. This reinforced the need for rapid public accessibility to information about social services via a centralized information and referral service.

Representatives of the Alberta Welfare Department (now Alberta Social Services and Community Health), the city Welfare Department (now Family and Community Support Services, the City of Edmonton), and the Council of Community Services met several times to examine both studies. There was immediate agreement on the necessity of establishing an information and referral service, and discussions centered on its structure and funding.

It was decided that the service should be a program of the Council of Community Services, *not* part of any government department. As such, the information and referral service would possess the autonomy needed for reporting any weaknesses or gaps in already existing programs—private or government. It was felt that this arrangement would also ensure the maximum cooperation from both private and public agencies.

The Alberta Welfare Department, the city Welfare Department, and the Council of Community Services agreed to cosponsor the information and referral service and to contribute funding on a 40-40-20 basis, with the Community Chest of Edmonton (now the United Way of Edmonton and Area) providing funding on behalf of the Council of Community Services. An advisory committee composed of two representatives from each of the sponsoring bodies was established to plan and provide direction for the new service.

Thus, with much fanfare, Welfare Information Service, the third information and referral service in Canada, officially opened in January 1960:

(1) To provide promptly and accurately welfare information and referral for the Edmonton region;
(2) To record information on the nature of the information requested and the referrals made;
(3) To provide an up-to-date file of welfare information on agency service, showing policies and conditions upon which services are rendered; and
(4) To make the service known thoroughly to the general public as well as to private agencies and concerned government departments.

During the first year of operation, Welfare Information Service addressed 5,119 inquiries. By its fifth anniversary, 55,535 inquiries had been processed.

Most contacts were by telephone, although people sometimes sought help in person or by letter. Frequent training sessions were held for staff of other agencies to provide both referral skills and information on available services. In 1964, Welfare Information Service assumed responsibility for publishing the *Directory of Community Services for Edmonton and District,* originally a task of the Council of Community Services.

By 1972, Welfare Information Service had grown sufficiently in size and stature to become an independent agency. A new name, AID Service of Edmonton, was selected. With the establishment of its own board of management, replacing the former advisory committee, AID Service of Edmonton became fully autonomous, with funding maintained as a blend of monies from the province, the city, and the United Way of Edmonton and Area.

THE DISTRESS LINE

At the same time AID Service of Edmonton was obtaining its independent status, another community need became evident. People in the helping professions realized that Edmontonians in distress had nowhere to turn for help after hours when social service agencies were closed. No one was available to listen to people's personal problems and offer information on community resources.

After several meetings of those concerned with the provision of an after-hours crisis service, plans were initiated for a "Distress Line"—a "hotline" people could call for help. Trained volunteers would be on duty to talk with those calling, to serve as sounding boards, and to provide appropriate referrals for professional help. To those planning the distress line program, it was logical that AID Service of Edmonton, the city's clearinghouse for information and referral on social service programs, be asked to be the sponsor. AID's board actively endorsed the concept of a crisis line as an adjunct to its already existing services and obtained funding to initiate the new hotline.

Thus, in 1972, AID began a much expanded program of volunteer involvement. Potential volunteers were carefully screened, then trained to answer both the new distress lines and the information and referral lines. This was a departure from previous policy; up to this point volunteers with Welfare Information Service had assisted only with directory publication.

AID's decision to staff the lines with trained volunteers was *not* made because the cost of the program would be too great if the lines were staffed by paid employees at all times. Rather, AID's board believed that the desired quality of service could be provided *only* by volunteers. AID recognized that carefully screened, well-trained volunteers could stress to callers that they are listening because they genuinely care and are donating their time to do so. In addition, volunteers would work only one four-hour shift per week, whereas paid staff would be required to work longer hours and therefore would be more subject to burnout. Volunteers might be less likely to "label" people; they would treat people as individuals rather than as "types."

The Distress Line began service to the public in 1972 from 8:30 a.m. to midnight, 7 days a week. By 1975, AID Service of Edmonton was providing 24-hour coverage, every day of the year, for crisis-oriented calls.

CORE (CRISIS OUTREACH AND REFERRAL EVALUATION)

In 1976, the report of the Task Force on Suicides to the Minister of Social Services and Community Health in Alberta discussed the magnitude of the problem of suicide in Alberta (Boldt, 1976). The report noted that:

> Even by official statistics, which, as we have shown, underreport such deaths, suicide ranks as the second leading cause of death between the ages of 15 and 34 [exceeded only by automobile accidents]. . . . Between the ages of 35 to 54, suicide ranks as the fourth leading cause of death, exceeded only by accidents, cancer and heart disease. In any year, four times as many people die by suicide than by homicide. When we make reasonable and appropriate correction for underreporting, by doubling the official figures, then suicide ranks as the leading single cause of death between 20 and 44 years of age. (Boldt, 1976)

In addition:

> Not only are there identifiable groups with high rates of suicide, but also there are identifiable geographic areas with a disproportionately high rate of suicide. For example, in Edmonton and Calgary [both in Alberta], suicide rates range from below 4 per 100,000 population in some of the better suburbs to above 30 in run-down areas adjacent to the downtown core. (Boldt, 1976)

As a result of this task force study, suicide prevention became a priority concern of the Alberta government. Funding suddenly was available for programs designed to attempt to decrease the suicide rate of high-risk groups.

AID recognized the need, via the nature of calls received on its lines, for a comprehensive program to link people who had already attempted suicide with helping resources. The task force study had already noted that "those who have a history of suicide [attempts] and non-accidental self-injury are one thousand times as (sic) likely to commit suicide than are members of the normal population." (Boldt, 1976) AID thus proposed CORE (an acronym for Crisis Outreach and Referral Evaluation), a program that would reach out to people in suicidal crisis, provide appropriate referrals, and evaluate whether or not the referrals were completed. Funding for this program was confirmed in 1978; however, it took until mid-1979 for CORE to become fully operational.

Since "studies show that the rate of voluntary participation in therapy reduces from approximately 65% when the individual is ap-proached during the immediate crisis to 10-15% if approached after the crisis has passed" (Boldt, 1976), it was decided to locate CORE workers in the emergency room of a major Edmonton hospital, where they could meet with people in suicidal crisis as soon as possible after an attempt had occurred. Because most interaction with people who had attempted suicide would be by trained volunteers, extensive negotiation was required with the participating hospital prior to pro-gram initiation.

Once a patient is referred to a CORE worker, the volunteer discusses with the individual those factors that precipitated the suicide attempt and provides personal support and appropriate refer-rals, among which may be the CORE follow-up program. After an individual is referred to CORE, either by the hospital volunteer or by a helping professional or agency, telephone contact is established to provide ongoing support and encourage the use of the appropriate services in the community.

In February 1982, a support group was initiated as a subprogram of CORE for those of its clients who are very isolated, have little (if any) family support, and find coping with daily stresses extremely difficult. While the program has not been a panacea for all participants, it has provided many of them with new coping methods and support sys-tems.

Still another sub-program of CORE began in November 1982, when Alberta Social Services and Community Health transferred the Edmonton Suicide Bereavement Program to AID (with the consent of AID's board of management). The purpose of this program is to help individuals and families move through suicidal loss towards acceptance and understanding.

AID IN THE 1980s

Overall Philosophy

AID's mandate is the same today as it was in 1960—"to help link people to resources." All of AID's programs and subprograms have that purpose, whether it is accomplished by referral to professional help or to a support program operated by AID (in which clients learn to reach out, as well as to be their own resources). No fees are charged for any of AID's programs, and none of the programs duplicate other community resources.

All of AID's work in the community is predicated on the premise that information and referral skills are essential for handling crisis intervention contacts and crisis intervention skills are essential for handling information and referral contacts. Thus, anyone contacting AID for help can expect empathic listening and understanding of whatever problem is presented, plus referral to appropriate community resources to meet specified needs. Moreover, all contacts are *confidential*.

Although AID's mandate has remained unchanged for more than two decades, the manner of service delivery has been adapted to include recent advances in technology and training methodology. Concurrently, statistical reporting and research have emerged as important adjuncts to all program areas (especially for pilot projects such as the support group for suicide attempters). Staff members provide accurate referral information and administrative support, while trained, supervised volunteers interact with clients. AID prides itself that volunteers, trained in listening and communication skills, are always available to listen to a person's problems. People who care are just a phone call away any time of the day or night.

As it is now, AID is a resource for people with questions about Edmonton's social service programs, people with personal and emotional problems (loneliness, depression, thoughts of suicide, and so on), suicide prevention, intervention and follow-up, and researchers monitoring social service trends. Future roles for AID will be discussed later in this chapter.

Information and Referral

Because of the nature of AID, it is difficult to isolate one area of program activities from the rest. Each program is strengthened by its interdependency with the others; none of the programs could stand alone without substantially increasing both cost and personnel.

The cornerstone of all of AID's programs is, however, the maintenance of accurate, up-to-date information on social service programs in Edmonton. Only when such information is readily available can AID rapidly link people to resources via its hotlines. In fact, it is the care and precision devoted to information and dissemination that has enhanced program development in the areas of crisis intervention and suicide prevention.

Two prime objectives of AID's Information and Referral Program are identical to those outlined by Long in 1972: "To increase the accessibility of human services and to maximize the utility of information and referral center data for the planning of human services." (Long, 1972) To accomplish these objectives, AID:

(1) Maintains a data base which includes information on social service and community programs in Edmonton and district;
(2) Publishes annually the *AID Directory of Community Services for Edmonton and District;*
(3) Provides a directory updating service to subscribers;
(4) Operates a telephone information and referral hotline from 8 a.m. to midnight seven days a week;
(5) Operates a telephone crisis hotline 24 hours a day, every day of the year;
(6) Maintains statistics on the types of calls received on its hotlines and on the referrals given;
(7) Maintains contact with Edmonton's neighborhood information and referral centers to develop an integrated approach to citywide service delivery;
(8) Keeps in touch with information and referral centers in Alberta, as well as throughout North America, to facilitate information exchange;
(9) Maintains contact with social service agencies in Edmonton to keep abreast of program changes; and
(10) Provides education and training on the effective use of information and referral services to the community.

Four types of activities will be described: The data base, the lines, data management, and community liaison.

The Data Base

The success of AID Service of Edmonton as a community information and referral service is largely dependent on, in addition to the listening skills of its volunteers, the reliability of its data base. AID's volunteers and paid staff *must* trust the information they provide to volunteer clients. AID's clients *must* be confident that they will receive only those referrals that meet their particular needs or circumstances and that the information obtained will be complete and accurate. Moreover, AID's funders *must* be assured that the data base is up-to-date for client referrals as well as for research and statistical purposes.

During the past 23 years, AID has worked hard to establish its credibility as an information and referral service. Many hours are spent by AID's staff checking the validity of services provided by agencies to ensure that each is accurately described for referral purposes. AID's information and referral staff are front-line workers who visit agencies to review all aspects of their programs and respond to any concerns service users express on the hotlines.

The 1984 edition of the *AID Directory of Community Services for Edmonton and District* marks AID's twentieth year of providing this service to the public. As principal user of the *AID Directory* (responding to over 5,000 calls per month), AID's staff has a great stake in its efficient organization as well as in the reliability of information included. Their dedication has earned the *AID Directory* the reputation of being "the Bible" for helping professionals in the community.

For the past three years, the data base for the *AID Directory* and all other file listings has been maintained utilizing SPIRES, a computer program that has the capability of text editing and searching in addition to information storage and retrieval. Through SPIRES and the cooperation of the Computing Services offices at the University of Alberta, AID is able to produce a camera-ready "master" copy of both the annual *AID Directory* and its updates, which AID sends to subscribers at six- to eight-week intervals.

Besides production of "masters," AID's computer program:

(1) Allows AID to control the collection, input, and dissemination of information to the community;
(2) Provides a flexible, easy-to-read format for the recording of information;
(3) Allows for the updating of information, simply, and rapidly; and
(4) Provides the ability to search for information with the use of specialized codes or key words (Olsen, 1983).

**TABLE 10.1   AID Service of Edmonton
Types of Calls (1982)**

Type of Call	Number of Information and Referral Lines	Number of Distress Lines	Total Number	Percentage of Total Calls
Information	17,210	2,956	20,166	37.8
Referral	13,267	2,370	15,637	29.3
Distress	1,581	5,770	7,351	13.8
Chronic	814	4,393	5,207	9.8
Miscellaneous	1,779	3,161	4,940	9.3
Totals	34,651*	18,650*	53,301*	100.0

*Error in data conversion is less than 5%.

AID eventually expects that its volunteer listeners will be able to request referral data directly from the computer via either its extensive coding system or its key-word indexing.

The Lines

AID makes no attempt to segregate its distress line service from its information and referral telephone service, since the programs are interdependent and possess many commonalities. In addition, there is considerable crossover in type of call on both lines; e.g., distress calls are received on the information and referral lines and vice versa (see Table 10.1). Thus, the same staff members (paid and volunteer) treat calls on both hotlines in a similar manner. Both hotlines provide assistance to people who need help, and the success of both depends on the ability of staff to combine crisis intervention skills with those of information and referral.

In 1982, 55,246 calls were received on AID's lines—approximately the same number of contacts responded to by Welfare Information Service during its first *five* years of operation. In the first six months of 1983, calls increased 20 percent over the same period in 1982. Most of the increase seemed to be the result of the recession, which had reached Alberta by this time, bringing with it the emotional and family problems caused by financial insecurity.

Calls on AID's hot lines roughly doubled from 1980 to 1983. In 1980, approximately 34,000 calls were received; in 1983, approximately 68,000. Such a rapid growth in the utilization of services led to a reactive management style, which attempted to predict the areas of stress before they occurred and secure additional resources before a crisis developed. This, in turn, led to a "team approach" within AID, with all staff (paid and volunteer) contributing to the solutions of problems caused by increased community needs and to the effective operation of *all* programs.

Data Management

AID's statistical recording is also managed by SPIRES and is compatible with AID's data base. Figure 10.1 shows the form on which data from each call to AID is recorded. Information and referral staff code each call to a five-digit number indicating the major category and/or subcategory of call (based on indexing in the *AID Directory*) as well as type of call (i.e., distress, information, referral, etc.). All referrals given are coded to seven-digit numbers based on listings in AID's data base. This information is then entered into the computer via a screen specially designed for simplicity of data entry, minimization of entry errors, and ease of data manipulation.

AID's statistical program permits the cross-tabulation of each category and subcategory of call as to length of call, number of calls, sex of caller, age of caller, and whether the call was received on the information and referral or crisis hotlines. Calls for a specific time period can be analyzed to determine quantity, duration of call, and specific time of day. The number of referrals to any social service program can be determined, as can the number of calls originating from outside Edmonton proper. In addition, requests for services nonexistent in Edmonton can be retrieved rapidly. There is, therefore, a wealth of information available both for agency management and city planning.

Table 9.1 provides a profile of types of calls received at AID in 1982 and an example of data collected via computer processing. Approximately twice as many calls were received on the information and referral lines as on the distress lines (65 percent to 35 percent). Most distress, chronic (alternatively defined as "repeat callers"), and miscellaneous (i.e., hang-ups, wrong numbers, calls from people unable to speak, and so forth) calls were answered on the distress lines than on the information and referral lines. Yet there was considerable crossover in each type of call; 22 percent of the distress calls were on the information and referral lines and 15 percent of the information calls were on the distress lines.

Table 10.1, by itself, gives a simple breakdown of call types; however, when compared with Table 9.2, a similar analysis of 1981 calls, changes in call patterns are evident. In 1982, calls on the distress lines increased 68 percent over 1981; calls on the information and

                                                                                    T I L

Date . . . .   LINE: AID 1   2   3   4   5   Out 1   2   3   4

Listener . . . .   DISTRESS 1   2   3   4   5

STATUS OF CALLER: ☐ Hosp./Health U.   TIME: from . . . . a.m./p.m.
  ☐ Agency/Comm. Org.   ☐ Individual
  ☐ Business/Labour   ☐ Other/N/A   to . . . . a.m./p.m.
  ☐ Church   ☐ School
  ☐ Gov't Dept.   ☐ Professional   TOTAL . . . . mins.

                                                                          SEX: M — F

CALLER . . . . Repeat: YES NO

ADDRESS . . . .

PHONE . . . . APPROX. AGE . . . . Y A S

CALLED BECAUSE:

COMMENTS:

Call Code	Referral

Figure 10.1: AID Service of Edmonton Call Sheet

TABLE 10.2   AID Service of Edmonton
              Types of Calls (1981)

Type of Call	Number of Information and Referral Lines	Number of Distress Lines	Total Number	Percentage of Total Calls
Information	15,493	1,210	16,703	37.5
Referral	11,946	1,842	13,788	30.9
Distress	2,504	4,239	6,743	15.1
Chronic	1,215	2,263	3,478	7.8
Miscellaneous	2,084	1,777	3,861	8.7
Totals	33,242	11,331	44,573	100.0

referral lines increased only 4 percent. In 1981, 37 percent of all distress calls were received on the information and referral lines, representing 58 percent more calls than in 1982. In 1982, 34 percent more distress calls were received on the distress lines.

Thus, AID has both a cross-sectional and longitudinal analysis of call types (i.e., a comparison of numbers of each call type within a given period and the comparison of the number of the same call type from year to year). This latter information provides feedback about the effect AID's policy changes have on utilization of services. For example, in 1982, the number of distress calls on the information and referral lines decreased significantly from the 1981 figure. Presumably, this difference occurred as the result of increased publicity about AID's programs and their respective contact phone numbers.

AID's statistical program is extremely useful in scheduling personnel for answering the hotlines. Call profiles for the past three years show that Mondays are typically the busiest days, followed by Tuesdays, Thursdays, Wednesdays and Fridays. Calls on the weekend days drop about 50%. March, October, November and December are normally the busiest months.

This information, together with Tables 10.3 and 10.4, provides guidance for volunteer management. Table 10.3 shows the number of calls on the information and referral hotlines during each volunteer shift. As expected, the majority of calls (77 percent) occur between 8 a.m. and 4 p.m. These calls are relatively short, averaging 2.2 minutes per call. Calls on the information and referral lines received during other shifts are longer, reflecting a high proportion of distress and chronic calls.

Table 10.4 shows that 28.2 percent of calls on the distress lines occur between 8 p.m. and midnight. These calls are, on the average,

TABLE 10.3   AID Service of Edmonton
         Number of Calls on Information and Referral Lines
         and Time Taken/Shift (January to December 1982)

Shift	Calls	Percentage of Total Calls	Minutes Spent	Percentage of Total Minutes	Minutes/ Call
Midnight - 4:00 AM	157	0.5	1,119	1.2	7.1
4:00 AM - 8:00 AM	165	0.5	738	0.8	4.5
8:00 AM - Noon	13,222	38.2	30,813	32.8	2.3
Noon - 4:00 PM	13,659	39.5	29,845	31.8	2.2
4:00 PM - 8:00 PM	4,803	13.9	16,825	17.9	3.5
8:00 PM - Midnight	2,573	7.4	14,552	15.5	5.7
Totals	34,579*	100.0	93,892*	100.0	2.7

*Error in data conversion is less than 5%.

13.1 minutes long. Only 9.1 percent of calls occur between midnight and 8 a.m., but these calls are relatively long, averaging 16 minutes per contact, reflecting the crisis nature of the call. These call patterns have remained virtually unchanged since 1980.

Therefore, volunteers who prefer to deal with distress calls may schedule themselves on shifts with a predominance of distress line work. Similarly, volunteers with a preference for working on the information and referral lines schedule daytime shifts. The volunteer manager ensures maximum coverage on the predictably busiest shifts.

What has not been discussed so far is the obvious role of AID as a barometer of social change in Edmonton. Since AID receives calls from all quarters of the city, reflecting people's problems and social service needs, any changes in the number of calls per category can provide an important social planning tool. Frequently, changes noted are in response to external conditions (i.e., changes in financial climate, social service policy, and so forth); however, many calls also indicate citizens' needs for unavailable services (i.e., a shelter for battered women without children, free legal advice on weekends and after normal working hours, and so on) and, as a result, reflect changing mores. Thus, by identifying community needs and concerns, AID plays an advocacy role in the development of social service programs.

Since AID's statistical format permits the recording of such a broad spectrum of data and therefore offers so many possible correla-

TABLE 10.4   AID Service of Edmonton
              Number of Calls on Distress Lines and Time Taken/Shift
              (January to December 1982)

Shift	Calls	Percentage of Total Calls	Minutes Spent	Percentage of Total Minutes	Minutes/ Call
Midnight - 4:00 AM	1,273	6.8	20,677	9.4	16.2
4:00 AM - 8:00 AM	427	2.3	6,567	3.0	15.4
8:00 AM - Noon	3,245	17.4	35,969	16.4	11.1
Noon - 4:00 PM	4,164	22.4	39,548	18.0	9.5
4:00 PM - 8:00 PM	4,274	22.9	47,786	21.8	11.2
8:00 PM - Midnight	5,263	28.2	68,969	31.4	13.1
Totals	18,646[*]	100.00	219,516[*]	100.0	11.8

[*]Error in data conversion is less than 5%.

tions, consideration must be given to the value of the information
gathered and its actual use. Certainly, AID's data provides useful
information for social planners and can be invaluable as a management tool. But the data cannot forecast unseasonal influxes in calls. In
other words, AID's statistical program cannot predict the unpredict-
able, and in an agency such as AID, which is involved in crisis
intervention, anything can and usually does happen.

In 1983, AID received a Canada Community Development Project grant to review its current statistical package to determine the
effectiveness of the format. This grant permitted the hiring of a
project manager and two information aides to streamline data collection and reporting.

Community Liaison

Edmonton's human service delivery system provides information
and referral on several levels. AID Service of Edmonton provides
citywide information on, and referral to, social service resources.
Neighborhood information and referral centers, on the other hand,
provide local information and referral as well as social service programs specifically for their communities. In addition, many social
services designed to serve a particular constituency have highly
specialized information and referral listings (such as Society for the
Retired and Semi-Retired, Gay Alliance Toward Equality, and Services for the Handicapped).

In February 1983, one of the Edmonton neighborhood Centers
received a Canada Community Development Project grant to inves-

tigate the coordination of neighborhood information and referral services with AID. Under the terms of this grant, a project manager and four field workers were hired to develop the basis of an Edmonton information and referral system involving:

(1) the development of a common data base for statistical recording;
(2) the identification of areas that require neighborhood information and referral services;
(3) the preparation of a strategic marketing proposal for information and referral services; and
(4) the determination of expanded funding sources.

Although all of the information and referral services in Edmonton (as well as one from an adjacent county) participate in the overall management of the project, the workers' home base is AID because of its access to computer equipment and expertise. The project staff members have familiarized themselves with the operation of each individual neighborhood center and devised a common coding system for all information and referral contacts. An annual statistical report is available (as of February 1984) correlating information and referral statistical data for all of Edmonton, and workers at each participating center will be trained to maintain that recording system.

In addition, AID provides education and training on the effective use of information and referral services to the community, and maintains contact with social service agencies in Edmonton to keep abreast of program changes, and with information and referral centers in Alberta, as well as throughout North America, to facilitate information exchange.

CORE

The CORE Program was initiated in 1978 to reduce the number of suicides in the Edmonton area by linking people who are suicidal to appropriate support resources. Among CORE activities are the following:

(1) makes contact in hospital emergency departments with people in suicidal crisis in order to provide personal support and appropriate referrals, including CORE's follow-up program;
(2) maintains long-term telephone contact with people who have been identified as "at risk" for suicide in order to provide personal support and appropriate referrals, as well as to help them reach out for assistance in time of crisis;

(3) operates, under the supervision of qualified professionals, a support group for selected people who have attempted suicide;

(4) operates, under the supervision of qualified professionals, a bereavement program for the survivors of suicide;

(5) trains all volunteer personnel at AID in the skills of suicide prevention, intervention, and follow-up;

(6) provides information on suicide prevention, intervention and follow-up, as well as on CORE itself, to professionals and the general public; and

(7) collects, records, and evaluates data on all CORE clients.

CORE's follow-up program serves, at any given time, between 80 and 100 clients. In 1982, a total of 143 clients were served by CORE. The majority (73 percent) were women. Although clients ranged in age from 13 to 61 years of age, the largest concentration was in the 20- to 29-year-old age range (37 percent). Approximately half (51 percent) of the client population was unmarried.

On the average, clients who made a commitment to CORE in 1982 stayed with the follow-up program for 6½ months and received 4 contacts per month. Of the referrals given to clients, 49 percent were completed.

Most clients (80 percent) identified depression as their primary problem, folowed by conflict, financial concerns, and alcohol, in that order. Of interest is the fact that only 34 percent of CORE's clients were employed in any capacity.

Since early 1982, CORE has been operating a support group for suicide attempters. Clients selected for this group are very isolated, have little if any personal support, find coping with day-to-day stresses very difficult, and have had little success with conventional helping services. The group experience provides a setting where its participants can

(1) develop their self-awareness and self-esteem;

(2) learn alternative methods of coping with stress, anxiety, and tension; and

(3) become comfortable about giving and accepting support.

Thoughts and feelings about suicide are openly discussed in the weekly meetings whenever a group member is experiencing a crisis. Topics discussed in any given session do vary, however, and relate directly to the experiences and feelings of those at the session.

Toward the end of 1982, CORE added the Edmonton Suicide Bereavement Program. Staff of the program (volunteer and paid) interview people grieving from suicidal loss. These clients are encouraged to express their feelings about the death of the suicide victim and are provided with appropriate community referrals, including AID's Suicide Bereavement Group.

The Suicide Bereavement Group meets one night a week for eight consecutive weeks. Those in the group are encouraged to work through their feelings of guilt, remorse, anger, stigma, and sorrow. Through the group, clients learn to accept their loss as one reality of their lives rather than the continuous focus for their future.

THE VOLUNTEER PROGRAM

As stated previously, AID's data base is the cornerstone of all its programs; however, it is the listening skills of its volunteers that are the conduit between the agency and the community. Thus, a great deal of agency time is spent nurturing volunteers and ensuring that they have sufficient skills and information to understand people's needs and problems as well as to offer appropriate referrals.

The main elements of the volunteer program include these:

(1) advertising, on a regular basis, for warm, caring, empathic, non-judgmental people to staff AID's hot lines;
(2) screening prospective volunteers for suitability;
(3) training volunteers, including the basic listeners' training course, advanced training, and in-service sessions;
(4) scheduling volunteers to staff the hot lines;
(5) monitoring and evaluating volunteers;
(6) maintaining statistics on volunteer involvement; and
(7) reviewing new methods to enhance volunteers' working relationship with AID to improve AID's service to the public.

When a potential volunteer contacts AID, information is provided describing the agency's programs and the nature of volunteer experiences available. The person, if still interested in volunteering, completes a detailed application form and is then interviewed by AID staff.

If accepted, the trainee attends a 50-hour training couse that includes information on the history and philosophy of the agency, listening skills, communication skills, suicide prevention and intervention skills, information and referral skills, information about CORE, alcoholism, and so forth. Extensive role-playing of actual calls is also included. Upon successful completion of the course, the new volunteer works the lines together with an experienced volunteer for a six-week probationary period. At the end of this time, barring any difficulties, AID has a full-fledged volunteer listener.

Listeners contract to work with AID for one four-hour shift per week for a minimum of six months. In 1982, volunteers spent 11,937 hours on the lines. This is equivalent to seven paid staff working full-time—a cost value of approximately $110,000. based on AID's 1982 salary scales.

Although there really isn't an "average" type of person volunteering at AID, several statistical inferences can be drawn to characterize the "typical" volunteer. An AID volunteer is twice as likely to be female than male (31 percent were male in 1982) and is an average of 32 years of age (61 percent were 32 or under in 1982). The average length of stay of a volunteer at AID is 19 months.

After working six months on the lines, volunteers are eligible to enter the CORE Program. After a screening procedure similar to that outlined for the listeners' program, prospective CORE volunteers take a 20-hour training course emphasizing advanced communication and suicide risk assessment skills. Those completing the course then become CORE hospital and/or follow-up volunteers. CORE volunteers also may elect to become volunteers in the bereavement program, interviewing individuals grieving from the loss of a relative or friend to suicide. This occurs only after successful completion of a 15-hour training course emphasizing interviewing skills, the grieving process, and suicide follow-up.

AID prides itself on the caliber of its volunteers and frequently reviews its training to clarify policy matters as well as new approaches to the types of interactions experienced with clients. The importance of good helping skills cannot be overestimated in any of AID's programs. These skills are essential to developing empathic relationships with clients and are reinforced through frequent in-service and advanced training courses.

Agency staff members also schedule and attend case conferences on selected "at risk" or "difficult" clients in order to formulate a coordinated approach to service delivery. Then, the results of the case conferences are summarized and included with the clients' histories as guidelines for future contacts. In addition, staff members rotate as resource leaders, providing 24-hours-per-day backup for line volunteers.

While information about clients is made available to all volunteers, strict confidentiality is maintained with respect to all client contacts. All staff members (volunteers and paid) sign an "oath of confidentiality" prior to working with the agency and obtaining access to client files. Violation of client confidentiality constitutes grounds for immediate dismissal, as does arranging to meet a client calling on either hotline. The anonymity of volunteers is paramount. Last names are *never* used when referring to a volunteer who has contact with clients. In this way, volunteers can feel secure that callers will be unable to identify them.

AID has created a rewarding, enriching volunteer experience for people who genuinely want to help other people. It is a delicate balance, with AID providing skills training and supervision and the volunteers supplying the caring and the time. Many volunteers eventually enter careers in the social services.

Interestingly, most of AID's permanent staff members were line volunteers prior to employment with the Agency. This means that AID's "professional" staff have an appreciation for both the philosophy and management of the Agency from a grass-roots level. Permanent staff also are committed to effective program operation through the use of trained volunteers and understand the support required for its success.

THE CHALLENGE

AID's purpose is to help link people to resources; yet as needs change, so must programs and methods of service delivery. AID *must,* therefore, *be reactive*—both to changing problems presented by clients and to changing services available within the community. The key to AID's development has been flexibility, tempered with an understanding of the political and social environment currently in force. AID's success has been dependent upon effective human resource management.

The challenge facing AID is not *what to do,* but rather *how to obtain the resources* to ensure all clients', and potential clients', needs are met. AID is a volunteer, non-profit agency, largely dependent upon government grants for its survival. Funding for its CORE Program is from Alberta Social Services and Community Health on the recommendation of the Suicide Prevention Provincial Advisory Committee. Funding for all other programs comes from Family and Community Support Services of the City of Edmonton, the United Way of Edmonton and Area, fees for service, publication sales, and miscellaneous revenue. Special short-term projects receive funding from federal or provincial grants available for the creation of job opportunities in the social services.

A large proportion of administrative time therefore, is, spent preparing and monitoring budgets and grants. Similarly, AID's board of directors, the policymaking body of the organization, spends many hours ensuring that sufficient operating funds are available for established programs and reviewing proposed program additions to determine priorities. AID's board is composed of volunteers from the community who donate their time to ensure the effective operation of the agency.

In a time of reduced government expenditures, it is difficult, if not impossible, to predict what the future holds for AID. However, AID's board is examining alternative methods of fund-raising at the same time as community groups are looking toward AID to provide additional programs to link more people to social service resources.

AID is, first and foremost, Edmonton's clearinghouse for social service information. It maintains an up-to-date computerized data base that many organizations, including the Province of Alberta and Edmonton's neighborhood information and referral centers, wish to access. Currently, staff and board are reviewing recent advances in computer technology to determine how best to provide this service. Should an in-house computer be obtained, with fees for service determined for usage by other agencies? Should the data base be expanded to cover other areas within the Edmonton region? Should "Telidon," Canada's videotex system, be considered as a viable option for service delivery?

The *AID Directory of Community Services for Edmonton and District* is the principle publication from the data base and is an established referral tool for those in helping professions. Computerization, however, makes it simple to prepare and publish "mini-directories" pertaining to specific services—i.e., youth services, services for the handicapped, day care services, and so forth. Is there a market for such "mini-directories"? Would publication be cost-effective?

AID's "Distress Line" service is accessible only to people within the toll-free area of Edmonton or to those who wish to dial long-distance and pay the resulting telephone charges. Many rural areas, over a hundred miles from Edmonton, have indicated the desire to cost-share this service with AID. It is obviously not feasible for each small town to have its own crisis line, nor would residents of sparsely populated areas feel comfortable talking about their problems with a volunteer who could be their neighbor. But can AID obtain the necessary social service information in each town to extend this program? Can AID train sufficient volunteers to ensure adequate coverage for such a program extension at all times? How should an appropriate fee structure be determined?

AID has been approached by members of the deaf community to consider initiating a message relay system for the deaf. This is a project that falls well within AID's mandate to link people to resources; however, AID's current resources are insufficient for ongoing program management. Can funding be obtained for equipment and staff for this project?

Meanwhile, CORE is currently receiving requests from clients and hospital staff for immediate face-to-face suicide crisis intervention at times and places when CORE volunteers are not on duty. Should CORE have a "Flying Squad"—i.e., a mobile crisis unit—to respond immediately, wherever and whenever needed, to people in suicidal crisis? What should the parameters of such a service be? Should CORE staff provide more public education in suicide prevention, intervention, and follow-up to schools, professionals, and community groups?

AID would like to respond positively to all of the above. AID has proven to be efficient, cost-effective, and well respected in the past and plans to maintain this image in the future. The challenge is great, but with a team approach from professional staff and volunteers, AID Service of Edmonton will continue to link people to resources to the limit of its own resources.

REFERENCES

Boldt, M. (1976). *Report of the Task Force on Suicides to the Minister of Social Services and Community Health.*

Long, N. (1973). Information and referral services: A short history and some recommendations. *The Social Service Review,* pp. 49-62.

Olsen, B. (1983). A decade of systems. *Information and Referral: The Journal of the Alliance of Information and Referral Systems.*

III

OTHER ACCESS SYSTEMS: VARIATIONS AND MODIFICATIONS

The primary rationale for the inclusion of these four chapters within the third section of the book is that they represent, to various degrees, the variability in design, structure, auspices, staffing, and funding, so that they neither fit ideally within the section on Citizen Advice Bureaus (CABs) nor within the section on Information and Referral (I&R). These reports represent an interesting geographic diversity, ranging from an eastern European country (Poland) to two Asian countries, one highly developed (Japan), and one a Third World country (India). The final chapter included in Part III is descriptive of an ombudsman system existing in a number of developed countries, such as France, the Federal Republic of Germany, Sweden, Finland, Denmark, New Zealand, Austria, and Portugal.

Consequently, the geographic dispersion also represents diversity in terms of the developmental stage of the country and the formality and the inclusivity of the social service system in general. The inclusion of these four chapters represents a series of unique modifications, or hybrids, of the previously described basic CAB and I&R models. For example, the Polish Access Services are described as not highly formalized and similar to generalized social work functions such as outreach, case-finding, and referral, while the Indian example of citizen advice bureaus presents a more formalized structure of service delivery but does not include some of the features of CABs as noted in Part I. Additionally, the Japanese Minsei-Iin System describes a very elaborate program for the recruitment and appointment of volunteers as well as a structured systemwide approach to provide wide coverage. Lastly, the ombudsman chapter focuses primarily on access to legal information and the legal system, and includes what for most access systems is a unique aspect, that of a watchdog function relative to other governmental bodies and governmental decision-making. Further elaboration on each of these four chapters might clarify these attributes.

Chapter 11, "Access to Health and Social Services in Poland," by Irena Sienko, presents an analysis of access services administered and supervised by the Polish Ministry of Health and Social Welfare, which represents the main field of professional and voluntary social work in Poland. Quite interestingly, compared to the development of the British CAB model or the North American I&R model, the system of "volunteer social counselors" did not emerge until 1959 in Poland, and, in fact, was not institutionalized in 1973-1974 at the time of national administrative reform and reorganization. The access system in Poland is viewed as part of the basic organizational structure for the delivery of social services at Social Work Centers, which conduct case-finding, identify community and client needs, and either deliver service directly or link clients to other resources.

According to legal regulations, however, social service delivery is restricted to specified groups, primarily persons who are not employed such as adults in retirement, physically handicapped or mentally retarded individuals. Other target groups include ex-prisoners and individuals as well as families in crisis. Consequently, many of the adult working population remain principally outside this system—unable to benefit from the various financial or social services presently available. Recent developments in the country have highlighted the inadequacy of this system and the insufficient means to provide services for newly emerging groups of people in economic crisis.

Since the majority of the beneficiaries are old or disabled persons and unable to reach institutional help, the social assistance system provides an active outreach program whereby the staff members are expected to be active case finders and referral agents, along with their usual responsibilities of direct casework service. Given this extraordinary demand on the social work staff, it is not surprising to find the increased use of volunteers as case finders and referral agents. Another important agent in case-finding and outreach in the Polish social service system is the community nurse. The interdisciplinary collaboration of nurse and social worker represents a unique professional partnership for the delivery of access services. More recently, the mass media has played an increasingly important role in publicizing access to human service information, an approach that is not atypical of other access systems reported on in this volume, Sienko describes the impact of several barriers of access to services in the Polish system, such as finances, shortage of trained staff, and technical skills.

The Japanese equivalent for the provision of access to essential human services is a well-organized and legally established national volunteer system that has developed since the early 1900s. Although between 1910 and 1950 questions of whether these community welfare volunteers were predominantly public or predominantly private remained ambiguous, a 1953 amendment established the volunteers' primary purpose as promoting social welfare in a community.

In Chapter 12, "Community Welfare Volunteers in Japan" Atsuko Matsuoka reports that volunteers are appointed without pay for a three-year period and can be reappointed. These volunteers provide four primary functions, which include surveying community conditions, promoting adequate help for those in trouble, keeping in touch with social welfare institutions, and cooperating in carrying out the work of public welfare and other related agencies. Thus, these volunteers go beyond many of the traditional access services and, like the Polish example, engage in a much more active outreach for case-finding than usually appears in North American I&R or the British CAB models.

Similar to the role we find and/or advocate for I&R agencies is that which the Japanese call "authentication"; that is, validating the existence of community needs and relevant community resources to meet these needs. Also similar to those that have been described elsewhere is the increased demand for information provision for the elderly and the physically handicapped in the Japanese system. Although this is predominantly a volunteer system, funds for training, authentication, and any other direct expenses are publicly underwritten. The goals of the Minsei-Iin system include developing support systems for people in need; encouraging citizen participation in movements for improving social welfare; and recruiting and organizing volunteers. One of the criticisms of this system is that access, linkage, and community organization efforts remain predominantly within governmental units and do not involve local voluntary agencies. The author concludes that the thrust of the system is toward the alleviation of individual poverty rather than the overall improvement of social welfare conditions through interagency collaboration.

The third chapter in this section, in which Ramesh Chandra Mishra and Meera Agarwal discuss the CAB in New Delhi, India, deals with a system that is more akin to the British CAB than are the Polish and Japanese systems. In fact, the founder of the New Delhi CAB conducted a thorough study of British CABs before the initiation of the Indian bureau. Consequently, it is not surprising to note a dual purpose of this organization: to advise citizens with personal problems as well as to ameliorate problematic societal conditions.

The New Delhi CAB is an independent, nonsectarian, nonpolitical, and nonprofit organization whose staff, mostly volunteers, represents a wide diversity of both professional and lay persons. Unlike the British prototype, it is privately supported but depends upon contributions, donations, and gifts. Because of its limited funding, it depends primarily upon the use of volunteers and operates on a limited schedule.

One of the major accomplishments of the New Delhi CAB is the spearheading of advocacy programs during the decade of the 1970s. Given this intended purpose of advocacy, an organization similar to the U.S. Common Cause was founded in the early 1970s and was a step toward the initiation of an ombudsman program, which, to date, has not been enacted. More frequently, advocacy occurs at the case level: landlord-tenant issues, income tax, sales tax, consumer concerns, and consumer grievances that are often negotiated out of court with the help of the CAB staff.

At the program advocacy level, a major feature of this CAB is its legal literacy program, with advocates that all citizens know their rights and protect themselves. This rather unique program component was launched by the New Delhi CABs in 1979 and, according to the authors, has made an enormous impact on mass literacy in the field of human rights and entitlements. The achievement has been accomplished with the collaboration of legal aid societies and citizen action groups and the cooperation of mass media, as well as through the distribution of specialized booklets and pamphlets, such as "Citizens and the Police" and "Women and the Law." In terms of policy advocacy, the CAB functions as an advisory body to governmental as well as nongovernmental agencies in submitting recommendations such as to universal and free access to schools and hospitals.

The last chapter in this section by Ulf Lundvik deviates from most of the other reports in this book in that it describes programs that may be included within generic access services, and are often described as an essential component of both CAB and I & R systems, but in the strictest sense are neither. However, the notion of the ombudsman is certainly not antithetical to class advocacy and informing citizens of their legal rights. Not unlike the traditional component of the Citizens

Advice Bureaus, the ombudsman system is an office established by constitution or statute headed by an independent high-level public official who is responsible to the legislature for receiving complaints from aggrieved persons against government agencies, officials, and employees, and who has the power to investigate, recommend action, and issue reports. The ombudsman model in its present day form developed in Sweden in 1809 and has been adopted and adapted internationally.

The ombudsman role is to identify discrepancies in litigation and erroneous interpretations in administrative procedures primarily through recommendations and reports. That is, the ombudsman cannot modify administrative rules and seldom can enforce recommendations. This is not to diminish the utility and effectiveness of the ombudsman system as a legally sanctioned critic of administration. The author therefore concludes that the impact of the ombudsman criticism not only impacts on the culprit, but that the public criticism also serves as a warning to other officials who may be confronted with similar problems.

An important facilitating device for the ombudsman, and one generally not available or permitted to access systems, is the legal right to obtain and review all pertinent files and information; to interrogate all officials concerned; to ask and receive assistance from agencies; and to legally enter premises of such agencies. The author distinguishes between the Scandinavian ombudsman role, which attempts to promote good administration through pronouncements of how laws should be interpreted and how administrative authorities should act, in contrast to the more circumscribed Anglo-Saxon role of the ombudsman, which concentrates more directly on individual case advocacy. In all countries, however, the ombudsman tends to assume an active role in the recommending amendments to existing statutes and legislation.

In conclusion, it should be evident that these four chapters further expand the notion of present access services worldwide as well as heighten the sensitivity to what might be achieved in the future: The Polish model of case finding and outreach as part of generic social work practice predominantly in the public sector; the Japanese model, which also includes active outreach collaboratively involving the private sector; the New Delhi illustration, which promotes although does not achieve the idea of class advocacy via an ombudsman model; and the fourth chapter, which provides blueprints for the development of a free-standing, legally sanctioned advocacy system. Taken together, these hybrid models represent imperfect but real and viable options for the delivery of essential information and access services across a variety of cultures and within a diversiy of political ideologies.

11

ACCESS TO SOCIAL SERVICES IN POLAND

IRENE SIENKO

The Constitution of the Polish People's Republic, in its Article 70, proclaims, "The citizens of the People's Republic of Poland have the right to the protection of health and to assistance in case of illness and inability to work." This constitutional right is intended to be fulfilled by the system of health and social assistance services managed and/or supervised by the Ministry of Health and Social Welfare.

Social assistance services constitute only a part of a wider social security system that also includes social insurance, health care, and rehabilitation of disabled (Karczewski, 1979). Other parts of the national social service system include education, housing, and employment programs. Numerous needs of children and adults are met outside the social assistance system referred to in the Constitution. Services delivered by schools, enterprises, or the social insurance system include meals for schoolchildren, recreation centers for workers and their families, and sickness and maternity leave benefits that are supervised and financed by other social sector ministries such as Labor and Social Affairs or Education. Unfortunatley, this separation of different areas of social services along bureaucratic lines is confusing, not only for an outside observer, but for a beneficiary as well.

The present analysis will refer only to the activities administered and supervised by the Ministry of Health and Social Welfare, which constitutes an important and separate organizational system in Poland and is identified by a separate name ("pomoc spoleczna"). This system refers to the main field of professional and voluntary social work in Poland.

DELIVERING SOCIAL ASSISTANCE:
THE SYSTEM AND ITS FUNCTIONING

Social assistance did not evoke particular attention from the state authorities during the first two decades after World War II. The initial mistaken assumption that socialism would eliminate the need for social assistance hampered the development of this field until 1958. In 1959 the institution of volunteer social counselors, which operated prior to the war, was reactivated on a large scale in urban and rural communities.

Although 1958 was the turning point in the official approach towards social assistance, its organizational development started in fact in the mid 1960s with the creation of social work centers and the establishment of schools of social work that offered a two-year training program. The present shape of the social assistance system, however, derives from the 1973-1975 national administrative reform, and the subsequent reorganization of the health care system to which the social assistance program is traditionally attached[1] (Wojciechowski, 1975).

The organizational structure of this sector is twofold. It consists of: (a) the professional structure of social work centers as basic units, affiliated at the local level with every Area Health Complex (ZOZ); and (b) the national administrative structure at the community (gmina) and province (wojewodztwo) levels. At each level the professional social assistance structure is doubly accountable to: (a) the higher professional level; and (b) the administrative bodies at the respective local level. This unique organizational structure is depicted in Figure 11.1.

The social work center as seen at the base of the chart is operated by social workers with the aid of volunteers. The staff is expected to conduct case-finding of people in need; to define their needs, and to order appropriate services to help them. The local administrative authority allocates community funds needed and accepts applications for social services. Since this local body also is able to refuse the grant of a benefit or to diminish its amount, the consequence is often a source of conflict between the local authority and the social worker, after leading to the ultimate dissatisfaction of the client.

Several voluntary associations operate as an auxiliary to this public system. Two of these organizations, the Polish Red Cross and Polish Committee for Social Assistance, are closely related to the state's social assistance system. On behalf of the social work centers, they provide professional nursing care for the sick at home (the Red

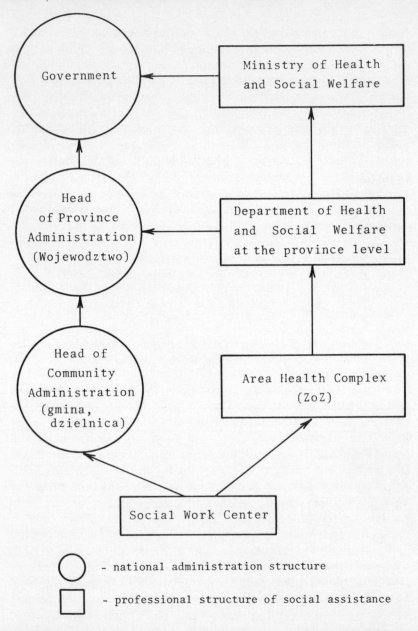

Figure 11.1

Cross) and organized professional or neighborhood home-maker services (the Polish Committee for Social Assistance). Although both associations are well financed by the Ministry of Health and Social Welfare, the cooperation between the two systems, the public state agencies and the voluntary associations, is not always achieved. In fact, coordination is often lacking. A residual role in delivering personal services is assumed by various other associations, including the Polish Scouting Union, the Women's League, and the Rural Housewives Circles. Their activity, entirely voluntary and unpaid, tends to be fragmentary, discontinuous, and generally not correlated with the above-depicted delivery system.

Three types of services are distinguished in the state's social assistance system:

(1) *Financial or economic support,* which includes permanent, temporary, and occasional benefits, as well as in-kind transfers;
(2) *Personal social services,* such as homemaker services, nursing care for the sick, home repair, bath and laundry services, meals, transportation, day care centers, counseling, and legal and advocacy services; and
(3) *Congregate housing,* which includes old-age homes and nursing homes for adults and for mentally retarded children.

According to existing legal regulations, the delivery of services is restricted to specified groups. The coverage includes persons unable to work, i.e., adults in post-retirement age, persons handicapped physically or mentally, children, and youth with profound mental retardation. Another group of recipients includes people who are able to work but are involved in exceptionally difficult situations. This group includes alcoholic families, persons released from prison or hospitals, and persons and families affected by tuberculosis or unexpected disasters (Oleszczynska, 1978).

Social services in this system are predominantly financial and are addressed mainly to the old-age and handicapped population. In 1980, social service expenditure reached the total of 2.8 billion zlotys, of which 2.2 billion were spent for financial and in-kind benefits, and only 600 million for personal services. At the same time, 80 percent of the recipients of all services were old or hanicapped people (Chrostowska, 1980).

This orientation reflects two major factors that influence the scope and functioning of social assistance in Poland:

(1) *The separation of different fields of social services administered by different authorities.* The adult working population remains

principally outside the described system, as the services for this group are mainly work-related and are delivered by the factory or enterprise. This is the reason for several gaps in the social service system, such as is the case of young families in temporary crisis caused by illness or accident. Except for a financial benefit for a special problem case, young families normally are refused any personal services, such as day care for children or homemaker services, and therefore have to rely on other family members, friends, or friendly neighbors help.

(2) *The demographic trend towards the aging of the society and the poor economic position of old or disabled people.* In 1981, 13.3 percent of the total population of the country was over 60. Approximately 40 percent of the retirement-age population (mainly in the countryside) has no independent source of income due to the gaps in the social insurance system that existed before its complex reform in December 1982. In addition, 30 percent of old people need supportive personal services and about 7 percent of them have to maintain another family member.[2]

Recent developments have illustrated the inadequacy of this system relative to the needs of the population. Insufficient means and lack of services for newly emerged groups of people in need became obvious in the current economic crisis (Izdebski, 1982). Therefore, the national government increased funds for social service expenditures from 2.8 billion zlotys in 1980 to 9 billion zlotys in 1982. New groups have been admitted to services provided by state agencies, including poor and "socially defective" families. This evolution created the Family Aid Fund in June 1982 with a budget of 2 billion zlotys for the calendar year 1982, designed exclusively for financial and in-kind benefits. Entitled to benefits from this fund were: (1) families with more than three children, (2) one-parent families, (3) families with a disabled member, (4) families affected by unexpected disasters, (5) student families in difficult economic situation, and (6) grandparents rearing grandchildren.[4] However, this fund expired at the end of the year and changed its main goals when reactivated in 1983 with diminished support for services. For example, a significant part of the budget now is assigned to finance services such as vacation camps for children.

II. PATTERNS OF ACCESS TO SERVICES

Organized access to social assistance services is influenced by the specific strategy of reaching people in need. As the majority of beneficiaries are old or disabled persons, it is assumed that they are unable to reach institutional help for their daily-life problems. Consequently, the social assistance system is conceived as unifying both functions: organizing access to services and delivering services within one overall structure. Its goal is described as "active social assistance," which means an active approach to reaching people in need (Chrostowska, 1980).

The staff members are expected to be the case finders and referral agents simultaneously with their basic task of delivering services. This approach requires the social worker to visit homes within the service district and involves interviewing people about their problems. This is contradictory to the approach applied in the majority of Western countries, which stresses the individual's responsibility in searching out help. This essential difference between both systems in organizing access to services results in a different type of information and referral operation.

In Poland, there is no separate and identifiable information and referral service conceived as an organized system to obtain information about the services available, provide information, and offer advice and referral. Nor is there a requirement that an adequate resource file be maintained, staffed by at least one part-time, paid worker in the agency (Levinson, 1978). In a social work center, a basic unit in the Polish system, these functions are incorporated in the overall social worker's tasks.

According to the outlines of the health care and social assistance systems, unified in the ZOZ, information and referral services are provided by a team of workers consisting of three persons: a district doctor (general practitioner), a community nurse, and a social worker, supported by volunteers.[5] All of these three professional persons are expected to perform other activities specific for their professional positions. The major practitioner in this team is the social worker, although the others, especially the community nurse and the volunteer, often serve as ad hoc advisers in personal and family problems.

The Social Worker: The Basic Link in Organized Access to Services

Regular duties of a social worker, defined in the official instruction, include providing a systematic diagnosis of needs of the inhabitants of his district, applying for benefits or services for clients at the local administrative authority, cooperating with voluntary associations, organizing and supervising activities of the volunteers, cooperating with district physicians and community nurses, collaborating with other institutions delivering social services, collecting agency data and statistics, and organizing "in-service" training for volunteers. This listing clearly indicates that administrative tasks predominate the "proper" function of a social worker—a fact that is a constant cause for complaints by social workers in Poland.

The actual tasks of the social worker also depend on numerous external factors, such as the number of inhabitants in the district, the number of volunteers working available, technical equipment at the center, and good or bad cooperation with local authorities. The new organizational model provides that each social worker will cover a population of one health-care district, i.e., approximately 3,500 inhabitants and 200 to 300 effective cases. To fulfill this plan, an increase in the number of employed staff is needed. The plan calls for approximately 11,000 social workers in 1985 and 14,000 in 1990.[6]

In order to strengthen local social work centers, a program to develop professional staff was launched in 1974 (Oleszczynska, 1980). It has brought a significant growth in the number of professional social workers, from 812 in 1974 to 5,240 in 1982, a total of workers who cover approximately 9,000 inhabitants.

A social worker's major responsibility is the determination of adequate needs, a difficult though essential task. Finding people in need is very similar to conducting a regular survey. Most frequently, social workers use police registers, voting lists, and disabled registers at the Medical Commissions for Disabled to identify addresses of people in old age, handicapped persons, or families with many children. Also, information on people in need is also collected from different institutions, such as schools, courts, and other agencies related to human services. Then clients are visited in their homes systematically by a social worker or a volunteer and their daily problems are discussed.

Another important aspect of this active strategy in reaching the population in need is the special arrangement of office hours by social workers, not necessarily at the agency but at the outpatient health clinic, where the social worker may be more available and accessible.

The Volunteer Worker: A Vital Aid
to the Professional Practitioner

Volunteers are predecessors of professional social workers in the Polish system. From 1959 until 1974 they were virtually the only practitioners in the country. In the early 1970s, their number reached a total of about 65,000 persons. Many of the volunteers are retired civil servants and professionals who live within the various areas of their activity, including villages, towns, and housing projects in large cities. They cooperate with social work centers on a regular basis and represent an important element in this generally professional structure. Volunteers act as case finders and referral agents establishing the linkage between the needy and the agency. Their tasks include collecting informations about the population within a specified area, determining target groups, and organizing access to services by notifying the social work center. Each social worker cooperates with 4 to 6 volunteers in towns and 8 to 10 volunteers in the countryside.

A survey conducted in Poland in 1974-1977 disproved the previously held opinion that the most volunteers were pensioners. The average age of volunteers was 46, and only 17 percent of them were retired. Only 29 percent were females, but the rate of persons with only primary education was high—55 percent (Kryczynska, 1978).

The professionalization of social work that started with the program launched in 1974 also changed the role of volunteer workers. The professional social worker assumed many of the previously held volunteer functions: the diagnosis of needs in the community, the organization of service delivery, and the planning of income maintenance (Marzec-Czaplicka, 1977). At the same time, volunteers showed a diminishing activity. Some of them died, some became too old to do their job, and some abandoned their usual functions as well as their assigned posts. Newly recruited volunteers were not numerous. In the course of these developments, the number of volunteer workers dropped from 65,000 in the early 1970s to 53,000 in 1980, with a subsequent increase to about 59,000 in 1982.

The primary tendency toward eliminating volunteers by replacing them with professionals proved to be shortsighted and erroneous. Since many of the workers tended to be young people with limited life experience and understanding to deal within crisis situations, the loss of volunteers, many of mature years and experience, proved unfortunate. In addition, the large size of most districts makes the help of volunteers indispensable for coverage. In general, social workers have appreciated the cooperation help, and advice of volunteers. Social workers also prefer to visit clients in the presence of the volunteer, who is often known in the assigned district. This process indicates that, although partly replaced by professionals, volunteers remain a characteristic and important feature of the Polish system.

The Community Nurse:
An Alter Ego of the Social Worker

The community nurse is another important service agent in the organized access to social services in Poland. Working in outpatient clinics, community nurses serve as visiting nurses as well as case finders for the social work center. Community nurses' duties include medical care of infants at home, home care of ill and disabled adults, simple medical treatment, communication between the patient and the clinic or hospital, dissemination of medical knowledge and good sanitary habits, and reports on patients' living conditions. Community nurses are highly qualified workers, having worked a minimum of three years previous experience as a regular nurse (preferably in a hospital) and completed a special two month training program. They cover a district of approximately 1,000 to 5,000 thousand inhabitants, depending on the area's demographic structure, the number of cases to be treated, and the geographical distance from the outpatient clinic. The employment program of community nurses was launched in 1966 and nurses were recruited in 1981.[7] As a consequence of these staffing problems, one community nurse has to serve an average of 5278 inhabitants in the countryside and 4509 in the towns, which exceeds the anticipated proportions by 2 to 3 times. Also, not every outpatient clinic employs a community nurse because of lack of a qualified cadre. All this results in a predominance of medical services over social aspects of the community nurse's job, and the latter tend to be only ancilliary to her main activity. This tendency seems to be approved by the Ministry of Health and Social Welfare.

Access to Services Provided
by Voluntary Associations

The Red Cross (PCK) and the Committee for Social Welfare (PKPS) delivery mainly in-kind services not only on behalf of the social work centers, but also in relation to their own clients. The Red Cross also provides financial benefits to people in need. Main channels of access in such cases are community institutions such as settlement committees, industry (mainly for its former workers), housekeepers, and neighbors. Some people come to the Red Cross offices on their own initiative, mostly because of media coverage on TV and in newspapers. A special role of the Red Cross Circles in schools and industry is in delivering some self-help services and acting as a referral agent. Similar patterns of access to services are utilized by the Polish Committee for Social Welfare.

Delivery of in-kind benefits by voluntary associations was not correlated with the services provided by social work centers for a long time. In order to eliminate duplication of services for more active or better-informed clients, a unified register for all services should be implemented and a closer cooperation between state and voluntary agencies should be established.

The Children's Friend Society cares exclusively for children, acting through its circles in schools, industry, and communities and using its own eligibility standards. The other associations mentioned above provide only occasional self-help services and some recreational programs for their members. Their activity is very loosely related to the social work center's services. However, they often inform people in need about the services available in the social work center, thus acting as a referral agent.

Outreach Information for the Needy

The "actively involved approach" toward the client may make outreach efforts appear less important than in other countries. However, the difficulty in locating persons in need, due to the limited number of staff and lack of sufficient organizational means, renders I&R outreach information extremely useful.

Until recently, mass media played a major role. TV and newspapers provided information about the services available. The daily *Kurier Polski* even made some efforts to organize new volunteer services, mainly for the winter season. Information about the nearest social work center is displayed in every housing project. In Warsaw, a special telephone hotline was maintained for a period of time to service people as an information and source. Brief information about the place and time to meet a social worker or a volunteer social counselor usually are displayed in outpatient clinics and at the entrance of houses where the volunteers live.

III. MODEL ISSUES VERSUS REAL PERFORMANCE

The formal model depicted above is only a framework that formally represents a process. Institutional channels are not always effective, so that informal referrals also play a significant role in access

TABLE 11.1

| Type of Referring Agent | Percentages and Ranges by Referral Source for Six Cities | |
	Percentage	Range
Client	28.2	15.6 - 37.6
Family	10.2	4.2 - 25.0
Volunteer worker	23.5	7.7 - 38.2
Social worker	16.0	1.9 - 30.3
Others-detail	22.0	13.5 - 29.9

to services. In a survey conducted in Warsaw in 1974-1975 it was found that only 17.5 percent of old people applying for a place in congregate housing used the direct help of a social worker or a volunteer. The rest made the application by themselves (53 percent) or, with the help of friends and neighbors (13 percent), children and relatives (7 percent), or the district physician (6 percent). This finding contributed to the opinion that the institutional channels to facilitate access and link clients to service do not function well, particularly since clients themselves apply for services.

Another survey conducted in 1977-1980 in the northern and central parts of Poland also proved that the proportion of volunteers and professional social workers in establishing the linkage between the client and the social worker center is rather low, as shown in Table 11.1.

Besides the heavy volume of their workloads, two factors explain the low position of volunteers and social workers in organizing access to services (averaging 25 percent to 60 percent of cases as reported above). The first is the overburdening administrative tasks incorporated in the social worker's job. The second is the shortage of means—financial resources and staff—to deliver home-help services and nursing care at home. Conscious of these limitations, social workers tend not to report all the cases in their districts, as they are not able to deliver services to everyone in need. These factors result in a high rate of "outsiders" reaching the social work center by informal channels.

In addition, the period of economic crisis opened new channels of access to social services. One of them is the wide dissemination of information regarding social services through the mass media. A vigorous campaign in favor of the needy was held in autumn and winter 1981-1982, encouraging many to seek social services or even to demand some benefits. Industry became the other channel of access, generally delivering some services of its own. In the new situation, as funds were still limited, industry would send lists of their present or former workers in need to the respective social work center or voluntary association. This concerned mainly pensioneers of the industry, families with many children and female-headed families.

The real picture of access to services is then strongly influenced by new tendencies. Very recently, in an ad hoc interview, two social workers in two different Warsaw districts arrayed the channels of access to services as follows:

District No. 1	District No. 2
(1) Community nurse and district doctors	(1) Clients themselves
(2) Social workers	(2) Volunteers
(3) Volunteers	(3) Social workers
(4) Enterprises	(4) Community nurse and district doctors
(5) Public and state authorities (clients asking for help at the Sejm, State's Council or local administrative authorities)	(5) Enterprises and voluntary associations
	(6) Public authorities and mass media (people writing to the TV and newspapers)

However, the question of access to social services may be analyzed in two respects: (1) as the process of establishing the linkage between consumers and service providers, or (2) as the effective delivery of direct services to the person in need.

There exist several barriers of access to services in the Polish system. The most important one is the shortage of financial means, trained staff, and technical base. The progress made during twenty years of development, although significant, is not sufficient if related to needs. In addition, the present system strongly prefers financial benefits over personal services as the easiest way to respond to one's needs. Also, centralization moves the system towards standardization and against the diversification of services. Frequently, financial benefits replace nonexistent, specialized personal services more suitable for the person in need. Clients, on the other hand, often are more interested in financial help.

Underdevelopment of personal services and their poor quality are principal problems of the Polish social service delivery system. The present system has proven to be inefficient. In addition to professional errors committed by the staff (Burawska, 1977), and troubled cooperation between the state and voluntary agencies, it shows a high degree of bureaucratization and lack of flexibility. It operates in typical situations, but does not respond to changing needs and emerging new social problems. The most significant failure of the present system is the almost total neglect of the drug addict and his needs. Although the number of drug addicts in Poland—exclusively young people—is increasing rapidly (their population is estimated at between 30,000 and 50,000), they can get only fragmentary services in psychiatric clinics and in only one voluntary association, not at the social work center.

The system evokes much criticism from the general public as well as from the professional milieu. Inadequate information, organizational patterns, and poor services have been criticized (Nowakowska, 1982). The new organization project stresses the need for developing new services for new groups of clients, improving the existing organizational structure, and changing some legal regulations hampering the delivery of services to persons in need. The present system most probably will evolve toward covering different needs of families in crisis situations and creating a continuous follow-up of clients' needs as an alternative to the life-cycle approach, thus dividing the competency and responsibility for delivering social services between three separate ministries.

This evolution, intended to develop new services and reach new populations at risk, probably will contribute to the development of specialized information and referral service. The variety of services provided and admission of many newcomers to the social service agencies will make organized access indispensable.

NOTES

1. The English reader may find a more comprehensive description of the Polish health care and social service system in: Wojciechowski, S. (1975), "Poland's New Priority: Human Welfare" in D. Thursz and J. L. Vigilante (eds), *Meeting Human Needs. An Overview of Nine Countries,* Beverly Hills, Sage Publications, and L. C. Millard (1982). "Health Care in Poland: From Crisis to Crisis", *International Journal of Health Services,* vol. 12, no. 3.

2. "Coordinated Social Welfare in the Years 1982-1985", (1982) Warsaw Ministry of Health and Social Welfare.*

3. "Protection of Families: Budget Against Economic Crisis" (1982), Rzeczpospolita, no. 34, 22. February.

4. "Ordinance of Ministry of Health and Welfare of April 30, 1982. Regulating Family Public Assistance", (1982), Warsaw, Ministry of Health and Social Welfare.

5. "General Activities of Regional and Local Health and Welfare Clinics", (1982), Warsaw, Ministry of Health and Social Welfare.

6. "Programs of Social Services as Projected up to the Year 1990", (1982), Warsaw, Ministry of Health and Social Welfare.

7. "Urban and Rural Employment of Nurses", (1982), Warsaw, Ministry of Health and Social Welfare.

*Title of an article in the weekly magazine.

REFERENCES

Burawska, E. (1977). Is our social service effective? *Opiekun Spoleczny, 4*.

Chrostowska, H. (1980). Some aspects of community social services. *Opiekun Spoleczny, 3*.

Grela, L. (1982). Social services for the elderly. *Studia i Materialy IPSS, 5*.

Izdebski, M. (1982). Social services and integrated programs of help for elderly and handicapped. In *Elderly in Poland: Their conditions and needs*. Warsaw: *Studia i Materialy IPSS, 16*.

Kahn, A.J. (1979). *Social policy and social services*. New York: Random House.

Karczewski, M. (1979). Social services. In A. Rajkiewicz (Ed.), *Political Science*. Warsaw: PWE.

Kryczynska, I. (1978). Summary report on the voluntary and professional manpower of social welfare in the Polish people's republic. Warsaw: Centrum Medyczne Ksztalcenia Podyplomowego.

Levinson, R.W. (1978). Helping the needy get help: The I&R services. *NASW News, 73*, 6.

Marzec-Czaplicka, H. (1977). Changing functions of voluntary social workers. *Opiekun Spoleczny, 4*.

Nowakowska, E. (1982). Six cooks dealing with one small pork chop. *Polityka, 15* (May 15)

Oleszczynska, A. (1978). Role of social worker in the social welfare system. Warsaw: IW CRZZ.

Oleszczynska, A. (1980). Social welfare in Poland in the perspective of 60 years. In I. Sienko (Ed.), *Origin Development and Perspective of Social Welfare in Poland*. Warsaw: Warsaw University Press.

Oleszczynska, A. (1982). Evaluation of social welfare experiment planned for 1990. *Opiekun Spoleczny, 1-2*.

12

COMMUNITY WELFARE VOLUNTEERS IN JAPAN
The Minsei-Iin System

ATSUKO MATSUOKA

In every town and village in Japan, a Minsei-Iin (community welfare) volunteer serves community residents who are in need, linking them to public social welfare organizations. The Minsei-Iin Volunteer System is well organized and nationwide. It is unique because, although it is a volunteer system, it has a special legal status. The national government subsidizes a prefectural government, which takes responsibility for funding the system in the prefecture. Each member is appointed by the minister of Health and Welfare, and the position is considered prestigious.

In the course of its nearly forty-year history, the Minsei-Iin Volunteer System has changed from an auxiliary agency to a cooperative agency for public social welfare. Today, it seeks a new direction that seems difficult to achieve. This chapter discusses the problems making these changes as well as the advantages of pressing toward change.

HISTORY

Two programs that developed prior to the Minsei-Iin volunteers were important precursors: the Saisei-Komon (relief advisor) system and the Homen-Iin (district volunteer) system.

In the 1910s Japan suffered a drastic rise in prices—especially in the price of rice—that culminated in countrywide rice riots in 1918. Thus a rise in the cost of living threatened the people's everyday lives.

In addition, the severe inflation after World War I produced chronic unemployment and an increase in the lower-income population.

The Saisei-Komon (relief advisor) system was established by the governor of Okayama Prefecture in 1917 to prevent poverty and improve the social environment. The governor instituted this system after a study revealed that there were more poor people than anyone had anticipated. A further study of remedies examined various systems of social welfare in other parts of the world, such as poor relief commissioners in Elberfeld, Germany, and probation services in the United States, and suggested several ways of dealing with social problems. The system that developed was composed primarily of relief advisors from the upper class.

Unlike the Saisei-Komon system, which was developed to solve the problems in rural communities like Okayama City, the Homen-Iin system, established by the governor in Osaka Prefecture in 1918, was intended to solve problems in urban communities. This system emphasized not only the prevention of poverty, but also a study of living conditions of the residents in a district, an evaluation of social problems, and the promotion of cooperative help from among residents. The governor chose Homen-Iin volunteers from among middle-class residents who knew their community well and could understand their local concerns.

From 1918 to 1921, programs and systems similar to the ones described above were established in many cities in order to cope with social problems, specifically poverty. The only legal provision for the poor at that time was the Poor Relief Regulation, enacted in 1874. The regulation provided assistance to the poor, aged, and sick who absolutely could not be cared for by their relatives or neighbors. Since most of the poor and needy were not eligible under this regulation, a great stigma was attached to it. Then, in 1928, a new Poor Relief Law was passed by the Diet, only to remain unenforced due to lack of funds. In response to this situation, the Homen-Iin, in league with other volunteers, lobbied for the enforcement of the law until the government finally implemented it in 1932.

Under this law, the Homen-Iin and other similar volunteers became auxiliaries to mayors in issuing poor relief. However, because the several volunteer systems varied in organization and role from place to place, there were difficulties in carrying out unified, standardized, and effective social welfare programs throughout the nation. Therefore, in 1936, the Homen-Iin Regulation proclaimed the Homen-Iin the officially recognized nationwide system.

The social action that led to the enforcement of the Poor Relief Law is a bright spot in the early history of the Minsei-Iin volunteer program. In 1937 the Military Assistance Law and the Mothers' Aid Law were enacted, and the Homen-Iin undertook services related to these laws. But during the war, the Homen-Iin became more of an agency that was subordinate to the national government than an independent volunteer system. Moreover, the Homen-Iin was involved in the Military Aid System and assumed leadership in military-related undertakings rather than in volunteer activities to help people in need.

After World War II, GHQ (General Headquarters of the Army of the Occupation) sent to the Japanese Government a memorandum that presented three principles of public assistance: equality, national responsibility, and guarantee of a minimum standard of living. This memorandum was an important landmark in the history of Japanese social welfare.

In order to enforce the principle of non-discriminatory equality, the GHQ forced the government to establish a nationwide agency for public assistance and prohibited the government from depending on the Homen-Iin System. In fact, the GHQ recommended that the system be abolished. However, the government and people in the social welfare field at that time did not understand the importance of the principle thoroughly (Yoshida, 1979: 272-274). Moreover, in the chaotic era after World War II the government could not afford to hire full-time public-assistance caseworkers (Nakamura, 1967: 198-200). Although the government abolished the Homen-Iin System, it was superseded by the Minsei-Iin Volunteer System under the Minsei-Iin Regulation of 1946. Both the Minsei-Iin Regulation and the Daily Life Security Law in 1946 (the latter of which established five categories of assistance for those in financial need) designated the Minsei-Iin system as an auxiliary agency, and the Minsei-Iin volunteers as determiners of eligibility for public assistance. This role prevented the three principles stipulated by the GHQ from being fully implemented. Therefore, although the new Minsei-Iin Volunteer System was established, the separation of public and private sectors had not yet been achieved.

In 1947 the Child Welfare Law made Minsei-Iin volunteers also Jido-Iin volunteers (volunteer workers in Child Welfare). A Minsei-Iin volunteer's average client load in 1948 was 20 to 25 public assistance households (Yoshida, 1979: 277), so it was impossible for the Minsei-Iin volunteer to also take an active role as a Jido-Iin volunteer (The National Council of Social Welfare (NCSW), 1975: 7).

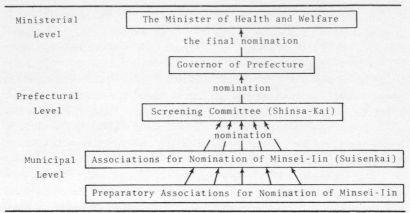

Figure 12.1: Nomination Process of Minsei-Iin Volunteer

In 1950, the Daily Life Security Law was amended and the status of the Minsei-Iin system was officially altered. Rather than serving as an auxiliary agency, it was now a cooperative agency for the Daily Life Security Law. In substance the change took place with the establishment of the system of social welfare officers under the Social Welfare Services Law in 1951. This change of role caused confusion among those Minsei-Iin volunteers who were deeply involved in public assistance work, which they had mistakenly thought was their only task. The relationship between public and private sectors was clarified when the Minsei-Iin Law was amended in 1953. The volunteers were now called "community welfare workers," and, as the name implies, they had to develop independent activities and revert to the original purpose of promoting social welfare in a community.

Appointment of Volunteers

A Minsei-Iin volunteer is chosen from among community members. (The process of nomination is shown in Figure 12.1). The governor of a prefecture nominates residents and the minister of Health and Welfare asks them to be Minsei-Iin volunteers. They are not obligated and are at liberty to decline the invitation. The Minsei-Iin Law of 1953 requires municipalities to form an Association for the Nomination of Minsei-Iin (Suisen-Kai), which must consist of seven to fourteen citizens who are members of the municipal government council, Minsei-Iin volunteers, workers in social work and related fields, or educators. The appointment is for three years. Some large cities use Preparatory Associations in smaller areas (for example, each school district) in order to help an Association for the nomination of Minsei-Iin choose appropriate volunteers.

The Minsei-Iin Law requires each prefecture to organize a screening committee (Shinsa-kai), which is to consist of, at most, ten citizens who have the right to vote for the prefectural government council. These ten members serve for three years. They are people who work in fields related to social welfare, who are members of the prefectural government council (maximum three members), or who are knowledgeable and experienced.

A screening committee examines the allotted number of nominations made by the Association for the Nomination of Minsei-Iin and makes the second and final judgment on nomination. The governor of a prefecture determines the final nominations, which are passed on to the minister of Health and Welfare.

According to the Minsei-Iin Law, selected volunteers must be people who:

(1) hold the rights of election for a given municipal assembly; specifically, those who are over 20 years old, hold Japanese citizenship and have been living in the immediate community for more than three years;

(2) embody personal development; that is to say, those who are willing to serve society and who have a rich life experience, well-rounded common sense, and a sense of justice combined with compassion and a keen insight into human nature;

(3) are enthusiastic about promoting social welfare and understand the problems of children, the elderly, and the handicapped; and

(4) can receive encouragement from their family for the Minsei-Iin activities (NCSW, 1978: 9-11).

The position of the Minsei-Iin carries no pay. An appointment is for a three-year period. Many Minsei-Iin volunteers take several consecutive appointments, because the work of the Minsei-Iin is demanding and they do not consider one term enough time to carry out their responsibilities as fully as possible. In 1980, new appointments made up 24.3 percent and reappointments made up 75.7 percent of the total number of volunteers.

While 49 percent serve between 3 and 9 years, only 30 percent serve less than 3 years. Since 1962, most volunteers have been between 50 and 70 years old and with new appointments in 1980, the average age rose to 57.3 years. The proportion of female volunteers increased from 26 percent in 1962 to 38 percent in 1980. The proportion of volunteers currently unemployed (i.e., housewives and the retired) has also increased, from 19.6 percent in 1965 to 30.4 percent in 1977 (NCSW, 1980: 1-7).

The change from the predominance of males to an equal male-female ratio, and the increase in the proportion of housewives who are Minsei-Iin volunteers, have added new and important human resources within the social welfare systems in Japan. Government policy emphasizes utilizing support from family members and developing community support through active participation by residents.

ORGANIZATION OF VOLUNTEERS

In order to increase the efficiency of their services within each prefecture, the Minsei-Iin volunteers have organized a council as required by law. This council operates autonomously and provides liaison with other agencies as well as among the Minsei-Iin volunteers themselves. The number of councils is determined by the governor, with advice from the mayors. Usually there is one council for every town, village, or jurisdiction within a city; one for every municipal; one for each prefecture; and one national council.

The functions of the council are to determine the district in which a Minsei-Iin volunteer takes charge; to coordinate the work of the volunteers with a social welfare office and other related agencies; to collect information and data; to encourage the Minsei-Iin volunteers to study and receive training; to deal with pertinent issues in order to make their work more effective; and to advocate the Minsei-Iin point of view to related ministries.

Members of a council of Minsei-Iin elect a representative from among their members, who acts as a director (Somu). The director arranges the work of the council and holds a monthly meeting to foster better communication among members of the council.

The number of Minsei-Iin volunteers is determined by the total number of households and the number of people needing services in a municipality. The proportions of volunteers to population are as follows: In such large cities as Tokyo, Osaka, Kyoto, Yokohama, Kobe, Nagoya, Kitakyushu, Sapporo, Hiroshima, Fukuoka, and Kawasaki, there is one Minsei-Iin volunteer for every 270 households; in a city with a population over 100,000, there is one volunteer for every 200 households; and in a city with a population under 100,000 there is one volunteer for every 120 households. (NCSW, 1982a: 178). The total number of volunteers increased from 124,318 in 1959 to 169,161 in 1980.

SERVICES AND ACTIVITIES OF THE MINSEI-IIN VOLUNTEERS

The Minsei-Iin Law of 1948 established Minsei-Iin as an agency to cooperate with other administrative agencies in order to promote social welfare in the community. The Minsei-Iin volunteers perform many activities, which may be categorized into three types, according to the relation they have to social welfare organizations:

(1) legally specified activities undertaken cooperatively with the Public Welfare Office;
(2) activities undertaken cooperatively with Councils of Social Welfare; and
(3) independent activities.

Legally Specified Activities Undertaken Cooperatively with the Public Welfare Office

The Minsei-Iin Law of 1953 states that the Minsei-Iin volunteers are to work with social welfare-related administrative agencies. One of the closest liaisons among the agencies is the one with the public welfare office, where cooperation can be classified into several types according to the related laws: six basic welfare laws (the Daily Life Security Law, the Law for the Welfare of the Aged, the Law for the Welfare of the Physically Handicapped, the Law for the Welfare of the Mentally Retarded, the Mother and Child Welfare Law, and the Child Welfare Law) and the Prostitution Prevention Law. The Minsei-Iin volunteers must cooperate with the director and officers of the Public Social Welfare Office regarding work related to these laws. All Minsei-Iin volunteers must maintain welfare cards as a part of their work. A welfare card is an official report that documents those who are in need; that is to say, the single-parent family, the elderly living alone, the bedridden elderly, the handicapped, the mentally retarded, and the recipients of public assistance. Although forms of the welfare cards vary according to the categories stated above, all the cards record the individuals in need, their living conditions, their relationships with other people, and additional salient items of information. Conversely, social welfare officers keep Minsei-Iin volunteers informed about the progress of specific clients' cases until these are concluded.

Under the Daily Life Security Law, as soon as Minsei-Iin volunteers find people in need, they inform the public welfare office. Whenever a resident or his relative, friend or neighbor asks a Minsei-Iin volunteer for advice and help, the volunteer provides information, offers advice, and helps the person to apply for assistance by making contact with the public welfare office or referring him to other agencies. When public welfare officers investigate the living conditions of the needy, Minsei-Iin volunteers supply the data available on the client; for example, data from welfare cards. A Minsei-Iin volunteer makes suggestions when public welfare officers are judging the need for protective custody or care, and when a daily-life guidance counsellor is making decisions about services given to public assistance recipients.

In carrying out the Law for the Welfare of the Aged, the Minsei-Iin volunteer informs every resident who is 65 and older of the annual medical checkup sponsored by the mayor's office. A Minsei-Iin volunteer provides counselling to elderly people who may need to be accommodated in an old people's home. The Minsei-Iin volunteer maintains liaison with personnel from agencies who provide services for the elderly in their own homes, such as home-helpers and telephone counselors.

Under the Law for Welfare of the Physically Handicapped, Minsei-Iin volunteers inform the public welfare office whenever they find people who need medical rehabilitation services or an identification booklet, or who are seeking an accommodation in a rehabilitation institution. The volunteer explains available support systems to adult handicapped persons and their families and, in cooperation with the public welfare office, counsels them to promote independence.

When the Minsei-Iin volunteers find a mentally retarded person, they inform the public welfare office and help the person to receive adequate welfare arrangements. They listen to the person and to family members about problems they face, and if necessary make contact with appropriate agencies. They help to improve the family relationships and the social environment, as well as to find jobs for the retarded. By publicizing the support system for the mentally retarded, the Minsei-Iin volunteers promote understanding among the neighboring citizens.

Under the Mother and Child Welfare Law, when the Minsei-Iin volunteers find single parents eligible for income security, they help them to receive it as soon as possible by cooperating with the public welfare office and providing necessary documents. They inform single parents about the Loans to Mothers with Dependent Children and, along with a public welfare officer, help them to go through the procedures of application and repayment. The Minsei-Iin volunteers inform and encourage pregnant women to get prenatal and postpartum guidance and remind mothers to take their three-year-old children for the standard medical examination.

The Minsei-Iin Law and the Child Welfare Law have placed every Minsei-Iin volunteer in the concurrent position of a Jido-Iin (volunteer worker in child welfare). When Minsei-Iin volunteers find children without a guardian or adequate care, or involved with juvenile delinquents and other children in trouble, they inform the public welfare office and help them to receive adequate assistance.

Under Section 37 of the Prostitution Prevention Law of 1956, a Minsei-Iin volunteer needs to collaborate with a counseling center for women whenever he finds women involved in prostitution. Preventive measures against prostitution also are taken.

The number of cases the Minsei-Iin volunteers handle under the six basic welfare laws has increased. Most notably, the number of cases under the Law for the Welfare of the Aged has increased 761 percent from 1970 to 1981. The second-highest increase 396 percent from 1970 to 1981) has been in the cases under the Law for the Welfare of the Physically Handicapped (NCSW, 1982a: 180).

The Minsei-Iin volunteers often help administrative authorities to carry out survey research on specific groups, such as single parents or the elderly. While engaged in cooperative research efforts, Minsei-Iin volunteers have a chance to meet with the residents and can find hidden needs in a community. Thus, the Minsei-Iin volunteers learn about the community. Because they themselves are residents of the community, they know community and neighboring citizens personally. For these reasons, the government asks the Minsei-Iin volunteers to authenticate concerns related to the six basic welfare laws and report other items of information such as unemployment, employment, family membership, residence, unemployment, and dependency (Hyogo Prefecture, 1982: 54).

Cooperative Activities with Councils of Social Welfare

The Councils of Social Welfare are quasi-government organizations that promote activities of private social welfare organizations. There are national, prefectural, and municipal councils of social welfare, all of which foster the efficient administration of social welfare in Japan. According to the Basic Survey on Welfare Services in April 1953, 2.04 million households, composed of 7 million individuals, had marginal incomes (Yoshida, 1979: 342). Recognizing the importance of assisting marginal income families to avoid poverty and dependency, a Minsei-Iin Family Rehabilitation System was formed, which the Prefectural Council of Social Welfare operates with the help of Minsei-Iin volunteers. This movement focuses on helping marginally poor people to achieve economic independence by providing adequate advice and guidance. Thus, the purpose of this movement was prevention of poverty and promotion of rehabilitation from poverty.

The Family Rehabilitation Loan System provides a variety of low-interest loans to low-income families and families with physically handicapped members to cover living expenses and reconstruction of homes so that these families can achieve economic independence. When an individual applies for this type of loan, a Minsei-Iin volunteer informs the Prefectural Council of Social Welfare. The volunteer writes a report on the applicant's living conditions and the necessity for the loan, after which the president of the Prefectural Council of Social Welfare decides whether the applicant will receive the loan.

The Minsei-Iin volunteers and the Councils of Social Welfare also collaborate in providing guidance counseling activities, which are available to all residents in a community. The Council of Social Welfare provides the office space for guidance counseling, and some Minsei-Iin volunteers fill the role of counselors. Counseling activities first started in 1951 in Ezu City in Shimane Prefecture and Onomichi City in Hiroshima Prefecture. By 1963, the number of Citizens' Counseling Service Bureaus had grown to close to 1,000 in Japan as the result of subsidies that the government provided between 1959 and 1963 to establish such bureaus. Since 1960, when the national government began to subsidize these activities, the number of bureaus open at least one day a week has risen to 2,972; and the number of Special Citizens' Counseling Service Bureaus, which are found in cities of 100,000 people or more and operate at least three days a week, has risen to 157 (NCSW, 1982b: 43).

Three different types of counselors work at a bureau. Part-time counselors elected from among Minsei-Iin volunteers work at least once a month. Full-time counselors are chosen from a pool of part-time counselors on the basis of their knowledge and experience, or from a group of Minsei-Iin volunteers who have experience and acquaintance with the law. A full-time counselor must be available during all office hours; he conducts the first interview and supervises part-time counselors. The third type of counselor is the professional counselor who can cooperate with a bureau on problems in law, education, or psychology. The municipal Councils of Social Welfare organize a training program for counselors and cover working and training expenses.

The total number of counselors decreased from 1980 and 1981 in spite of the increased numbers of bureaus. Since 1976, the number of full-time counselors has gradually decreased, but the number of part-time counselors has increased. Although the National Council of Minsei-Iin volunteers encourages local bureaus to furnish full-time counselors, the trend tends to be otherwise in favor of part-timers and professionals.

Statistics on case management and outcome show that approximately 66 percent of the cases are resolved within the bureau, 11 percent are ongoing cases, and 23 percent are referred to other resources. The most frequent problems referred to the bureaus from 1976 to 1981 were, in order of decreasing frequency, living expenses, property, family problems, legal problems, and old-age-related problems.

Independent Activities

The Minsei-Iin volunteers frequently carry out surveys. For example, they have carried out large-scale surveys on victims of traffic accidents, pregnant women, and handicapped children. They work to eliminate "found-deaths" among the aged (that is, situations in which no one knows that a person is dying and the person is later "found dead"). They not only visit older people who are in poor health and living alone, but ask neighbors and members of senior citizens' clubs to visit or keep up contacts with these older people. Among the vanguard activities, recently initiated by Minsei-Iin volunteers are Meals on Wheels and Meals in a Center, both of which are mainly for the elderly. The number of these meal services carried out by the Minsei-Iin volunteers has been increasing.

FUNDING

The Minsei-Iin Law, Section 26, states that the prefecture is responsible for financing Associations for the Nomination of Minsei-Iin volunteers, screening committees and councils of

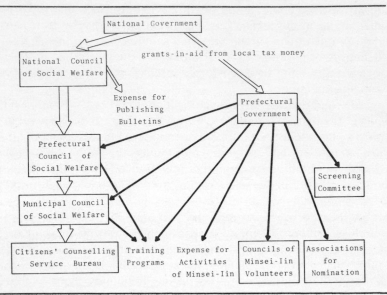

Figure 12.2: Funding

Minsei-Iin. The prefecture also supports training programs for Minsei-Iin volunteers, and, in fact, all activities of Minsei-Iin volunteers. According to Section 28, the national government subsidizes prefectures with grants-in-aid from local tax money on items determined by the minister of health and welfare determines, such as the activites of Minsei-Iin volunteers, the publishing of Minsei-Iin bulletins, and guidance and counseling (see Figure 12.2). Therefore, the budget varies among prefectures. The Osaka prefecture, for example, paid only ¥1,000 (approximately $5) to each council of Minsei-Iin volunteers in 1982, and provided ¥27,000 for each Minsei-Iin volunteer screening committee. The Osaka prefecture asked the Prefectural Council of Social Welfare to run training programs for Minsei-Iin volunteers; and in 1983 the prefecture set up a budget of ¥10.4 million for this purpose. Because this fund includes training expenses for social welfare officers, a separate figure for Minsei-Iin volunteers is not available.

The national government funds the activities of the Citizens' Counseling Service Bureau. The National Council of Social Welfare receives the funds from the national government and allocates a portion to each Prefectural Council of Social Welfare. In 1979, the total fund was ¥213.9 million. Every municipal council allocated over ¥174,000 for Citizen's Counseling Service Bureau, and over ¥480,000 for a Special Citizens' Counseling Bureau. The national subsidy amounted to ¥580,900 for each counseling bureau and ¥160,000 for each Special Counseling Bureau (NCSW, 1982: 102-103).

FUTURE DIRECTIONS

Since 1946, when the Minsei-Iin Volunteer System was established, the Minsei-Iin volunteers have worked closely with governmental agencies and quasi-governmental organizations. Unlike the disorganized and chaotic era after World War II, various levels of government have since employed full-time public welfare officers, and Japanese citizens have organized many groups to help others meet their own needs. In 1977, when the Minsei-Iin volunteers celebrated their 60th anniversary, the National Council of Minsei-Iin Volunteers (NCMV) proposed a policy that implies two future directions for the Minsei-Iin Volunteer System. On the one hand, the Minsei-Iin volunteers will continue to serve mainly people in need. On the other hand, they will also respond to the needs of all local residents by helping them take active roles in social welfare by organizing citizens and developing leadership among them so that they can advocate measures in their own interest.

NCMV emphasizes the second direction more than the first. To move in the second direction, Minsei-Iin volunteers are required to cooperate in discussions about local concerns, express opinions and formulate recommendations on behalf of the local residents, and move beyond the specific assignment set at the beginning of the Homen-Iin System. I will examine whether the second direction is feasible, focusing on these requirements as criteria.

For nearly 40 years the Minsei-Iin Volunteer System has served mainly people who are in need. Although the system was established after World War II, its target groups still are similar to those that existed prior to the war. Because these people in need receive services from the Minsei-Iin volunteers in a passive way, Minsei-Iin volunteers tend to be social controllers of certain groups of people, rather than value guardians for the community. In this sense, they are moving in a direction contrary to their goal of working for the benefit of all local residents. In fact, the Minsei-Iin volunteers have not moved beyond the original assignment.

According to the 1981 report by the National Council of Social Welfare and the National Council of Minsei-Iin Volunteers, in 1979 only 7 percent of all Municipal Councils of Minsei-Iin volunteers made recommendations and requests to the municipal governments.

The most frequent requests concerned the .administration of local Councils of Minsei-Iin Volunteers, specifically, financial assistance for the volunteers to carry out their activities, improvement in training programs for themselves and changes in the membership of the volunteers in a district. The second most frequent request was for social welfare services to the elderly (NCSW, 1981: 95). Interest in better services for the elderly is growing in communities. However, since the average age of the Minsei-Iin volunteers was 57 in 1980, their most frequent requests relate to their own self-interest and those of similar cohort groups, rather than to the needs of local residents.

Almost all the liaison activities of Minsei-Iin volunteers take place between governmental agencies and the local residents in need (see the section on activities and services). But they do not focus their activities on other local voluntary organizations and the residents who could become a part of a human-service network. In other words, they are still aiming their activities and services toward the alleviation of individual poverty rather than balancing that concern with the improvement of social welfare in their local communities through the formation of alliances and organizations.

However, there are quite a few organizations in each neighborhood that strengthen community solidarity by providing information and fostering interactions among the local residents (for example, children's clubs, women's associations, seniors' associations, and district or neighborhood associations). When Minsei-Iin volunteers collaborate with these organizations, they help community organizations to negotiate policies and resolve conflicts. The role of negotiation may be too demanding for the Minsei-Iin volunteers, not only because they are part-time, unpaid workers who carry a large load of activities and services with public agencies, but because they are appointed in ways that can produce conflicts of interest.

Social work scholars and government welfare officers have often questioned whether the recommendation of a specific candidate fairly represents the interest of residents in general rather than the interest of a select group (Ogura, 1965; Santomi, 1977; Ueda, 1967; NCSW, 1968). A committee for nomination may serve, in effect, as a screen for preventing those with an ideology different from the committee's from becoming Minsei-Iin volunteers. A committee that discriminates against specific ideologies may create an unfavorably strong connection with a certain political party, and thus encourage interference with the activities of some voluntary organizations rather than cooperation. Another problem in the appointment process is the issue of reappointment. As long as Minsei-Iin volunteers are carrying out their work properly there are few reasons for rejecting volunteers should they be recommended again. If Minsei-Iin volunteers are to improve welfare by organizing the community, they may need to serve for a longer time. However, serving more than four terms (each term consists of three years) without an adequate input of new knowledge results in stultification of the activities. In short, the Minsei-Iin volunteers face a great difficulty in circumventing politics in a local community.

The present activities of the Minsei-Iin volunteers and their appointment process do not indicate any change toward the second direction of serving all local residents. Unlike public officers who cannot work beyond the domain of their specialized departments, the Minsei-Iin volunteers do not need to limit their services to specific groups, e.g., the elderly, the lower class, or the handicapped. Therefore, the Minsei-Iin volunteer System provides a broad base for welfare services because it is officially recognized and established throughout Japan.

Although Japan is moving from an industrial society to an informational society that provides Japanese people with better access to telecommunication systems, they cannot necessarily obtain immediate help in cases of emergency, such as stroke, heart attack, and accidents at home. Relatives, friends and nearby neighbors have been the traditional source of such direct help in Japan. Because the Minsei-Iin volunteers serve their immediate neighborhood, they can react to emergencies among the local residents at any time, even at night or on weekends, when such help is difficult to obtain in any other way. Furthermore, serving their own communities makes it possible for Minsei-Iin volunteers to develop services in accordance with the needs of the local residents. Apparently, the Minsei-Iin Volunteer System has not shifted toward the second direction, that of improving the social welfare of total communities. If the Minsei-Iin volunteers can see beyond their present problems and roles, the system has good potential to expand the services and the human resources of the community.

REFERENCES

Hyogo Prefecture (1982). *Minsei-Iin Jido-Iin Kankei Shiryosyu.*
Nakamura, Y. (1967). Kotekifujo Taishyosya no Shyogu. Pp 195-206n Nihon Shakai Jigyo Daigaku (Ed.), *Sengo Nihonno Shakai Jigyo.*
National Council of Social Welfare. (1968). *Minsei-Iin no Kaisen ni Noxonde:* 63-64.
National Council of Social Welfare. (1975). *Minsei-Iin no Katsudo.*

National Council of Social Welfare. (1978). *Minsei-Iin Ho no Kaisetsu.*

National Council of Social Welfare. (1980). *Minsei-Iin Jido-Iin Issei Kaisen Jokyo.*

National Council of Social Welfare. (1981). *Minsei-Iin Jido-Iin Kasudo Shiryoshyu.*

National Council of Social Welfare. (1982a). *Syakai Fukushi no Doko:* 177-184.

National Council of Social Welfare. (1982b). *Zenkoku Shinpai Goto Sodansyo Kenkyu Kyogikai Togishiryo.*

National Council of Social Welfare. (1982c). *Shinpai Goto Sodansyo Nenpo 1981.*

Ogura, J. (1965). Minsei-Iin no Ishiki Jyokyo nitsuite. *Doshisya Daigaku Jinbun Gakkai, 83* (September), 105-117.

Santomi, N. (1977). Minsei-Iin no Kaikyuteki Kiban. *Ritsumeikan Keixaigaku, 26,* 3, 517-518.

Ueda, K. (1967). Minsei-Iin Seidoron Jyosetsu. *Bukyodaigaku 1* (September), 1-24.

Yoshida, K. (1979). *Showa Shakai Jigyo Shi* (5th ed.) Mineruba-Shobo.

13

CAB IN NEW DELHI, INDIA
"In the Service of the Citizen"

RAMESH CHANDRA MISHRA
MEERA AGARWAL

In carrying out its stated mission "in the service of the citizen," the Citizens Advice Bureau (CAB) in New Delhi conducts a vigorous advocacy program. In addition to serving as a committed advocate for the individual citizen, CAB has been instrumental as a catalyst in generating a series of joint advocacy organizations during the decade "in the service of weaker sections of society."

This chapter will deal with the origins of CAB, its structure and staffing, and its program of services dating from its inception in 1966. The central role of the CAB as citizen advocate is apparent in its own range of services and its leadership role in the founding of advocacy organizations such as Citizen Action and the Council of Legal Aid and Advice. CAB efforts to establish an ombudsman system also are related to its advocacy stance.

The major content of this chapter will deal with CAB involvement in the relation to case advocacy as well as aspects of program and policy advocacy. But first a brief overview of CAB beginnings and its esteemed founder, Shri D. D. Diwan.

CAB: COMMITMENT TO SERVICE AND ADVOCACY

The suggestion for CAB in India was first proposed by Shri D. D. Diwan at the India International Center, Delhi, on Nov. 6, 1960. The lecture was well attended and presided by Shri Morarji Desai, exprime minister of India. Shri Diwan ended his lecture with an appeal for altruism and a quotation from Dr. Albert Schweitzer, Nobel Prize winner:

> It is not enough merely to exist. It's not enough to say, I am earning enough to live and support my family. I do my work well. I am a good father. I am a good husband. I am a good Church man. This is very well. But you must do something more. Seek always to do some good—somewhere. Every man has to seek in his own way to make his own self more noble and to realize his own true worth. You must give some time to your fellowmen. Even if it is a little thing, do something for those who have need of man's help, something for which you get no pay but the privilege of doing it.

HISTORY

Following a thorough study of CABs in England, Shri D. D. Diwan set up a Citizens Advice Bureau in East Patel Nagar, New Delhi, patterned at the CAB in England. Diwan was well aware that while CABs were originally set up to meet the post war needs of rehabilitation after World War II, they became established as vital bases for linkages to human services.

Diwan became committed to the notion of operating a CAB in New Delhi, which could be staffed by "good samaritans who have sympathy for individual problems and public ailments." Thus, the CAB that was registered in 1967 (under the Societies Act XXI of 1860, Punjab Amendment Act, 1957) was designed to accomplish a dual purpose: (a) to advise the citizens with their personal problems, and (b) to help redress their grievances against "red-tapism, Draconian Laws, inefficient and pathetic government machinery, sometimes bordering on corruption and maladministration."

STRUCTURE AND STAFFING

The CAB is an independent, nonsectarian, nonpolitical, and non-profit organization. The staff consists of a devoted band of advisors and volunteers drawn from a wide cross-section of the society and different walks of life, i.e. jurists, lawyers, doctors, engineers, educators, psychologists, paralegal and paramedical personnel, so-cial workers, and housewives. These advisors offer free and expert advice to the citizens and are under an oath of confidentiality which reads as follows:

> I, _____, solemnly affirm and declare that I shall maintain the secrecy of the facts which come to my knowledge as an advisor and worker of CAB and shall render the services in advisory capacity without expectation of personal gain.

Volunteers are selected on the basis of their mature judgment, fund of knowledge, and ability to render sound advice, in confidence, to any member of the public on any question "that may be a cause for trouble or worry."

The main office of CAB is located in a community hall and is administered by Shri D. D. Diwan, founder and director/chairman, among others. Working hours are between 5:30 p.m. and 7:30 p.m. The hours are scheduled for the convenience of the citizens, who are usually free in the evening to attend to their personal problems. A few other community halls in the metropolis as well as the offices of certain advisors also are utilized for limited periods by prior appointment. The inquirers are required to fill in a case card, the contents of which are as follows:

> Case card . . .   Confidential.
>
> (The advice given has no legal binding or any other liability.)
>
> Name of Advisor: Subject head
>
> Name of Enquirer: No.
>
> Record of Interview/
>
> Correspondence etc.
>
> Signature of Enquirer.

CAB is supported financially by subscriptions from members, voluntary contributions, donations, and gifts from India and abroad. Donations to CAB are exempted from income tax under the Indian income tax rules. Some grants-in-aid also are available from various statutory bodies.

One of the major accomplishments of the CAB has been its dynamic role in spearheading advocacy programs through its own range of activities and through joint action with other advocacy agencies, which it helped to create during the decade of the 1970s. The following discussion on advocacy encompasses CAB's agency program and the advocacy programs in which CAB has participated as a catalyst and collaborator.

CATALYST FOR OTHER ADVOCACY ORGANIZATIONS

CAB and "Citizen Action"

Encouraged with the positive response from the citizenry in regard to the utilization of CAB advisory services, Shri D. D. Dowan conceived the idea of an organization similar to the program platform of Common Cause in the United States to help the citizenry in redressing their grievances. Following Diwan's visits to Europe and the United States, the notion of a citizens action organization based on the precepts of Common Cause seemed very desirable.

Thus, Citizen Action (CA) was brought into existence in December 1973, founded "on the faith that the rights and obligations of citizenship can be fulfilled only by an aware, vigilant, and concerned citizenry."

Citizen Action was registered in July 1974 under the Societies Act of XXI of 1960 and operates as a close associate of CAB. It is committed to foster and inculcate a widely shared sense of civic responsibility. Common Cause endeavors to maintain public vigilance against "inroads from any quarter." It was noted that Citizen Action stands for secularism, democracy and social justice, and strives to ensure justice and fair play for the underpriviledged and "weaker section of the society" while preserving the administration of democratic process.

Similar to CAB, Citizen Action is a nonpolitical voluntary organization staffed by volunteers, both professional and non-professional, who are selected on the bases of "competence, mature experience, and social commitment," Citizen Action aims at making authorities, administrators, and legislators responsive to the people by facilitating representation and attempting to redress the legitimate grievances of the citizen. By promoting law reforms, social change, and legal aid and advice to indigents, Citizen Action seeks to fulfill its mission "for the common cause of common man."

The role of the CA-CAB collaborative program in promoting case and policy advocacy will be discussed in greater detail in the following section on advocacy.

CAB and the Indian Council of Legal Aid and Advice

Through its Chairman, Shri D. D. Diwan, the New Delhi CAB was also instrumental in founding the Indian Council of Legal Aid and Advice in 1975. The founding president was Shri H. R. Gokhale, then law minister of India; Shri D. D. Diwan also was a founding council member. The council is housed on the Supreme Court premises and offers free legal aid advice, particularly to the poor.

Through its operational program, CAB has become aware of discriminatory legislation, which appears to be inimical to the interest of the citizens in regard to some of the current acts, rules, and regulations. Thereupon, a Legal Reforms Panel has been set up to study and suggest amendments or changes to these in order to make ongoing legislation more responsive to the needs of the public. At present this panel is engrossed in examining laws which on prima facie evidence "appear to be pro-establishment and anti-public and also a heritage from the colonial past."

CAB and the Institution of Lokpal and Lokayuktas (Ombudsman)

As early as 1968, Shri D. D. Diwan submitted evidence before the Joint Committee of Parliament in regard to the advisability of establishing an Ombudsman System (Lokpal and Lokayuktas). A model draft of the bill was sent to the central government through the Administrative Reforms Committee, with which Diwan was associated at that time. The Government of India has deliberated over the provision of Lokpal and Lokayuktas, which would be charged to follow up the complaints of citizens against the administration. However, successive bills have been allowed to lapse over the years.

CAB is currently trying to function in a twofold capacity: (1) to look after the complaints of citizens against the administration; and (2) to help the individual citizens in solving day-to-day problems. Thus the two institutions (Ombudsman and CAB) have quite different functional fields through which they redress the grievance of the public.

CAB is looking forward to that day when the Government of India passes a law creating the institution of Lokpal and Lokayuktas based on studies conducted by the Institute of Public Administration, which is concerned about citizen-administration relationships. Thus, the role of CAB as a guide and helper of citizens can be expanded considerably, given a working relationship with the institution of Lokpal and Lokayuktas.

ADVOCACY PROGRAMS (CAB AND JOINT PROGRAMS)

Case Advocacy

The cases dealt with by CAB are of a diverse nature, but relate primarily to personal, domestic, and financial-economic problems in household management as well as at the workplace. It has been acknowledged that"succor to the distressed" may imply "acting as a safety valve through the simple act of listening sympathetically."

In relation to marriage and dowry, CAB staff also offer advice on separation, maintenance, and divorce. CAB advisors succeed in arranging marriages without dowry and, in some cases, where the marital harmony is disrupted, the husband and parents-in-law of the brides are persuaded to terminate the marital bond and return the dowry (when taken) to the brides.

Legal information and advice to individual inquirers is a major investment of CAB activities. Disputes between landlord and tenant dealing with lease, rent and repairs are handled by CAB frequently. Tax on earned or unearned income allowances as well as sales taxes are handled by CAB, as are questions concerning property tax and land ownership.

Requests for information on life, property, and household insurance are made to CAB often. When problems arise that involve clarification and legal action on consumer purchases, credit sales, and conditions of employment, a significant number of court cases are withdrawn by the litigants at the insistence of CAB advisors or have been settled amicably out of courts.

CAB guidance is particularly helpful in providing information and follow-through on service and veteran benefits; also pensions that may or may not be service-connected. CAB is also responsive to the requests of citizens regarding jobs and employment, as well as opportunities for education and training. Information on health and medical problems and appropriate referrals to health agencies are vital areas of CAB involvement that have led to public health campaigns for environmental health, anti-pollution measures, and food protection.

Case advisors from CAB have arbitrated successfully in numerous cases among the members of public who aproached CAB for this purpose. At times, CAB has resorted to action in order to establish greater equity among employees of various companies.

For example, intervention on behalf of the employees of Martin Burn Railways, a private company, was initiated by CAB after its nationalization and merger with Eastern Railways to bring to par the seniority, salaries, and other facilities of the employees of Martin Burn Railways with that of the employees of the Eastern Railways.

Advice rendered to persons in distress often centers on the appropriate agency to approach. Advisors also help in filling out required forms and help in understanding the rules, regulations, and social laws, which are often complex. CAB also engages in the redressal of citizens' grievances and even files writ petitions as public interest litigation.

Program Advocacy

A major feature of CAB is its legal literary program, which urges citizens to "know your rights and protect yourself." Legal literacy programs were launched by CAB in 1979 and have subsequently made an enormous impact on mass literacy in the field of human rights and entitlements.

CAB has worked closely with Legal Aid Societies and Citizen Action in the production of a series of booklets that deal with information on citizen rights and benefits. These booklets are distributed throughout the country and have been translated in many respective regional languages.

The booklets, before publication, are screened by a panel of legal experts and also by Shri D. D. Diwan, director of CAB, who examines them from the citizen's point of view to see that the language is easily understood by laymen.

It is important to note that the Delhi Legal Aid and Advice Board, a government body that also provides free legal aid to the public, has adopted these booklets and published as many as 10,000 copies of each booklet in a second edition, which is available in English as well as Hindi language. These booklets are distributed free of cost to all citizens to apprise them of their legal rights. Several provinces of India also have shown keen interest in adopting the booklets, which are cosponsored by CAB and other advocacy agencies. Thus, the Legal Literacy Programs of CAB are reaching every corner of the country.

The credit for launching this program of providing informative literature to the citizen is given to D. D. Diwan, who is referred to as "a moving spirit of the common cause of public vigilance and participation."

Following is a brief description of the first four pamphlets that have been circulated "with the faith that the spread of civic awareness and the dissemination of legal literacy will strengthen the sinews of (our) democratic system."

The first booklet, entitled "Citizen and The Police," was authored by Dr. N. R. Madhava Manon, secretary of the Bar Council of India Trust and member of the Committee for Implementation of Legal Aid (a statutory body).

This booklet, written in a simple and direct question-and-answer format, emphasizes "the service role of police in modern times." Attention is called to the legal and constitutional limitations of the police as well as the restrictions of police power. Some possible remedies are offered to a citizen "when aggrieved by the unjust expertise of police powers." The pamphlet serves as a primer for the citizen in dealing with "the most important enforcement agency of the government, namely the police." Taking a strong advocacy stance, N. R. Mandava Menon, convener and editor of the Legal Literacy Project under CAB auspices, insists that "every policeman is a citizen in uniform and every citizen is a policeman without uniform."

To direct the citizens for further action if indicated, referral agencies are listed in each of the pamphlets for contact "if you have any legal/departmental problem and your annual income from all sources does not exceed *R's* 5000/ or you belong to a scheduled caste/ scheduled tribe or you are a woman or child."

The second booklet, entitled "Compensation to Victims of Road Accidents," was authored by Shri T. U. Mehta, ex-chief justice of Himachel Pradesh High Court, India, and now senior advocate of the Supreme Court of India.

Because road accidents constitute the greatest single source of death and maiming of human beings in India today, and because in the majority of cases the killed or injured belong to the lower socioeconomic strata in society who are often uninformed about "just compensation of loss," this booklet explains the rights of citizens involved in road accidents. The provisions of the Motor Vehicle Act (Act IV of 1939) are presented in a question-and-answer format that is in "language free from professional jargon."

As is noted in the foreword of the pamphlet, the plethora of laws that already exist are of little value, if not know or understood. In fact, it is stated that "if legislative work can usher in an era of plenty, this ancient land would have long become the Ganges of milk and honey."

Therefore, it is important that legal literature assume a high priority to make citizens conscious of rights and obligations.

The third booklet in the series, entitled "Women and the Law," was co-authored by Dr. Meera Agarwal, advocate of the Supreme Court and member of the Governing Council of the Indian Law Institute, and Dr. N. R. Madhava Menon, Secretary, under the joint auspices of CAB and CA. This brief pamphlet presents the complex theme of the rights of women in matrimony in a simple and intelligible format.

In the introduction of this publication, it is stated that the laws have been enacted to protect the rights of women in marriage. However, "in the present social set-up, women stand to lose more on broken marriages." Moreover, different marriage laws pertain to different religious groups. Although Article 44 of the Constitution proposes a uniform civil code, and the Special Marriage Act of 1954 enables persons belonging to different religious groups to opt for a Civil Marriage, women are still bound to the rigid codes of divorce laws, customs, and religions and are often unaware of their matrimonial rights.

For example, whereas giving a dowry had been a widely prevalent practice at the time of marriage, today giving and accepting dowry is a serious offense, punishable under the Prevention of Dowry Act of 1962. Although 13 legislative acts are listed in the pamphlet, dating from 1869 to 1973, it is acknowledged that "due to lack of awareness of the legal provisions and problems relating to access to justice, these benefits have not reached the bulk of Indian women."

The fourth booklet authored by Shri J. C. Batra, Bar-at-Law and Advocate Supreme Court of India, was entitled "Landlord/ Tenant Relationship Under Delhi Rent Control." D. D. Diwan notes in the preface to this pamphlet that fifty percent of the CAB's cases relate to tenant/landlord problems and that both tenants and landlord are generally unaware of their rights and obligations. The content of this little booklet, written in a simple, clear style, relates specifically to salient aspects of the laws that affect landlords and tenants under the Delhi Rent Control Act. As the rent laws vary from state to state, citizens residing outside Delhi are advised to consult lawyers regarding the legalities that pertain to their respective areas. The hope expressed by the chief justice of the Delhi High Court is that through legal literacy, more disputes will be settled out of court for the mutual benefit of the parties involved. Thereby courts can also be spared from the flood of litigation that so often occurs.

Another publication currently under consideration is a booklet entitled "Health and Nutrition for the Poor." Related to the campaign for legal literacy is the consumer protection movement CAB has fostered through a separate ministry of consumer affairs, which it has helped to create, called the ministry of Civil Supplies. As a consequence of CAB consumer advocacy, some of the suggestions of CAB have already been implemented, resulting in the following:

(1) Better rationed articles are supplied to the public;
(2) Market prices of essential consumer items are published in the newspapers, telecast on television, and broadcast on radio;
(3) Price tags are fixed to the articles for sale.

"Q" System at the Bus Stops

An important aspect of CAB's program is its involvement with interagency activities in cooperation with social welfare organizations operating in various parts of the country. Some of these agencies are concerned with the plight of women in India, i.e., the All-India Housewife Federation (Women's Vigilance Committee, Mahila Dakshita Smiti), the Women's Protection Committee (Nari Rasksha Samith), and Friends of Women (Saheli). CAB is also closely associated with consumer organizations such as the New India Movement, Federal of Consumer Protection Societies, and the Consumer Education and Research Center. Members of the CAB managing committee also maintain links with other vital social agencies such as the Delhi Social Welfare Advisory Board and the Delhi Municipal Corporation.

To promote the CAB program, the CAB director is frequently called upon to deliver lectures, conduct seminars, and participate in public broadcasts and other mass media in India and in many countries abroad. For example, ongoing communication has been established with the National Association of Citizens Advice Bureaus in London, the Center for the Study of Responsive Law in Washington, D.C., and numerous social welfare organizations in Indonesia, Hong Kong, Singapore, and Israel.

Policy Advocacy

In addition to providing actual and practical help to the individual citizen, CAB is involved in the process of redressing grievances as a class action and projecting a plan for improved social conditions. Working closely with the Citizens Action, CAB has succeeded in functioning as an advisory body to governmental as well as non-governmental agencies in the interest of trying "to better the lot of a downtrodden and oppressed class of society" and "to make their day-to-day existence rather less of a struggle."

Therefore, a series of 14 recommendations were submitted by CAB and CA to the Honorable prime minister of India who, finding the suggestions noteworthy, referred the program to the Planning Commission for scrutiny and report on September 10, 1974. These points dealt with the creation of a "cooperative society" and are summarized below:

> All lands (Government and surplus) be brought under Co-Operatives. Individual will be lessees in perpetuity or 99 years. The allottees can also lease out to the Society their lands, in accordance with the law of primogeniture. The society should also possess a part of land, the profits of which should also be shared equally by all members and their dependents having prior right to work on the Co-operative farms.

> All welfare services like schools, hospitals etc. will be free as also watch and ward. The local police will function through the Society and no civil suit will be taken to the court.

The plan proposed creation of small model towns that would be tax-free and could provide joint utility services at cheaper rates. It was also suggested that community kitchens be established to save national time lost in cooking the whole day by each family. To finance the Cooperative Society, areas should be earmarked on the fringe of the town for light industries to be established with the help of industrialists.

The educated people should be made supervisors in the training of unskilled labor and also implement the program of "Each One Teach One" to promote total literacy.

To keep housing functional and at reasonable prices, local materials should be used for the contruction of inexpensive houses such as durable barracks, which may be well maintained because of pride in individual ownership. The aim of the Cooperative Society should be toward self containment and self-sufficiency (by utilizing local supply of water, power, and fertilizer) and to be least affected by either strikes or even catastrophes such as war.

While the above recommendations are at the present time proposals, the CAB has involved the Parliament to give consideration to them. It is especially important to note that CAB is quite often invited by different parliamentary committees to express its views and "tender evidence" on bills under review such as the Lokpal (Ombudsman) Bill, the Prevention of Food Adulteration Act, Rent Control Acts, the Dowry Prohibition Act, and the Amendment to the Hindu Marriage Act regarding the irretrievable breakdown of marriage.

On the other hand, CAB has taken the initiative to apprise Parliament of problems that require policy changes and legislative action to improve socioeconomic conditions of the citizenry, provide better nutrition and health for the poor, and "tackle the grievances of the citizens" in a wide variety of public concerns such as traffic problems, atmospheric pollution, poor sanitation, as well as measures to prevent waterlogging on the streets and the explosion of gas cylinders.

Also, CAB has urged the banning of "Kesari Dal," a kind of lentil, which is also known as "Killer Dal."

CAB has also urged governmental action against pharmaceutical producers to control the price of medicines, and also to reduce repair charges on TV sets. In general, it can be concluded that CAB's cooperation with government serves as a window through which authorities can see the effect of their laws, rules, and regulations.

CONCLUSION

The future of CAB will continue to rely on the quality and charisma of its executive leadership, which has proved to be vital in its initiation, implementation, and operation. Above all, however, CAB will be dependent on the combined services and commitment of professional advisors and volunteers who constitute the lifeline of CAB.

"They alone live who live for others" (an axiom from the Vedanta).

14

THE OMBUDSMAN
Watchdog of Legality and Equity
in Administration

ULF LUNDVIK

Even in the most democratic of all countries there is a danger that the administrative authorities, in their zeal to achieve the goals set out for their activities or from other less respectable motives, may exceed their jurisdiction and encroach upon the rights and liberties of the citizens. More and more responsibilities appear to be entrusted to the formal authorities and, consequently, administration becomes unwieldy. All administrators are not competent, and some are overzealous, unfair, or even dishonest. No wonder that the questions of how to control the administration, and how to oversee the officials to ensure that they respect the principles of legality and equity have become universal problems.

THE RIGHTS OF APPEAL AND REVIEW

Various approaches to achieve these principles have been explored. In many countries there exists, generally or in specific cases, a right of appeal from one level of administration officials to the next higher level, and so on to the top. Administrative tribunals sometimes serve at lower administrative levels, while sometimes they hear cases only on appeal. When they hear appeals, administrative tribunals can be considered as an external means of controlling the administration.

Almost everywhere, the administration is also subject to some form of judicial review. In the common law countries this review is exercised by the ordinary courts of law and is mainly restricted to questions of legality. Common law courts do not consider the wisdom or merits of discretionary decisions. In other countries, such as France, the Federal Republic of Germany, Sweden, and Finland, the review is exercised by special courts for administrative law. These courts usually consider not only questions of law but also questions of fact and expediency.

There is, however, another totally different system of external control of the administration, which has attracted considerable attention in recent decades and has been adopted by a great many countries in various parts of the world. This is the system of the ombudsman, which is the subject of this chapter.

THE OMBUDSMAN—HISTORICAL BACKGROUND

The ombudsman institution has been defined as an office established by constitution or statute and headed by an independent high-level public official who is responsible to the legislature. He receives complaints from aggrieved persons against government agencies, officials, and employees, or acts on his own motion, and has the power to investigate, recommend corrective action, and issue reports (Bernard Frank: "The Ombudsman and Human Rights-Revisited," in *Israel Yearbook on Human Rights,* vol. 6/1976).

While there were counterparts to the ombudsman as far back in history as the Han dynasty in China (202 B.C.-A.D. 221) and under the reign of the Caliph Omar (A.D. 634-644) in Arabia and the kingdom of Aragon in medieval Spain, the institution in its modern form originated in Sweden. The constitution adopted in 1809 in that country contained a provision for the election by Parliament of a "Justitieombudsman" (ombudsman for justice). He was to be a man "of known legal ability and outstanding integrity."[1] His duty was to supervise, in his capacity as a representative of Parliament, the observance of laws and statutes by all officials and judges.

The constitution was to be supplemented by an act of instruction to the ombudsman. Once this was passed, Parliament on March 1, 1810, elected the first ombudsman, Baron L. A. Mannerheim, who held office until 1823. The ombudsman supervised all state officials, both civil servants and officers of the armed forces until 1915, when a separate office was created for a military ombudsman. In 1957 the ombudsman's jurisdiction was enlarged to include municipal officials. In 1968 the offices of the ombudsman and of the military ombudsman were merged into one office consisting of three ombudsmen, all of equal status. Since 1976, the office has been made up of four ombudsmen, one of whom has status as administrative director of the office or chief ombudsman.

Meanwhile, the ombudsman system had expanded. In 1919, Finland, upon gaining its independence from the rule of the Russian czar, established an ombudsman office closely following the Swedish model. The new Danish constitution of 1953 contained provisions for the election of an ombudsman and in 1955 the first Danish ombudsman, Professor Stephan Hurwitz, was elected. He soon began to write and lecture in English about his office and thus stimulated an interest in the concept of the ombudsman in the English-speaking world. At the request of the United Nations, Professor Hurwitz wrote a paper about the ombudsman system for the seminar on "Judicial and Other Remedies Against the Illegal Exercise or Abuse of Authority," which was held at Kandy, Ceylon, in 1959.

In New Zealand, the problem of how best to control the administration had been discussed even before Professor Hurwitz assumed office as ombudsman in Denmark. Hurwitz's paper for the Kandy seminar was read by prominent New Zealand lawyers and politicians, as some of his previous articles had been. When preparing for the general elections of 1960, the National Party included in their party platform the establishment of an ombudsman office. The party won the election, formed the new government, and in 1962 New Zealand became the first country outside Scandinavia to introduce the ombudsman system. The system soon proved its worth in the hands of the skillful first incumbent, Sir Guy Richardson Powles. When it was found that an ombudsman could work with success in a common law country, the institution began to spread throughout the world rapidly. In 1967, Great Britain adopted the system in a modified form and two of the Canadian provinces appointed ombudsmen. Australia and other British Commonwealth countries soon followed suit. Also, countries outside the English speaking world adopted the system, including France, Switzerland, Austria, and Portugal. Today, ombudsmen are to be found in nearly every part of the world, although as yet not in every country. They work on the national, state, provincial, or regional level, and some ombudsmen operate on a city level.

As ombudsmen work under many different conditions and in diversified settings, a total overview is beyond the scope of this discussion. This chapter will concentrate mainly on the Scandinavian ombudsmen (particularly the ones in Sweden and Finland), and the ombudsmen in the British Commonwealth.

(1) The Scandinavian Model

It was previously mentioned that the Swedish ombudsman was—and still is—authorized to supervise judges of the courts of law. The jurisdiction of the Finnish ombudsman also includes judges. However, in both countries, the main emphasis now is the supervision of the administrative authorities.

In Denmark and, subsequently, in all other countries which have adopted the ombudsman system, the courts of law are exempt from the ombudsman's jurisdiction. Administrative tribunals are usually, although not everywhere, exempt from the ombudsman's supervision. Other differences in the various ombudsman's purview may be mentioned. Some supervise municipal authorities, while military authorities in most countries are excluded from the ombudsman's supervision. In some countries, there is a special ombudsman for supervision of the armed forces, and for other administrative settings. In some countries the ombudsman can initiate an investigation on his own motion, particularly in Sweden and Finland, where many cases are self-initiated. In most countries, however, the ombudsman has not or does not exercise such a right to any great extent.

The role of the ombudsman as a watchdog of legality can be seen clearly in the wording of the present Swedish constitution of 1974, where, in Chapter 12, Article 6, it is said that Parliament shall elect one or more ombudsmen for the purpose of supervising, under instructions determined by Parliament, the application in the public service of laws and other statutes. Similar words are used in the Finnish constitution. The Danish constitution states briefly that the ombudsman shall supervise the civil and military government administration. In Norway it is clearly defined by statute that the ombudsman "shall endeavor to ensure that the public administration does not commit any injustice against any citizen and that civil servants and others in the service of the administration do not commit errors or neglect their duties." In the newly enacted rules for the ombudsman of the Kanton of Zurich in Switzerland, general guidelines note that "the ombudsman oversees that administrative authorities proceed legally and equitably."

(2) The Anglo-Saxon Model

In the Anglo-Saxon countries, the statutes are differently worded, yet their purport is essentially the same as that of the statutes mentioned above. The New Zealand Ombudsmen Act 1975 (a consolidation and amendment of the first act of 1962, which served as a model for most other Anglo-Saxon ombudsman acts) indicates in section 13, subsection 1, that

> it shall be a function of the Ombudsmen to investigate any decision or recommendation made, or any act done or omitted, whether before or after the passing of this Act, relating to a matter of administration and affecting any person or body of persons in his or its personal capacity, in or by any of the Departments or organisations named or specified in Parts I and II of the First Schedule to this Act, or by any committee (other than a committee of the whole) or subcommittee of any organisation named or specified in Part III of the First Schedule to this Act, or by any officer, employee, or member of any such Department or organisation in his capacity as such officer, employee, or member.

and in section 22, subsections 1 and 2 it is specified that

> (1) The provisions of this section shall apply in every case where, after making any investigation under this Act, an Ombudsman is of opinion that the decision, recommendation, act, or ommission which was the subject-matter of the investigation
>
> (a) Appears to have been contrary to law; or
>
> (b) Was unreasonable, unjust, oppressive, or improperly discriminatory, or was in accordance with a rule of law or a provision of any Act, regulation, or bylaw or a practice that is or may be unreasonable, unjust, oppressive, or improperly discriminatory; or
>
> (c) Was based wholly or partly on a mistake of law or fact; or
>
> (d) Was wrong.
>
> (2) The provisions of this section shall also apply in any case where an Ombudsman is of opinion that in the making of the decision or recommendation, in the doing or omission of the act, a discretionary power has been exercised for an improper purpose or on irrelevant grounds or on the taking into account of irrelevant considerations, or that, in the case of a decision made in the exercise of any discretionary power, reasons should have been given for the decision.

And finally, in section 22, subsection 3 it is stipulated, inter alia, that

> (3) If in any case to which this section applies an Ombudsman is of opinion
>
> (a) That the matter should be referred to the appropriate authority for further consideration; or

(b) That the omission should be rectified; or

(c) That the decision should be cancelled or varied; or

(d) That any practice on which the decision, recommendation, act, or omission was based should be altered; or

(e) That any law on which the decision, recommendation, act, or omission was based should be reconsidered; or

(f) That reasons should have been given for the decison; or

(g) That any other steps should be taken

The Ombudsman shall report his opinion, and his reasons therefor, to the appropriate Department or organisation, and make such recommendations as he thinks fit.

The New Zealand Act also contains the provision that if the ombudsman's recommendations are not followed, the ombudsman may notify the prime minister and Parliament, thus making the recommendation public.

Most Anglo-Saxon countries, states, or provinces have provisions that are essentially similar, though significant differences are to be found. It should, however, be mentioned that in the United Kingdom of Great Britain and Northern Ireland all acts containing provisions for parliamentary commissioners, commissioners for local government, and the Northern Ireland Commissioner for Complaints restrict the ombudsman's right to intervene in cases where "injustice has been caused to the person aggrieved in consequence of maladministration." The health service commissioners for England and Wales may intervene when the person aggrieved has suffered injustice or hardship in consequence of a failure or in consequence of maladministration. These provisions have been the subject of much controversy. The expression "maladministration" is currently, however, given a very wide interpretation and the difference in this respect between the ombudsman in the United Kingdom and those in New Zealand, Australia, and Canada is hardly perceptible.

COMMON TASK AND OBJECTIVES

All ombudsmen tend to pursue a more or less impossible task, that is, to promote legality in the administration. They even go a step further than that by trying to raise the standards of the administration in the interest of fairness and equity. The Hon. Mr. Justice Carl Clement, in an address to the First International Ombudsman Conference, held in Edmonton, Alberta, Canada in September 1976, clearly pointed out that "there has been now created a new area of jurisprudence, . . . guided by principles that go beyond those of the human activity."

The ombudsmen, in fulfilling their mandate, are not empowered to quash or modify an administrative decision. Generally, an ombudsman can only recommend that the matter be reconsidered, that some kind of remedial action be taken, or that existing rules or regulations be amended. An ombudsman's authority is, therefore, primarily a moral one. To what extent he can succeed depends largely upon the respect that he commands.

The ombudsman of the City of Zurich in Switzerland has, in a paper presented at a meeting of the Legal Affairs Committee of the Council of Europe (Paris, April 18-19, 1974), set out the objectives he seeks to achieve as follows:

> Informatory control: the Ombudsman keeps himself informed of what is going on with the secondary purpose of making the administrative authorities aware that they are being observed;
>
> Corrective control: the Ombudsman seeks to rectify faults on the part of the administrative authorities by recommending the competent bodies to alter the decision;
>
> Directive control: The Ombudsman urges the official concerned not to repeat his error or ineptitude.

While these objectives could be said to be the common objectives of all ombudsmen, some differences in their priorities and their general approach to the problem can be discerned.

(1) The Scandinavian Model

Originally in Sweden, the ombudsman was mainly a prosecutor—a man whose duty it was to prosecute before the competent court of law any official who had committed a fault. The constitution of 1809 expressly said that the ombudsman should supervise the application of laws and other statutes by judges, government officials, and other civil servants, and prosecute those who in their official capacity had committed offenses or neglected to fulfill their duties. During the nineteenth century, prosecution was the ombudsman's main weapon against bureaucracy. This system must be seen against the background of the then existing penal rules, which made it a criminal offense for a civil servant to neglect his duties. Gradually, however, prosecution was instituted less frequently. A difference of attitude on the part of courts and that of the ombudsman became apparent. In the case of a minor offense, the courts had begun to acquit the offender, saying that while he had behaved or acted wrongly, his behavior still did not amount to a criminal offense for which he should be punished. The ombudsman then in similar cases found it not worthwhile to prosecute; instead, he closed the file with a "reminder" or an "admonishment" to the official, expressing the ombudsman's criticism.

Finally, in 1975, an amendment of the Penal Code was made (to become effective from Jan. 1, 1976) specifying that faults such as breach of duty or neglect of duty are punishable only if the fault was intentional or due to gross negligence and committed in the exercise of public authority. Therefore, in many cases brought before the ombudsman, prosecution was no longer possible. Instead of prosecution, the ombudsman could now institute disciplinary proceedings. So far, however, this weapon has not been wielded to any great extent. The main source of strength of the ombudsman is his right to criticize the actions or omissions of the administration when he finds that matters have not been handled in the way that they should have been. He can, of course, also recommend that the matter be rectified in one way or another.

Finland's ombudsman system closely follows the Swedish model. The ombudsman is authorized to institute prosecutions and disciplinary proceedings. So far there have been no amendments of the penal rules reducing the ombudsman's option of resorting to prosecution, as there has been in Sweden. Yet the tendency in Finland has been not to prosecute except in cases of very gross misdemeanor. The ombudsman's main responsibility is to criticize any official found at fault.

When the ombudsman system was transferred to Denmark, it was adopted in a slightly different form. As has been mentioned already, the ombudsman was not given jurisdiction over the courts of law, nor was he authorized to act as a prosecutor. However, he can order a prosecution to be entered and he can, furthermore, order the competent authorities to institute disciplinary proceedings. Such orders have to date been issued only on a few occasions. (The ombudsman's unrestricted right to criticize constitutes his major action.)

In Norway, the ombudsman cannot even *order* prosecution or the institution of disciplinary proceedings. The only thing he can do in that direction, apart from expressing criticism, is to *recommend* that prosecution or disciplinary proceedings be instituted. Likewise, in all other countries that have adopted the ombudsman system, the ombudsman has not been empowered to act as a prosecutor or to issue orders that disciplinary proceedings be instituted. In almost all countries he can, however, make recommendations, and such a recommendation could be for the institution of prosecution or disciplinary proceedings. Moreover, in most of the acts modeled after the New Zealand pattern, there is a provision (here quoted from the Alberta Ombudsman Act) that

> if, during or after an investigation, the ombudsman is of opinion that there is evidence of any breach of duty or misconduct on the part of any officer or employee of any department or agency, he shall refer the matter to the deputy minister of the department or the administrative head of the agency, as the case may be. (Alberta Ombudsman Act)

The purport of such a referral is clearly seen in section 28 of the New South Wales (Australia) Ombudsman Act, where it is said that the ombudsman shall report his opinion when he finds "that a public authority is or may be guilty of misconduct in the course of his functions to such an extent as, in the opinion of the ombudsman, may warrant dismissal, removal or punishment".

In this context it should be mentioned that the Northern Ireland Commissioner for Complaints Act 1969 contains a unique provision of the following content, when the ombudsman (commissioner for complaints) finds that a complainant has suffered injustice in consequence of maladministration, the complainant can secure redress by going to the county court, which will award him damages on the basis of the ombudsman's report.

The fact that the Swedish ombudsman originally was a prosecutor still affects his approach to the cases. Upon the referral of a case, the Swedish ombudsman—as well as his colleagues in Finland, Denmark, and Norway—will ask, when confronted with a case where injustice seems to have been done, who is responsible and what action shall be taken. As has already been said, the Scandinavian ombudsmen's main weapon is "criticism." As this criticism is pronounced in a public document and more often than not printed in the ombudsman's annual report to Parliament, which is widely read in administrative circles, the impact of the ombudsman's criticism is considerable and far-reaching to the culprit and the public at large. The criticism also serves as a warning to other officials who may be confronted with similar problems. The main empahsis is thus the judgment of whether the action or omission of action was right or wrong, and therefore subject to the ombudsman's criticism. This does not mean, however, that Scandinavian ombudsmen are indifferent to the sufferings a citizen may have sustained through wrongful actions or interactions of the administration. They occasionally recommend that remedial action be taken. That such recommendations are not more frequent is mainly due to the fact that the administrative authorities usually rectify the matter on their own motion as soon as they become aware of the fault committed and—it should be added—aware that the matter has been referred as a complaint to the ombudsman. Moreover, as will be explained subsequently in more detail, the ombudsmen frequently make general recommendations for the promotion of good administration. For instance, they may recommend the amendment of existing laws and regulations.

The Scandinavian ombudsmen's attitude has its background in old traditions and, in Sweden and Finland, in the particular penal responsibility of civil servants and judges.

(2) The Anglo-Saxon Model

Traditions are different in the Anglo-Saxon countries. The theory seems to be that the civil service is anonymous, and that therefore the administrator is the sole responsible person who has to bear the blame if something goes amiss. At least publicly, the individual civil servant should not be criticized for an error of judgment. The ombudsman's interventions are therefore supposed to be directed against the department or agency concerned, not against an individual. This can be illustrated by the words of the attorney general of New Zealand, when speaking for the government at the first reading of the Ombudsman Bill (Aug. 29, 1961).

> The first duty of the (Ombudsman) is to investigate decisions and recommendations, and not actions of individuals. He is not a Gestapo. If he finds out something that a public servant has done or should not have done that is not primarily his business. His duty would be to report to the head of the Department concerned, and let him take action. He is not concerned with discipline within the service. He is concerned with decisions in so far as they affect an individual outside.

Under these circumstances it is understandable that Anglo-Saxon ombudsmen have quite a different approach to problems. Instead of asking, "Who is responsible for the fault committed and what action should be taken against him?" they are likely to say, "My complainant surely has suffered injustice; what can I do to set the matter right again?" A study of various Anglo-Saxon ombudsmen's annual reports indicates that they seldom pronounce criticism, particularly not against an individual official, but that they frequently recommend remedial action (if such has not been already taken during the course of the investigation) such as the reconsideration of an application, the payment of a sum of money as a compensation, or merely the sending of a written apology. They also quite frequently make general recommendations for furthering good administration. The recommendation of punishment for an official found at fault is seldom implemented.

The effects of the Anglo-Saxon ombudsmen's interventions in individual cases are, no doubt, highly satisfactory to the persons aggrieved. Very often, redress is obtained at an early stage of the investigation without any formal recommendations being made by the ombudsman. Whether such interventions can be said to promote legality and equity in the administration in a wider sense remains to be discussed. The agency conceding that it has committed an error that is now being rectified is, of course, not likely to repeat the error. The criticism that although not openly expressed, underlies the recommendation normally will be brought to the attention of all public servants who are confronted with similar problems. However, the carefully worded criticism contained in a recommendation by an Anglo-Saxon ombudsman can hardly be expected to have the same direct and widespread impact as the open criticism pronounced by Scandinavian Ombudsmen.

POWERS GRANTED TO OMBUDSMEN

To enable the ombudsmen to fulfill their mandate, legislators have appropriately accorded them certain powers. They generally have the right to see all pertinent files, interrogate all officials concerned, ask for assistance from the competent agencies, and enter the premises of any agency that is subject to the investigation. Some ombudsmen, for example in Sweden and Finland, have an unrestricted right of access to documents, however secret they may be. Normally, however, documents may be withheld from an ombudsman for reasons of state security or national defense.

In many instances, administrative decisions can be subjected to judicial review by means of appeal or through other avenues. This might, of course, cause conflicts of jurisdiction between the courts and the ombudsman. The problem has attracted the attention of legislators in the Anglo-Saxon countries. When the ombudsman system was introduced in New Zealand, a provision was inserted in the Parliamentary Commissioner (Ombudsman) Act 1962 that the ombudsman was not authorized to investigate

> any decision, recommendation, act, or omission in respect of which there is, under the provisions of any enactment, a right of appeal or objection, or a right to apply for a review, on the merits of the case, to any Court, or to any tribunal constituted by or under any enactment, whether or not that right of appeal or objection or application has been exercised in the particular case, and whether or not any time prescribed for the exercise of that right has expired.

Subsequently when the Parliamentary Commissioner Act of 1967 was passed in Great Britain, a similar provision was inserted. However, it was added that the commissioner might conduct an investigation

> notwithstanding that the person aggrieved has or had such a right or remedy if satisfied that in the particular circumstances it is not reasonable to expect him to resort or have resorted to it.

The same or strikingly similar words are used in the Northern Ireland Parliamentary Commissioner and Commissioner for Complaints Acts; in the rules for the health service commissioners for England and Wales; in the Local Governments Acts of 1974 for England and Wales and 1975 for Scotland; in the Ombudsman Acts of some Canadian provinces; and in the act establishing the office of the Commonwealth Ombudsman in Australia and in the Ombudsman Acts of most Australian states. Subsequently, the New Zealand Ombudsman Act has been amended so as to give the ombudsman a right to investigate notwithstanding that the complainant has or had a right to appeal if by reason of special circumstances "it would be unreasonable to expect him to resort or have resorted to it." It may also be mentioned that in the Australian states of Queensland and Victoria, the ombudsman may conduct an investigation notwithstanding that the aggrieved person had a right of appeal, provided that the ombudsman considers that the matter merits investigation *in order to avoid injustice*.

In several of the Canadian provinces, such as Alberta, New Brunswick, and Ontario, the ombudsman is precluded from investigating *until after* the right of appeal or objection or application for a review of the merits of the case has been exercised in the particular case or *until after* the time prescribed for the exercise of that right has expired.

In the Scandinavian countries no similar rules exist. Yet the ombudsmen will not normally intervene while there is still a possibility of appeal. Nor will they intervene while a case is pending in court or, for that matter, while an administrative agency is reviewing the merits of the case. Sometimes, however, the complaint concerns minor issues not likely to be dealt with by the authority to whom the appeal may be lodged, and then the ombudsman will intervene if he feels this action is appropriate.

Another aspect that should be noted in this context is that, while in the particular case brought before the ombudsman no court action is likely to be taken or even is possible, the same problem may come up in another similar case and then be brought before a court of law. Most material problems can, at least theoretically, become the subject of litigation. In the Scandinavian countries, particularly in Sweden and Finland, the ombudsmen have felt that the mere fact that the matter complained of involves a problem that can be brought to court must not impede their intervention. In most cases it is not probable that the complainant will go to court if the ombudsman takes up the case, nor is it likely that a similar case will be brought to court by anybody else. The ombudsmen have felt free under these circumtances to pronounce an opinion on how the law should be interpreted. Sometimes the answer to the question raised by the complainant is perfectly obvious, there being, for instance, clear precedents from the Supreme Court. But even when the question is a more difficult one, the ombudsmen have on several occasions given a ruling. It has happened that subsequently a similar case has been brought to court. While a court is by no means bound by what the ombudsman has said, his opinion has usually been upheld. A contributing fact is that all Scandinavian ombudsmen have legal training; many of them have been high-ranking judges prior to their appointment. It may be added that in Sweden, upon occasion the ombudsman has been confronted with difficult problems, usually related to the interpretation of tax statutes, which concern a great many people. Since many years may pass before a ruling is obtained from the Supreme Court, the ombudsman, to promote uniformity of decisions, has recommended that the administrative authorities, pending a decision from the Supreme Court, interpret the statutes in the manner suggested by him.

This practice in Scandinavia seems not to have been adopted by other countries. A study of various ombudsman reports indicates that the

Scandinavian ombudsmen, in their attempts to promote good administration, are more apt to pronounce opinions on how the laws should be
interpreted and how administrative authorities should act under given
circumstances, while ombudsmen in other countries concentrate more
upon the individual case brought before them and endeavor to have the
complainant's grievances redressed.

In all countries, however, the ombudsmen have been active in
recommending amendments of existing laws and statutes in the interest of fairness and equity. Even in the first Swedish Act of Instruction
to the Ombudsman, passed in 1810, it was stated that the ombudsman
should report to Parliament on the state of laws and statutes and
suggest such amendments as he found necessary. In nearly all statutes
subsequently issued to establish ombudsman offices, the ombudsman
has been authorized and encouraged to suggest amendments of existing rules when possibly such amendments would promote a good
and fair administration or otherwise be to the benefit of the citizens.
The French ombudsman (mediateur) particularly has been active in
this field. In 1978, the French Parliament passed an enactment containing numerous amendments of various statutes, all of which had
been recommended by the ombudsman. Maybe it is merely a coinci-
dence, but the new ombudsman (protecteur du citoyen) in Quebec,
Canada, also has shown a great interest in combating inconsistencies
in legislation.

CONCLUSIONS

The ombudsmen all supervise the administration. Their main
concern is to oversee administrative authorities by ensuring that they
proceed legally and equitably.

They cannot, however, quash or modify an administrative decision. Generally they can do nothing more than recommend that the
matter be reconsidered, that some kind of remedial action be taken, or
that existing rules or regulations be amended. As an ombudsman's
recommendations in individual cases are nearly always made public, his
interventions have a considerable direct impact. The mere fact that
the ombudsman has received a complaint from an aggrieved person
often causes the administration to redress the grievance immediately.

The Scandanavian ombudsmen are more likely to publicly criticize
officials found at fault and to express their opinions as to how the law
should be interpreted than are the Anglo-Saxon ombudsmen, who seem
to favor a more low-profile approach. While much can be said in favor

of the latter method, it is a matter of some doubt whether the Anglo-Saxon ombudsmen's interventions have the same effective widespread impact as those of their Scandinavian colleagues.

NOTE

1. The constitution of 1809 *did* prescribe that the Justitieombudsman be a *man*. It was not until 1941 that the word "man" was replaced by "citizen," thus making it possible to elect a woman to be Justitieombudsman. So far no woman has been elected to that office.

ADDENDUM
The International Ombudsman Institute

RANDALL E. IVANY

The Internatinal Ombudsman Institute was established in 1978 at the University of Alberta, after years of discussion and planning. As early as 1969, Dr. Bernard Frank, chairman of the Ombudsman Committee of the International Bar Association, raised the idea of a university center at the Bangkok World Conference on World Peace Through Law. Dr. Frank approached many organizations with the purpose of promoting the establishment of such a center. Among those approached were the Canadian ombudsmen, at their annual conference in September, 1975. A formal submission (on which I, as ombudsman for Alberta, worked) by the University of Alberta's Faculty of Law was prepared and presented to the then existing International Ombudsman Steering Committee in May 1977. The proposal was accepted and the International Ombudsman Institute was established.

OBJECTIVES

The International Ombudsman Institute is incorporated as a non-profit organization under the Canada Corporation Act. Its objectives include, *inter alia,* to promote the concept of ombudsmanship and encourage its development throughout the world; to encourage and support research; to develop and operate educational programs associated with ombudsmanship; and to collect, store, and disseminate information about the institution of ombudsman.

Any project of this magnitude takes time to develop. It took nine years to go from an idea to an actuality, and there was much work to be done to achieve the objectives set out at the institute's inception.

During the first two years, progress was continuous but slow. An office was established in the law school at the University of Alberta along with a library collection of close to 1200 books and articles, legislation from 75 ombudsmen offices, and reports from 95 ombudsmen and complaint-handling offices throughout the world. Many hard to get and out of print materials are housed in the Institute's library collection. The flow of new additions is ever increasing.[1]

PUBLICATIONS

Two mammoth projects that consumed most of the first year of operations were the compilation of a comprehensive bibliography and a mailing list. In April 1979, the first issue of the bibliography was published. Approximately 2,000 entries were recorded on the bibliography computer data base at that time. Indexing on the bibliography computer program permits searches to be done for author, title, and subject area. An extensive mailing list was also built up during 1978-1979.

Sir Guy Richardson Powles, former ombudsman for New Zealand, was the first ombudsman-in-residence during the summer and fall of 1978. He prepared several occasional papers and aided in the startup process.

1979 marked the beginning of the International Ombudsman Institute publications. Volume 1 of the *Newsletter* was circulated to ombudsman offices, as were Occasional Papers Nos. 1-5, by Sir Guy Powles, Stanley Anderson, Yvan Gagnon, and Larry Buillot. "The Eighth Annual Survey of Ombudsmen and Other Complaint Handling systems" was published in conjunction with the International Bar Association Ombudsman Committee.

Ulf Lundvik was the second ombudsman-in-residence during the summer of 1979, at which time he prepared several papers on ombudsman offices in Europe.

The winter of 1979-1980 was spent updating the bibliography, with the first supplement published in April 1980; preparing a "key words out of context" index for all materials in the institute library; and answering research questions submitted to the institute. Research areas studied included the confidentiality of ombudsman proceedings; removal from office provisions; crown solicitor restrictions; ability to take a reference to court on questions of jurisdiction; and an overall comparison of ombudsman legislation in the commonwealth. Workmen's compensation rating charts were collected from North American jurisdictions for an ongoing study.

Ramawad Sewgobind, ombudsman for Mauritius, was ombudsman-in-residence in July, 1980. I became acting executive director in July replacing Peter Freeman, and executive director at the October Board of Directors' meeting. Mrs. Priscilla Kennedy, associated with the institute for a number of years, continued to be the person involved at all levels and is the "powerhouse" of activity.

CONFERENCES AND SEMINARS

"Court Cases of Interest to the Ombudsman Institution" was published in July 1980. The long-awaited "Sydney Conference Proceedings of the I.B.A. Ombudsman Committee" came out just in time for the Berlin Conference. "The Sixth Annual Canadian Ombudsman Conference Proceedings" came out just in time for the meeting held at the Second International Ombudsman Conference. "The Third Annual United States Ombudsman Conference Proceedings" were prepared in time for the Fourth Annual Conference.

A major event in the life of the institute was marked by the official opening at the Van Leer Foundation in Jerusalem on Oct. 28, 1980, during the Second International Conference. The Herzliya Seminar following the International Conference was a first for the Institute. Future seminars are now in the planning stages. In particular, one was held in Stellenbosch, South Africa, in March 1982.

Publications of the *Newsletter* and Occasional Papers have occurred on a regular basis since the summer of 1980. Occasional Paper No. 6, "Brief on the Office of the Ombudsman," was published in August of that year; No. 7, on the New Zealand ombudsman, appeared in September; No. 8, on the Mauritius office, came out in October; and No. 10, Dr. Frank's address for the opening of the institute, appeared in December, 1980.

PROGRAM DEVELOPMENT

During the fall of 1980, assistance was provided to the governments of the Netherlands and Ireland to prepare for legislation and the beginnings of their respective ombudsman offices, and has continued in 1981. Research for the Central Vigilance Commission of Pakistan, on the question of whether any ombudsman possesses the power to stay another official agency's investigation that occurs during the ombudsman's investigation, was completed late in 1980. The Ninth Annual Survey was ready for distribution in November 1980.

The Commonwealth Legal Secretariat published "Ombudsmen in the commonwealth: A Survey Prepared and Researched by the International Ombudsman Institute" in late October 1980.

CURRENT ACTIVITIES (1981-1983)

January 1981 brought the conclusion of research for the region of Emilia-Romagna, Italy. Requests requiring research received in 1981 included questions relating to ombudsmanship in the Third World; the history, function and goals of the ombudsman movement; comparisons of North American offices; jurisdiction over government-funded organizations; and ombudsmen in the health services area. Requests for materials necessary to evaluate United States offices in light of budgetary restrictions have researched. Numerous bibliography search requests are also received each month.

Publication in 1981 has mushroomed.[2] Two books have been prepared: Stanley Anderson's *Ombudsman Readings* and Randall Ivany's *Readings in Ombudsmanship*. Both are intended to provide an overview and introduction to the ombudsman area. A cumulative revised bibliography, containing over 4,000 entries, was distributed to institute members in June. After years of work, the first run of "The Ombudsman Office Profiles" was printed. Occasional Papers by Ulf Lundvik, Joseph Berube, and Dr. Jacques Vontobel were published. Occasional Paper No. 12 was published in English and French. Efforts were made to continue this effort in bilingualism in future publications. The Tenth Annual Survey and Volume I of the *Ombudsman Journal* was published in the Fall. A directory of ombudsmen is now completed and issued annually. In September 1982, Volume 2 of the *Journal* was published along with a book on Canadian ombudsmen.

NOTES

1. All inquiries regarding publications and the institute's library collection should be directed to Randall E. Ivany, Executive Director, International Ombudsman Institute, Law Centre, University of Alberta, Edmonton, Alberta, Canada T6-G2H5.

2. Since 1981, Occasional Papers 13-21 have been published, and include articles by Dr. Bernard Frank, Mr. Ulf Lundvik, Mr. Kenneth Bratton, Professor Larry Hill, Herr Karl Wilhelm Berkhan, Mr. Brian Goodman, Herr Klas Lithaer and Professor Donald Rowat—an international survey of materials on the world ombudsman scene.

CONCLUSIONS

RISHA W. LEVINSON
KAREN S. HAYNES

This volume represents the first compilation of cross-national reports that focuses on organized access systems of human services. These fourteen reports from nine different countries reflect the enormous diversity of access systems and the multiple levels of development at which various entry systems operate. While there are marked differences in the organizational structure, range of services, staffing, funding patterns, and policy-planning capabilities in the reported CAB and I&R systems, it is apparent that these systems also share significant commonalities. Some of these salient common elements and diversities merit further elaboration.

Regardless of the stage of development of any single access system, a common goal of all access systems is to link the person in need of helping services to available and appropriate resources. Whether stated implicitly or explicitly, all access systems aim to provide direct services to the citizen-client at the closest point of consumption. It is also important to note that organized access systems are vital to human service agents who provide information, referral, advice and advocacy, and other service functions that facilitate access to human services.

Of equal importance, though not always clearly delineated, is the utilization of the capabilties of an organized system as a base for planning, research, and social action. Based on the availability of a resource file, the compilation of service statistics, and funds of client data, access systems can provide linkages for the effective operation of a service network.

The strategies to develop these linkages may vary; however, the effectiveness of an access system, whether it is a CAB or an I&R operation, is dependent upon the degree of interagency cooperation that exists. The efforts involved in securing the cooperation of relevant health and social service organizations are documented by the British authors in their description of alliances and working agreements with various social organizations. The interagency aspects of cooperation also are strongly stressed by the authors of the New Delhi CAB system as well as the reporters on the New Zealand and Japanese access systems. In fact, one of the major criteria stipulated by Gargan and Shanahan in their selection of model I&R systems in the United States is the level of interorganizational collaboration within I&R networks.

Another feature shared by organized access systems is the dual responsibility of an access system to provide a generic program of services to the total population as well as the provision of specialized services or appropriate referral to specialized services. The conceptual framework designed by Doron and Frenkel suggest the presence of total and target populations that relate to general and specialized services.

The problem of limited resources is a common concern of all the reported access systems. Support is usually sought from multiple funding sources that include public and private funding sources. The extent of governmental initiative in the promotion and support of access systems varies considerably, from direct funding by central government, as reported by the British National Association of Citizens Advice Bureaus, to individual state grants as provided for special training in I&R programs under Title XX of the U.S. Social Security Act.

While the information systems and information technology reported in this volume demonstrate diverse levels of sophistication, the general trend is toward increased interagency collaboration in the centralization of operating information systems concurrent with the decentralization of local service delivery. This trend toward expanding centralized service networks is evident in the reports on I&R systems in North America as well as CAB operations in the United Kingdom and New Zealand.

It is clear that each of the access systems presented in this volume reflects the socioeconomic and cultural conditions of its respective country. These social factors may explain the hesitancy of the newly arrived Israeli immigrant to use the CAB services in Israel, and may also help to explain the lack of community readiness on the part of Cyprian leaders to establish a CAB system in their country. The priority of legal literacy for the Indian citizen, for example, is also indicative of a social priority based on the need for citizen self-advocacy in a country with a record of low literacy.

All of the reported access systems have highlighted the paramount role of the volunteer as the direct service agent. Whether the volunteer operates with a high degree of autonomy, as reported in the British CAB system, or collaboratively with public service agents, as described in the Japanese Munsei-Iin system, or concurrently with social workers, as presented in the Polish social welfare system, the consensus is that a well-organized training program is central to the operation of an effective volunteer program. In fact, the effectiveness of an access system is viewed as contingent upon systematic training programs for volunteers as well as for all levels of staff.

The report on the International Ombudsman Institute in the final chapter is an example of an international organization that represents an alliance of access systems designed to promote advocacy in the administration of human service agencies. The development of this multinational institute offers cross-national exchange and communication between access systems that promote the ombudsman function in human services organizations.

The expansion of organized access systems, as reported by the contributors for their respective countries, points to the growing recognition of the need to facilitate universal access to human resources.

INDEX

Access systems
  diversity of, 15-16
  expansion of, 16, 21
  goals of, 17
  literature on, 21-22
  origins and purpose of, 16
Advocacy services, 39-40, 81, 90, 129, 280-86
Aged/aging. *See* Elderly, services to
AID Service of Edmonton, 217-37
  accessibility, 217-19, 223
  confidentiality procedure, 222, 234-35
  funding of, 235-36
  origins of, 217-19
  purpose and philosophy of, 222-23, 235, 236
  services and activities of, 222-31
    CORE (Crisis Outreach and Referral Evaluation), 220-22, 231-33, 237
    data base accuracy, 224-25
    data management, 226-30
    Distress Line, 219-20, 226, 228, 236-37
    neighborhood centers, 230-31
    suicide intervention, 220-22
  staffing, 219-22, 225, 233-35, 244
Alliance of Information and Referral Systems (AIRS), 136, 169*n*
Appeal and review, rights of, 287-88
Area Agency on Aging, 148

Canada. *See also* AID Service of Edmonton; Citizens' Inquiry; Community Information Center of Metropolitan Toronto (CICMT); Community Information Centers (Ontario); CORE (Crisis Outreach and Referral Evaluation)

Alberta Ombudsmen Act, 295
  functional illiteracy in, 212
  International Ombudsmen Institute, 303-6
Case integration, 129, 132
Centralization, 20, 106, 108-9, 149-50. *See also* Poland (*pomoc spoleczna*)
Child welfare services, 129-30, 217, 266-67
Citizens Advice Bureaus. *See also* Community Information Project; Community Information Project (CIP); Cyprus Citizen Advice Bureaus; Israeli Citizen Advice Bureaus; New Zealand Citizen Advice Bureaus
  client population, 47-48
  comparative analysis of, with I & R services, 17-20
  expansion of, 49-50
  functions of, 29-30, 36-42
    feedback/prevention, 40-41
    information and advice, 37-39
    mediation/advocacy, 39-40
    specialist advice services, 41-42
  funding of, 23, 48-50
  future directions of, 53-55
  membership requirements, 36
  networking by, 50-53
  organizational structure of, 34-35
  origins of, 16, 30-33
  principles of, 33-34
  purpose of, 23-24
  staffing of, 42-53
  standards of service, 35-36
Citizens' Advice Bureaus (New Delhi, India), 275-86
  accessibility to, 277
  advocacy programs, 280-86
    case, 280-81

policy, 284-86
    program, 281-84
case card reporting, 277
confidentiality procedures of, 277
funding of, 277
interorganizational cooperation, 278-
    80, 284
legal literacy programs, 281-83
organization structure of, 276-78
origins of, 275-76
purpose of, 276, 285
staffing of, 276-78
Citizen's Inquiry, 209-10
Client-volunteer relationships, 115-17, 128
Community Information Center of Met-
    ropolitan Toronto (CICMT), 205-9
accessibility to, 204, 206, 208
client population of, 206
delivery modes, 206, 208-9
establishment of, 200-201, 205
funding of, 207
resource file bank, 206-7
services of, 205, 206
    Blue Book, 206, 207
staffing of, 206, 207-8
Community Information Centers (Ontar-
    io, Canada)
accessibility to, 204
functions of, 205
funding of, 202-3
origins of, 200-201
staffing of, 204-5
Community Information Project (CIP),
    57-76
achievements of, 24-25, 66-75
Advice Services Alliance (ASA), 75
Cambridge Community Council proj-
    ect, 67
Citizens Advice Bureaus project (East
    Anglia), 67-68
community resource centers, 74
computer use by, 72-73
current status of, 75-76
functions of, 57
general development work of, 70-71
information dissemination procedures,
    61-63
Know How, 71
libraries cooperation with, 66-67, 73
mass media use by, 73-74

networking, 63-64, 74-75
On the Road, 71-72
origins of, 57, 58-66
principles of, 60
research projects of, 65-66, 68-69, 70
South Molton Project, 69-70
Village contacts, 73
Westminister libraries project, 66-67
Computer/communications services
Broward County (Florida), 172, 182
cable television, 184-85, 213
Community Information and Referral
    Services (Phoenix), 190-191
Community Service Planning Council
    (Philadelphia), 189-90
Computer Assistant Information & Re-
    ferral Network (CAIRN) of Boston,
    173, 182
Crisis Clinic, Inc. (Seattle), 191-92
Greater New York Fund/United Way,
    193-95
KEYFACTS, 184-85
locations of, 188
Mile High United Way I & R Service,
    153, 166
Service Agency Inventory System
    (SAIS), 194
SPIRES, 224, 226
TELIDON, 185-86, 207, 208, 209, 210-
    11, 213
United Way of America Service Identi-
    fication System (UWASIS), 21
United Way of Texas Gulf Coast
    (Houston), 195-96
videotex, 185-86
Videotex, 185-86, 209
word processing, 208-9
Computer/communications technology,
    171-98
applications of, 173-84
    ancillary, 192
    file cards, 181
    information dissemination, 175-81
    microfiche, 177, 180-81, 192
    online inquiries, 181-82
    printed directories, 175-77, 178,
        179, 180
    resource file maintenance, 174
    statistical analysis, 183-84

vacancy control program, 182-83,
189, 191
batch processing, 174, 192
costs of, 172-73, 182, 189, 190, 191, 195
functions of, 137
glossary for, 196-97
hardware, 171
mainframe, 195
microcomputers, 68, 172, 190
minicomputers, 191
Information Center of Hampton Roads
(southeastern Virginia), 167
limitations of, 212, 214
Mile High United Way I & R Service,
153, 166
obstacles to, 137, 171-73
on-line interactive input, 174, 193, 194,
195
protocols system, 191-92
software, 171-72
taxonomies for, 172
variables, 190, 191, 195
Confidentiality procedures, 19, 34, 36, 80,
87, 110, 116-17, 202-3, 222, 234-35
oaths, 234-35, 277
Consumer services, 284
CORE (Crisis Outreach and Referral
Evaluation), 220-22, 231-33
Counseling services, 268-69
Cyprus Citizen Advice Bureaus, 95-103
administration of, 99-100
funding of, 101-102
networking by, 101
problems and constraints of, 102-3
proposal for, 95-98
publicity for, 100-101

Decentralization, 20, 81, 150-51, 153
Directories, printed, 175-76, 190, 206, 224,
236

Elderly, services to
Area Agency on Aging (AAA), 148,
151, 163, 164, 165-66, 168
funding of, 168
information and referral
need for, 160-61
Interdepartmental Task Force on Information and Referral, 159
in Japan, 266

National Insurance Institute (Israel),
131-32

Family services, 249, 268

Handicapped services, 213, 266
Hotlines, 219-20, 225, 226, 228, 236-37. See
also Info Line(s)
Distress Line, 219-20, 226, 228, 236-37
Zenith Ontario, 210-11
Housing services, 85-86, 283, 285

Illiteracy, functional, 212, 281-83
Immigrant services, 105-7, 122, 202-3
Info Line(s)
of Connecticut, 149, 151, 152, 156, 162
of Los Angeles County, 150, 152, 157,
165, 169n
of Summit County, 158, 164
Information and referral services. See also
Model Systems Project
Information and referral services. See also
Canada
capacity levels of, 143-44, 146
comparative analysis of, with CABs,
17-20
computerization of. See Computer/
communications technology, 000
conditions for, 144, 146
in-place policies for system concerns, 156-58
quality coverage, 148-53
quality support systems, 153, 156
contextual determination of, 147-48
ecological approach to, 211-12
effectiveness of, 152
elderly's need for, 160-61
elements of, 142-43
expansion of, 158-59
fragmentation of, 159
funding of, 147, 148, 149, 159-61, 159,
159-60, 161, 163, 164, 168, 169n
generic vs. specialized, 152, 153, 168
networking/linkage, 149-51, 161
organizational structures
centralized, 149-50, 151, 162
decentralized, 150-51, 153, 165
disaggregated, 151
moderately decentralized, 150, 165
origins of, 16

as political issue, 159-60
priority of, in CABs, 54, 58-59
problem areas in, 141, 147-48
Information dissemination, 115-16
computerized, 175-81
by consulting services, 61-62
by mass media, 63, 73-74
by publications, 62-63, 70-73, 92-93, 162, 394-5, 306
International Ombudsmen Institute, 303-6
IRMA (Information and Referral Manual), 193-94
Israeli Citizen Advice Bureaus, 105-34
conceptual model for, 122-26
confidentiality procedures, 110, 116-17
delivery of services
levels of, 124
types of, 123-24, 125-32
funding of, 107-8, 109
history and development of, 105-9
immigrant services, 105-7
information services, 115-17
objectives of, 109-10
ombudsmen services, 109
organizational structure, 110-17
centralization, 106, 108-9
front line work, 112-17
office set, 111-12
service channels
Citizen Advice Bureaus network, 120-21, 126-27
emergency health care, 130-31
Jerusalem Municipal Information Office, 125
local information bureaus (LIBs), 121-23, 127-29
National Insurance Institute, 131-32
police, 125-26
specialized, 122
well-baby clinics, 129-30
staffing, 111, 112, 112-17

Japan, 259-74. See also Minsei-Iin volunteer system (Japan)
Child Welfare Law of 1947, 261
Citizens' Counseling Service Bureaus, 268-69, 270-71
Daily Life Security Law of 1946, 261, 262, 266

Family Rehabilitation Movement, 268
GHQ (General Headquarters of the Army of the Occupation) principles of social assistance, 261
Homen-Iin (district volunteer) system, 259, 260
Homen-Iin Regulation of 1936, 260
Jido-Iin volunteer, 261, 267
Law for the Welfare of the Aged, 266
Law for the Welfare of the Physically Handicapped, 266
Military Assistance Law of 1937, 261
Minsei-Iin Law of 1948, 265
Minsei-Iin Law of 1953, 262, 265
Minsei-Iin Regulation of 1946, 261
Mother and Child Welfare Law, 266-67
Mothers' Aid Law of 1937, 261
Poor Relief Law of 1924, 260
Poor Relief Law of 1928, 261
Poor Relief Regulation of 1874, 260
Prostitution Prevention Law of 1956, 267
Saisei-Koman (relief advisor) system, 259, 260

Legal advocacy services, 280-86
Libraries, role of, 66-67, 163-64, 204
Linkages, 128-29
benefits of, 63-64, 156-58, 161
computerized, 214, 215
local and area, 50-51
national, 51-53, 64-65, 74-75
systems approach to, 143
vertical vs. horizontal, 156-57

Microfiche, 177, 180-81, 190, 192
Minsei-Iin volunteer system (Japan), 259-74
appointment/nomination process in, 262-64, 272-73
Councils of Social Welfare, 264-65, 267-69
funding of, 269-71
future directions of, 271-73
history of, 259-62
limitations of, 271-73
local focus of, 271-73
origins of, 259-62
services and activities of, 265-69
to aged, 266, 269

child welfare, 266-67
    to families, 268
    guidance counseling, 268-69
    to physically handicapped, 266
    to single parents, 266
    to women, 267
    welfare cards in, 265
Model Systems Project, 141-70
    conditions of, 143-44
        in-place policies for systems con-
            cerns, 156-58
        quality coverage, 148-51, 148-53
        quality support functions, 153, 156
    criteria for, 144-47
    definition of concept, 142-43
    development histories of, 161-69
        Humboldt/Del Norte I & R system
            (northern California), 167-68
        Info Line of Akron/Summit Coun-
            ty (Ohio), 164-65
        Info Line of Connecticut, 162
        Information Center of Hampton
            Roads (southeastern Virginia),
            167
        Los Angeles I & R system, 165-66
        Memphis (Tennessee) Library In-
            formation System (LINC), 162-
            64
        Mile High United Way I & R Ser-
            vice (Denver, Colorado), 166
    development of, 141-44
    findings of, 147-48

Networking. See Linkages
New Zealand Citizen Advice Bureaus, 77-
    93
    administration of, 88-89
    client population of, 85-87
    code of ethics, 83
    functions of, 79-81
    funding of, 87-88
    future directions of, 91-93
    networking by, 89-91
    ombudsmen services, 290-92, 295, 296,
        298
    origins of, 78-79
    publications of, 91-92
    staffing of, 81-85

Ombudsmen services, 109, 287-301
    authority of, 293, 297-300
    definition of, 288
    historical background to, 288-92
    in India, 279-80, 279-80
    International Ombudsmen Institute,
        303-6
    models of
        Anglo-Saxon, 290-92, 296-97
        Scandinavian, 290, 293-96
    tasks and objectives, 292-97
        disciplinary, 295
        offering of criticism, 295-96, 297
        prosecutorial, 293-94, 295
        recommendatory, 294-96, 297

Poland (pomoc spoleczna), 245-58
    access barriers to, 256-57
    access channels, 249-56
        community nurse, 253
        informal referrals, 254-55
        social worker centers, 246, 251, 252,
            254
        social workers, 250-51
        voluntary associations, 246, 253-54
        volunteer workers, 246, 251-52
    Area Health Complex (ZOZ), 246, 251
    client groups served by, 248-49, 250
    constitutional rights to social service in,
        245
    funding of, 249
    inefficiency of, 249, 254-55
    information and referral services in,
        lack of, 259
    organizational structure of, 246-49
    outreach in, 254, 255
    scope and functioning of
        active social assistance, 250
        factors influencing, 248-49
    services delivered by, 248, 249, 253
Polish Committee for Social Assistance
    (PKPS), 246, 248, 254
Polish Family Aid Fund, 249
Polish Red Cross (PCK), 246, 248, 253-54

Reporting systems, 129
    computerized, 201-2
Resource files
    computerized, 174, 206-7

Service opening registry (SOR), 182-83, 189
Social action/policy roles, 53-54, 96, 124, 131-32, 133, 285
Social workers, 88-89
    in New Zealand, 84-85, 87, 88-89
    Polish, unique role of, 250-51
Suicide intervention, 220-21, 231-35, 237
System
    definition of, 142
    elements of, 142-43
    model, 145-47

Telephone call sheet, 226, 227
Telephone services. *See* Hotlines

Unemployment services, 158
United Way
    of Akron/Summit County, 158
    of Connecticut, 151, 162
    Greater New York Fund/United Way, 193-95

of Humboldt/Del Norte counties, 168
of Los Angeles County, 165
of Memphis, Tennessee, 163
Mile High, 148, 151, 153, 166
of Texas Gulf Coast (Houston), 195-96
United Way of America Service Identification System (UWASIS), 21

Volunteer-client relationships, 115-17
Volunteer programs, 111, 112-17. *See also* Minsei-Iin volunteer system (Japan)
    screening procedures, 234, 263
    selection procedures, 43-44, 84, 113-14, 219-20
    training programs, 20, 36, 45-46, 82-84, 103, 113-14, 116, 222, 225, 233-34, 262-64
Volunteer social counselors, 251-52

Women, services to, 261, 266-67, 283, 284

ABOUT THE AUTHORS

MEERA AGARWAL is an Advocate, Supreme Court of India. She serves as a member of the Executive Committee of Citizens Advice Bureau and Citizen Action, New Delhi, India. Dr. Agarwal holds a Ph.D. in English Literature as well as an LL.B. from Agra University. She has practised in the Trial Court, High Court, and Supreme Court of India, New Delhi and argued before the Indian Parliament issues related to dowry and marital breakdown. She has published for the CAB, two booklets entitled, "Women and the Law" and "Fundamental Rights and State Police."

YEMINA BARNEIS is a National Information Officer with the CAB Ministry of Labour and Social Affairs, Israel. Ms. Barneis holds a B.A. in English Literature and Sociology from Hebrew University, Jerusalem, Israel, as well as a B.A. in Environmental Design from the Bezalel Academy of Art and Design, Jerusalem, Israel. Previously Ms. Barneis was employed by the Edinburgh Council for Single Homeless, in Edinburgh, Scotland.

DONALD F. BELLAMY is Professor and Coordinator of Graduate Studies, Faculty of Social Work, University of Toronto, Ontario, Canada. Dr. Bellamy holds a D.S.W. from Columbia University, an M.S.W. from the University of Toronto, and a B.A. from the University of Western Ontario. Dr. Bellamy has conducted evaluative studies of information and referral services, conducted experimental developments in computer networks of information and referral centres using the concept of shared visual and acoustic space, and has been a member of a team which developed a research design for the videotex system. He has published several articles relative to these projects.

ABRAHAM DORON is Associate Professor at the Paul Baewald School of Social Work, The Hebrew University of Jerusalem. Dr. Doron obtained his Ph.D. in Social Administration from the London School of Economics and Political Science and has an M.A. from the University of Chicago in Social Service Administration. Dr. Doron has written several articles on social services and information services.

ALEX EASTABROOK is Development Officer of the National Association of Citizen Advice Bureaux. NACAB is the major independent national organization with over 900 bureaus in the United Kingdom. Mr. Eastabrook has been the series editor of fifteen papers published under the NACAB Occasional Papers Series. He holds a B. A. in Philosophy from the University of Sussex, England.

OFRA FISHER is the National Director of the CAB Ministry of Labour and Social Affairs, Israel. This CAB is a national government service, which offers the public accurate and updated information about citizens' rights and guidance in using these rights. Ms. Fisher holds a teaching degree from Kibbuz Seminary, Israel.

DONALD J. FORGIE is Associate Professor in the Faculty of Library and Information Science, University of Toronto, Ontario, Canada. Mr. Forgie received his Masters in Library Science from the University of Western Ontario and holds a Masters in Communications from the University of Toronto. He has taught course related to theoretical and practical aspects of access to information, technological considerations and community services. He was principal investigator for a research design for Telidon Systems and has worked with experimental developments of computer network of I & R centers.

ELI FRENKEL is the Deputy Director of the Paul Baerwald School Work at the Hebrew University in Jerusalem, Israel. He earned both his undergraduate degree (B.S.W.) and his master's degree in Social Work (M.S.W.) at the Hebrew University: He was awarded a Ph. D. degree from Brown University in Providence, Rhode Island in 1982. Dr. Frenkel's publication on "The Local Social Service Delivery System" is included in the series of Cross-National Studies of Social Services Systems, edited by A. J. Kahn and S. B. Kamerman at Columbia University, New York.

JOHN J. GARGAN is Associate Professor of Political Science at Kent State University, Kent, Ohio. He holds a Ph. D. in Political Science from Syracuse University. He has published articles dealing with I & R policy, strategic planning, and local government capacity building.

WILLIAM GARRETT is the Assistant Vice President, United Way of Tri-State, New York, New York. Mr. Garrett received a Masters of Science in Social Work and an M.B.A. from Columbia University, New York. He was previously the Director of the Service Agency Investing System of Greater New York Fund/United Way. This system designed and developed a computerized, detailed listing of human service organizations for the City of New York. He has been an Adjunct Professor at Fordham Graduate School of Social Science teaching computers to social welfare managers. He has been the guest editor of a special issue of computerization of the *Journal of the Alliance of Information and Referral Systems.*

KAREN S. HAYNES is Associate Professor, School of Social Work, Indiana University and President, The National Alliance of Information and Referral Systems. She holds a Ph.D. from the University of Texas at Austin in Social Welfare Policy and Planning, and an M.S.W. from McGill University, Montreal, Quebec, Canada. She has written numerous articles in the area of taxonomic systems for human services, I&R data for planning, and served on the National Advisory Board to the U.S. Administration on Aging's Model Systems Project. Dr. Haynes was the Editor of the *Journal of the Alliance of Information and Referral Systems* from 1980-1983. She has been a consultant with the Egyptian Institute for National Planning for two years and conducted comparative international research.

RANDALL E. IVANY is currently Ombudsman, Province of Alberta, Canada, and Executive Director, of the International Ombudsman Institute. Dr. Ivany received his LL.D. from the University of Alberta, Edmonton and holds several degrees from Wycliffe College, University of Toronto. He has written numerous articles on the subject of Ombudsmanship.

RISHA W. LEVINSON is Associate Professor of Social Policy and Director of the Service Development Division at the Adelphi University School of Social Work in Garden City, N.Y. She holds a D.S.W. degree from Columbia University and a master's degree in Social Service Administration from the University of Chicago. She has written numerous articles on professional training and program development, in information and referral services, and has been a strong proponent for linking health and social services through I&R. During her sabbatical year (1980-1981) she made extensive site visits to CABs throughout the United Kingdom, under the guidance of the National Association of Citizens Advice Bureaus (NACAB). Dr. Levinson is the author of a forthcoming book, *Doorways To Human Services: Information and Referral* scheduled for publication by Springer Publishing Co. in 1985.

ULF LUNDVIK is currently a Judge and was formerly Chief Parliamentary Ombudsman and President of the International Ombudsman Institute. He holds a Bachelor of Law from the University of Uppsala (1942). He has written several articles on law and the Ombudsman system and has a book entitled *The Ombudsmen in the Provinces of Canada*.

ATSUKO MATSUOKA is currently involved in the Ph. D. program at the Faculty of Social Work at the University of Toronto, Canada and is Community Welfare Volunteer in Japan—The Minsei-Iin System. She has conducted research in Amagasaki and Nishinomiya and has been involved in the meals on wheels program in Osaka. She received a B.A. from the University of Toronto, and an M.A. from the Graduate School of Kwanseinakuin University. She has published the results from her research on life conditions in Amagasaki and Nishinomiya.

RAMESH CHANDRA MISHRA is currently Advocate, Supreme Court of India, New Delhi, and Advisor of Citizens Advice Bureau and Citizen Action. She received her B. A. and Bachelor of Law from Allahabad University, India. She has written several articles on citizens' legal rights and provides free legal services to those who cannot pay for services.

GRAINNE MORBY is currently an Information Officer with the Community Information Project. She was formerly a Senior Information Officer with the National Association of Citizens Advice Bureaus. As an Advice Worker, she has had experience in working in both the public and voluntary sectors of the social services.

BARBARA ANN OLSEN is the Executive Director of the AID service of Edmonton, Alberta, Canada. Following her undergraduate studies at Bryn Mawr (B.A.) and her graduate studies at Yale University (M.Sc.), she earned a Ph. D. at Brown University in Chemistry. As administrator for the AID Service, she has developed a crisis intervention service as well as a public education program. In addition to her published scientific papers, Dr. Olsen has contributed various articles on I&R related to suicide prevention and information systems.

JAMES L. SHANAHAN is a Professor in the Department of Urban Studies at the University of Akron, Ohio, and is also the

Acting Director of the Center for Urban Studies at the university. His major professional interests as reflected in his extensive publications are planning and development, cultural economics, and human services, with a special research interest in information and referral systems. Dr. Shanahan was the principal investigator in a *Model Information and Referral System Demonstration Project* that was granted to the Alliance of Information and Referral Systems, Inc. (AIRS) by the U.S. Administration on Aging, Department of Health and Human Services (1983). During his tenure as President of AIRS, he was also instrumental in the production of a new national I&R Directory and, in collaboration with the United Way of America, promoted the publication of newly revised I&R Standard. He is currently the Executive Editor of *Information and Referral: The Journal of the Alliance of Information and Referral Systems, Inc.*

IRENE SIENKO is an adjunct professor at the Institute of Social Policy at the University of Warsaw, from which she received her Master Degree in Economics (1968) and a Ph. D. degree in Political Science (1975). In addition to her teaching and research activities, Dr. Sienko has published numerous articles in Polish scientific journals on social welfare policy and social assistance in Poland.

NEIL SMITH serves on the National General Committee of the New Zealand Association of Citizens Advice Bureaus. Prior to his current retirement, he worked as a clinical social worker and a community development worker with the Auckland City Council and the affiliated CABs. Mr. Smith received his bachelors degree (B. A.) and Diploma in Social Work from Victoria University.

ELENI WILTCHER, a native of Cyprus, has received most of her professional education and training in Great Britain. She is a registered mental health nurse and has also earned a certification of qualification in Social Work. Ms. Wiltcher completed a CAB Training Course in London, where she is currently working toward a Social Sciences Degree at the Open University. She is currently affiliated with the Social Services Department in London. Her previous work experience involved placement at a refugee camp in Cyprus.